SOCIAL SECURITY
What Every Taxpayer Should Know

A. Haeworth Robertson

Retirement Policy Institute
Washington, DC

For further information and to place purchase orders please address:

Retirement Policy Institute—Publications Division
P. O. Box 240242
Charlotte, NC 28224

This publication is designed to provide accurate and authoritative information in regard to the subject matter covered. It is sold with the understanding that the publisher is not engaged in rendering legal, accounting, or other professional service. If legal advice or other expert assistance is required, the services of a competent professional person should be sought.

From a Declaration of Principles jointly adopted by a Committee of the American Bar Association and a Committee of Publishers and Associations.

In this book, the masculine pronoun "he" has occasionally been used to refer to both sexes for the sake of simplicity.

Manufactured in the United States of America

Printed by Science Press, Ephrata, Pennsylvania

First Printing: May 1992

Cataloging in Publication Data

Robertson, A. Haeworth. 1930–
  Social security: what every taxpayer should know.
  xxvi, 326 p. : ill. ; 23 cm.
  Includes bibliographical references and index.
  1. Social security—United States. 2. Social security—United States—Finance. 3. Medicare. I. Title.
HD7125.R62   1992   368.4'3'00973   92-80166
                                            AACR2
ISBN 0-9632345-4-4

Chart 2.C
Old-Age, Survivors, and Disability Insurance Program
Beneficiaries as of December 31, 1989 and
Amount of Benefits in Fiscal Year 1989, by Type of Beneficiary

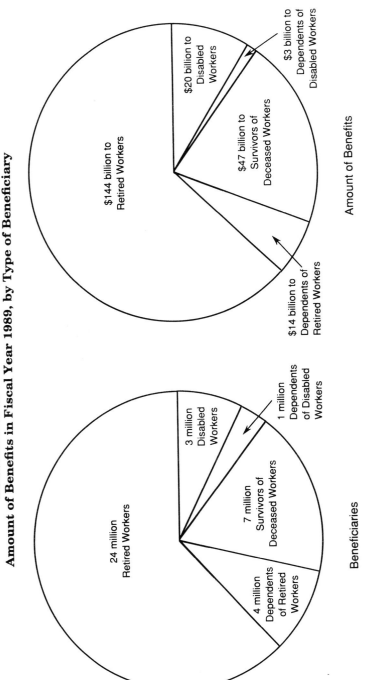

$144 billion to Retired Workers

$20 billion to Disabled Workers

$3 billion to Dependents of Disabled Workers

$47 billion to Survivors of Deceased Workers

$14 billion to Dependents of Retired Workers

Amount of Benefits

24 million Retired Workers

3 million Disabled Workers

1 million Dependents of Disabled Workers

7 million Survivors of Deceased Workers

4 million Dependents of Retired Workers

Beneficiaries

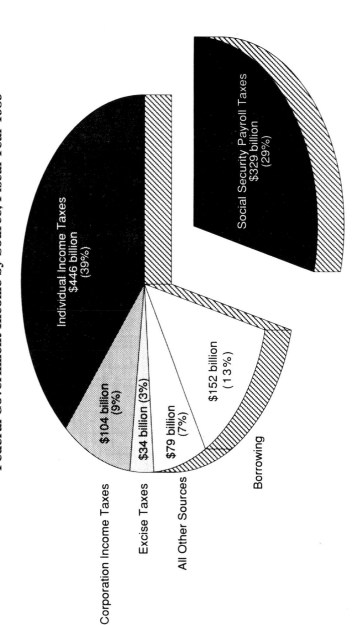

Chart 5.A
Federal Government Income by Source, Fiscal Year 1989

Social Security Payroll Taxes
$329 billion
(29%)

Individual Income Taxes
$446 billion
(39%)

Corporation Income Taxes
$104 billion
(9%)

Excise Taxes
$34 billion (3%)

All Other Sources
$79 billion
(7%)

$152 billion
(13%)

Borrowing

Fiscal Year 1989 Total: $1,143 billion

Chart 7.C

Projected Expenditures for Old-Age, Survivors, Disability, and Hospital Insurance Programs Combined under Alternative Demographic and Economic Assumptions,[a] and Tax Income[b] Expressed as a Percentage of Taxable Payroll[c]

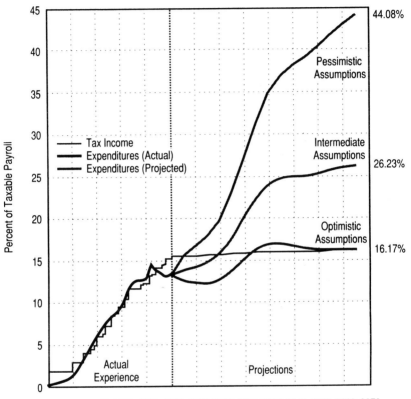

[a] See Chapter 10 and Appendix I for discussion of alternative sets of assumptions.

[b] Tax income includes OASDI and HI payroll taxes and revenue from the income taxation of OASDI benefit payments. Figures shown are based on the intermediate II-B assumptions. Estimates under the alternative assumptions differ slightly.

[c] "Taxable payroll" consists of the total earnings subject to Social Security taxes, after adjustments in applicable years to reflect (i) deemed wages based on military service, and (ii) the lower tax rates on self-employment income, tips, and multiple-employer "excess wages." This adjustment is made to facilitate both the calculation of tax income (which is thereby the product of the tax rate and the payroll) and the comparison of expenditure percentages with tax rates. This taxable payroll is slightly different for OASDI and HI because of past differences in the tax treatment of self-employed persons and current differences in coverage of employment; however, these differences do not materially affect the comparisons.

Chart 7.E

Projected Expenditures for Supplementary Medical Insurance Program under Alternative Demographic and Economic Assumptions[a]
Expressed as a Percentage of Taxable Payroll[b]

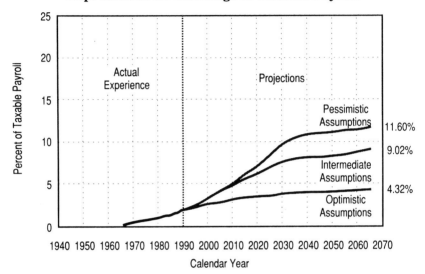

[a] See Chapter 10 and Appendix I for discussion of alternative sets of assumptions.

[b] Although the SMI program is not financed by payroll taxes, its cost is shown for comparative purposes as a percentage of payroll that is taxable for HI purposes. Participation in SMI is optional and is financed by premiums paid by the enrollees, and by general revenues.

In contrast to the procedures for the OASDI and HI programs, a long-range actuarial balance for the SMI program is not officially calculated or even defined. The SMI actuarial deficit could well be considered to be the amount by which projected future expenditures for benefits and administration exceed the projected income from premiums paid by the participants. Under this theory, future general revenue would not be taken into account since it has not been earmarked in any way to ensure its availability. Using such a definition, the actuarial deficit over the next seventy-five years would average approximately 5.74 percent of the payroll taxable for HI purposes. Expressed as a single-sum amount, this actuarial deficit is about $7,600 billion as of January 1, 1990.[9]

inflation is not slowed, these combined systems will probably play a smaller role in meeting retirement needs than they do now.

The baby boom was followed by a baby bust beginning in the 1960s. The decline in the size of the pool of workers entering the work force is already evident and employers are turning to older workers to meet their needs.

Effect of Increased Longevity and Improved Health

Additional factors that will influence the nation's average retirement age are the continued increases in life expectancy and improved health at the higher ages.

Life expectancy measured from birth has increased but this is not relevant to the question of retirement age since much of this increase has been attributable to decreased infant mortality. It is the increase in life expectancy measured from age 65 that is of interest in considering the question of retirement age. Table 20.1 compares the remaining life expectancy for a 65-year-old person in the past with that for such a person in the future based upon the

Table 20.1

Remaining Life Expectancy, Past and Projected

Calendar Year	*Remaining Life Expectancy for Persons Reaching Age 65 in Designated Calendar Years*[a]	
	Male	*Female*
(1)	(2)	(3)
1910	11.4	12.1
1930	11.8	12.9
1950	12.8	15.1
1970	13.1	17.1
1990	15.0	18.9
2010	16.0	19.9
2030	16.8	20.8
2050	17.6	21.7

[a] Projections are based on the intermediate set of assumptions.

Chart 4.B
Past, Present, and Projected Covered Workers, Retired Workers, and Other Social Security Beneficiaries

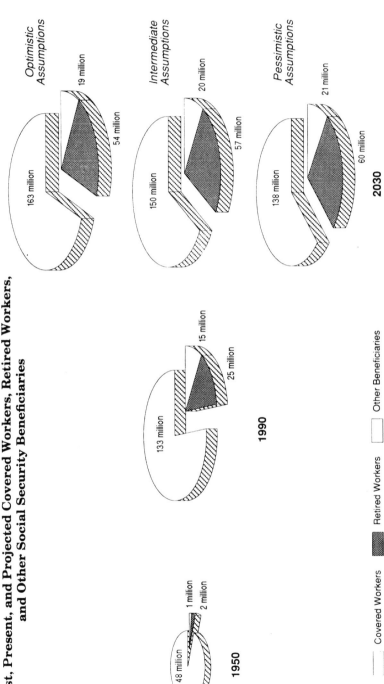

Optimistic Assumptions

19 million
54 million
163 million

Intermediate Assumptions

20 million
57 million
150 million

Pessimistic Assumptions

21 million
60 million
138 million

2030

15 million
25 million
133 million

1990

1 million
2 million
48 million

1950

═══ Covered Workers   ▓ Retired Workers   ☐ Other Beneficiaries

Chart 6.A

Projected Expenditures and Tax Income for Old-Age, Survivors, and Disability Insurance Program under Intermediate Assumptions,[a] Expressed as a Percentage of Taxable Payroll[b]

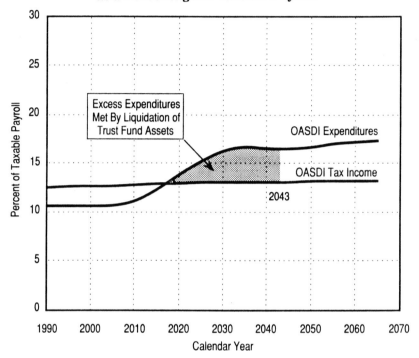

[a] See Chapter 10 and Appendix I for discussion of alternative sets of assumptions. Tax income includes OASDI payroll taxes and revenue from the income taxation of OASDI benefit payments.

[b] "Taxable payroll" in 1990 and later consists of the total earnings subject to Social Security taxes, after adjustments to reflect (i) deemed wages based on military service and (ii) the lower tax rates on multiple-employer "excess wages." This adjustment is made to facilitate both the calculation of tax income (which is thereby the product of the tax rate and the payroll) and the comparison of expenditure percentages with tax rates.

Disability Insurance part of Social Security, this would entail a combined employee-employer payroll tax rate increase in 2043 from 12.4 percent (as currently scheduled in present law) to about 16 percent under the intermediate assumptions.

This phenomenon is illustrated in Chart 6.A, which shows the expenditures (for benefits and administration) and the

For an individual who meets the statutory definition of blindness, only the fully insured requirement need be met. In addition to the insured status requirements, other conditions must be met before benefits will be payable to you or your dependents. These will be mentioned later when the various specific benefits are discussed.

Normal Retirement Age

When Social Security was adopted in 1935, the normal retirement age was set, rather arbitrarily, at age 65. If benefits commence prior to this age they are reduced; if benefits commence after this age they are increased.[1]

In 1983, Social Security was revised to provide a higher normal retirement age for persons born after 1937 and who, therefore, reach age 65 after the year 2002. An individual's normal retirement age now depends upon his year of birth, as shown in the following table. The normal retirement age applies not only to the primary beneficiary but also to a spouse who may be eligible for benefits. (The normal retirement age schedule is slightly different for widows.)

Year of Birth	Normal Retirement Age
1937 or earlier	65
1938	65 years, 2 months
1939	65 years, 4 months
1940	65 years, 6 months
1941	65 years, 8 months
1942	65 years, 10 months
1943–1954	66
1955	66 years, 2 months
1956	66 years, 4 months
1957	66 years, 6 months
1958	66 years, 8 months
1959	66 years, 10 months
1960 or later	67

Amount of Benefits

The amount of monthly cash benefits paid by Social Security is based principally upon the following factors:

the benefit values used in preparing Table 11.3. While these examples may not be typical of persons covered by Social Security, they do show that it is only by sheer coincidence that a worker receives benefits that are equivalent to the taxes that he or she pays. This statement is true whether we consider employee taxes only, employee and employer taxes combined, or taxes of the self-employed.

It should be noted that the calculations shown in Table 11.3 are strictly theoretical, and it cannot be assumed that an individual or a group of individuals with the characteristics indicated in Table 11.3 can duplicate Social Security benefits by means of private savings and insurance for the costs that

Table 11.3

Theoretical Tax Rate Payable by Workers and Employers, Each, If Taxes Are to Be Equivalent to Benefits for Selected Workers Entering the Work Force[a] in 1990

Brief Description of Worker[b]	Tax Rate Payable by Worker (with Matching Rate Payable by Employer)
Unmarried male who enters work force at age 21, works in steady employment at the maximum taxable earnings under Social Security, remains single, retires at age 70	4%
Unmarried female who enters work force at age 21, works in steady employment at the average earnings level for all workers covered by Social Security, remains single, retires at age 67	7%
Married male with dependent wife and two children, who enters work force at age 21, works in steady employment at about the federal minimum wage, retires at age 67	16%
Married male with dependent wife who enters work force at age 55, works in steady part-time employment at high salary (that produces about the same annual income as full-time employment at the federal minimum wage), retires at age 65	29%

[a] In employment covered by Social Security.

[b] Retirement age shown in each example represents age at which worker is assumed to retire if he or she has not died or become disabled prior to that age.

a divorced spouse aged 60 or older (50 or older, if completely disabled), if the marriage lasted at least ten years; or

dependent parents aged 62 or older.

The amount of the benefits and the conditions for payment are based upon a seemingly endless set of conditions. These conditions are discussed briefly here and in more detail in Chapter 3. Eligibility for some death benefits requires that

Table 17.2

Ratio of Initial Social Security Survivors Benefits to Deceased Worker's Average Earnings Prior to Death for Illustrative Surviving Families

Earnings Level of Worker[b]	Replacement Ratio[a] Where Worker's Death Occurred at...	
	Age 25	Age 50
(1)	(2)	(3)
	Surviving Spouse and Two or More Children	
Low	92%	91%
Average	83	82
Maximum	54	47
Twice Maximum	27	24
	Surviving Spouse and One Child (or Two Surviving Children)	
Low	92%	91%
Average	69	67
Maximum	46	40
Twice Maximum	23	20
	One Surviving Child	
Low	46%	45%
Average	34	34
Maximum	23	20
Twice Maximum	12	10

[a] Replacement ratio equals the survivors benefits payable in the first year divided by the deceased worker's average earnings in the last three full years prior to death. In each example the worker is assumed to have died in January 1990.

[b] "Low" and "average" denote earnings in each year equal to 45 percent and 100 percent, respectively, of the average wage for all employees. "Maximum" and "Twice Maximum" refer to the level of the maximum contribution and benefit base under Social Security.

marry (except if you marry another disabled child aged 18 or over who is receiving child's benefits, or if you marry a person entitled to old-age, widow's, widower's, mother's, father's, parent's, disability, or divorced spouse's benefits).

These comments about whether and whom to marry, taking into account the Social Security benefits that may be gained or lost, may appear to be somewhat overdrawn. There is, perhaps, an element of satire in the exposition in the sense it is "used for the purpose of exposing folly." Consider, however, Chart 18.A, which is a copy of page 303 of the following government publication: *Social Security Handbook 1988*, U.S. Department of Health and Human Services, Social Security Administration, SSA Publication No. OS-10135, October 1988.

Whether (or When) to Divorce

A divorce at any time will result in a potential loss of future benefits. A divorce *prior* to ten years of marriage can result in the *total loss* of benefits a person may have become eligible to receive based on the other person's coverage by Social Security. A divorce *after* ten years of marriage will result in a *partial loss* of such benefits. From the standpoint of receiving Social Security benefits, it is obviously preferable to divorce after ten years and one month of marriage rather than after nine years and eleven months. The difference in a few days could amount to a loss of more than one hundred thousand dollars.

Consider, for example, a recently divorced wife, aged 30, with one child aged one month, whose former husband died in January 1990 leaving her with maximum Social Security benefits. The actuarial value of these benefits at the time of the former husband's death would be:

Divorced Mother's benefits	$ 142,000
Divorced Widow's benefits	137,000
Child's benefits	156,000
Total	$ 435,000

The actual dollar amount payable over the years would be more than six times these amounts.

The Projected Cost of Medicare

Previous chapters present the projected cost of Medicare, sometimes alone but usually as an inherent part of the total Social Security program. This chapter shows Medicare costs alone, separately for the HI and SMI segments.

Hospital Insurance

Chart 21.A and Table 21.1 illustrate the range of projected expenditures for the HI program under the optimistic, pessimistic, and intermediate "II-B" sets of alternative assumptions used in the 1990 Trustees Reports. The expenditures

Chart 21.A

Projected Expenditures for Hospital Insurance Program under Alternative Demographic and Economic Assumptions,[a] and Tax Income, Expressed as a Percentage of Taxable Payroll[b]

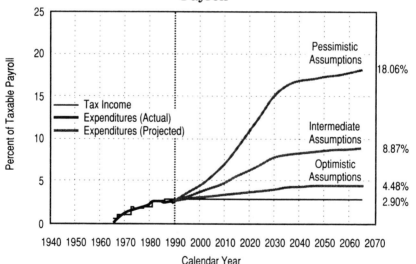

[a] See Chapter 10 and Appendix I for discussion of alternative sets of assumptions.

[b] "Taxable payroll" consists of the total earnings subject to Social Security taxes, after adjustments in applicable years to reflect (i) deemed wages based on military service, and (ii) the lower tax rates on self-employment income, tips, and multiple-employer "excess wages." This adjustment is made to facilitate both the calculation of tax income (which is thereby the product of the tax rate and the payroll) and the comparison of expenditure percentages with tax rates.

Chart 21.C

**National Medical Care Expenditures in Calendar Year 1987
by Source of Payment**

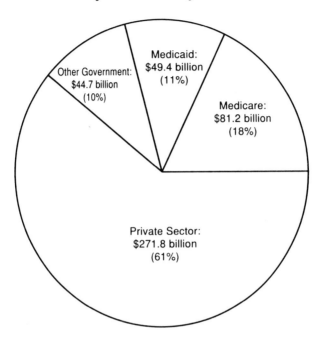

according to some studies—is attributable to qualitative and technological improvements; but it is nonetheless an increase in costs.

Medicare Costs Relative to Total National Medical Care Expenditures

Many of the factors that have increased the total cost of Medicare over the years have also increased the cost of other national health care expenditures: that is, primarily for the population that is less than 65. Total national expenditures for health care have increased from 6 percent of the Gross National Product in 1965—when Medicare was adopted—to 12 percent in 1989. This cost is expected to rise to between 15 and 18 percent of the Gross National Product by the year 2000 and to 30 percent or more by the year 2030 when all the

To Help Increase Understanding of Social Security

Social Security: What Every Taxpayer Should Know is for everyone concerned about the role that Social Security will play in their own future financial security, as well as the financial security of the nation.

If this book has given you facts and perspectives that help you understand Social Security better and thus enables you to take a more informed position in the ongoing public debate about the future of the system, perhaps you would consider giving copies to your friends and neighbors. People tend to pay more attention to a book if someone they know recommends it or gives it to them. One thing seems certain: more widespread understanding of Social Security is essential if we are to have a system that is considered to be fair and reasonable by the majority of our citizens.

Additional copies of this hardcover edition of *Social Security: What Every Taxpayer Should Know* are available at the following prices:

Single copy	$ 40.00	5 to 9 copies	$ 30.00
2 to 4 copies	35.00	10 to 24 copies	25.00
	25 or more copies	$ 20.00	

FREE shipping for orders pre-paid by check or credit card.

Mail order form to:
RPI Publications • P.O. Box 240242 • Charlotte, NC 28224

Please send me _____ copies of *Social Security: What Every Taxpayer Should Know* for a total of $ _____ .

I understand I may return books within 15 days for a full refund if not satisfied.

[ ] Check enclosed   [ ] Visa   [ ] MasterCard

Card#_____ Exp. Date_____

Signed_____

Name _____

Address _____

_____

City _____ State _____ Zip _____

SOCIAL SECURITY
What Every Taxpayer
Should Know

A selection of other works by A. Haeworth Robertson

The Cost of Social Security: 1975-2050 (1975)

OASDI: Fiscal Basis and Long-Range Cost Projections (1976)

The Outlook for Social Security: 1977-2051 (1977)

Social Security—Prospect for Change (1978)

The Challenge in Long-Range Pension Commitments (1979)

A Commentary on the 1979 Advisory Council Report on Social
Security (1980)

The Coming Revolution in Social Security (1981)

The Underlying Problems of Social Security (1982)

The National Commission's Failure to Achieve Real Reform in
Social Security (1983)

Social Security's Bleak Future (1984)

Is the Current Social Security Program Financially Feasible in
the Long Run? (1985)

The Crisis in the U.S. Medicare System (1986)

What Is in the Future for Public Retirement Systems? (1987)

Financing the U.S. Military Retirement System (1988)

1989 Trustees Report on Social Security's Financial Health:
Good News for the Elderly, Bad News for the Young (1989)

SOCIAL SECURITY
What Every Taxpayer Should Know

A. Haeworth Robertson

Retirement Policy Institute
Washington, DC

For further information and to place purchase orders please address:

Retirement Policy Institute—Publications Division
P. O. Box 240242
Charlotte, NC 28224

This publication is designed to provide accurate and authoritative information in regard to the subject matter covered. It is sold with the understanding that the publisher is not engaged in rendering legal, accounting, or other professional service. If legal advice or other expert assistance is required, the services of a competent professional person should be sought.

From a Declaration of Principles jointly adopted by a Committee of the American Bar Association and a Committee of Publishers and Associations.

In this book, the masculine pronoun "he" has occasionally been used to refer to both sexes for the sake of simplicity.

Manufactured in the United States of America

Printed by Science Press, Ephrata, Pennsylvania

First Printing: May 1992

Cataloging in Publication Data

Robertson, A. Haeworth. 1930–
    Social security: what every taxpayer should know.
    xxvi, 326 p. : ill. ; 23 cm.
    Includes bibliographical references and index.
    1. Social security—United States. 2. Social security—United States—Finance. 3. Medicare. I. Title.
HD7125.R62   1992   368.4'3'00973   92-80166
                                              AACR2

ISBN 0–9632345–4–4

This edition is dedicated to the actuaries of the Social Security Administration and the Health Care Financing Administration who endeavor tirelessly to provide the financial information needed to ensure that Americans will be able to keep the financial promises that one generation imposes upon another.

Contents

CONTENTS

PART THREE
COMMENTARY ON SELECTED TOPICS

CONTENTS

List of Charts

List of Tables

xv

Preface

In 1975, only six months after becoming Chief Actuary of the United States Social Security Administration, I concluded that the most important problem confronting Social Security in the immediate future was the widespread lack of understanding of the program—its basic rationale, the type and level of benefits it provides, the method of financing, the significance of its high future cost, and the tenuous relationship between taxes paid and benefits received by an individual. For the most part, people's ideas about Social Security were wrong. It was natural, therefore, that the program could not satisfy their expectations. Furthermore, it was evident that as taxes continued their inexorable rise this frustration and disenchantment would get worse and not better.

Immediately I began trying to clarify those issues by talking with anyone who would listen to me—inside or outside the government. People were thirsting for knowledge about Social Security, yet there was no single source of written information concerning the many questions being asked. As time went by and I developed simplified answers to these never-ending questions, I decided the most effective way to communicate with a broad audience would be to write a book on the subject—a book that could be read and understood by nontechnicians. Accordingly, I wrote *The Coming Revolution in Social Security* (Reston 1981).

Following the Social Security Amendments of 1983, questions about Social Security abated for a while. But recently, public interest in Social Security has increased as Social

Security taxes have continued to rise and as the economic reality of the accumulating Trust Funds has been increasingly questioned. Baby boomers, in particular, are asking more questions as they approach their 60s—an era that begins only fourteen years from now.

This book is an attempt to answer the many new questions I have heard asked about Social Security, as well as the older questions that are still being asked but not always answered correctly. The book is a revised and updated version of my earlier book except that it excludes the portions of that earlier book, particularly Part IV, that called for significant revisions in Social Security. The purpose of this present book, therefore, is merely to provide a ready source of information, as well as some uncommon perspectives, on what Social Security is and how it works. Any calls for specific reforms can more appropriately be made elsewhere once the basics of the present system are more widely understood.

Many people encouraged and assisted me. I wish to acknowledge the cooperation of the actuarial staff of the Social Security Administration, headed by Chief Actuary Harry C. Ballantyne and Deputy Chief Actuaries Richard S. Foster and Francisco R. Bayo, and the actuarial staff of the Health Care Financing Administration, headed by Roland E. King, Chief Actuary. The actuarial work performed by these staffs is crucial to ensure that we are able to honor our commitments to future generations.

Although it is not practical to acknowledge everyone who helped me with this particular work as well as with prior endeavors that made this book possible, I would mention a few individuals who were of particular assistance: Maynard I. Kagen, Chief Actuary, Railroad Retirement Board; Richard G. Schreitmueller, Senior Research Actuary, Alexander & Alexander Consulting Group, Inc.; Carolyn L. Weaver, Director—Social Security and Pension Project, American Enterprise Institute for Public Policy Research; Sandra Costich, who provided valuable editorial assistance; and Barbara L. Wilmoth, who painstakingly typed the manuscript. Mary K. Robertson, my daughter, provided the important talent needed to coordinate and produce an accurate and consistent manuscript. The views expressed herein are strictly mine, of course, and not necessarily those of anyone who helped me.

It is unfortunate that the public perception of Social Security has been allowed to grow so far apart from the reality. This has created a serious dilemma for Social Security. If public misunderstanding is allowed to persist, confusion and disappointment will worsen because Social Security will continue its failure to match most of the public's expectations; and this could result in a frenzied cry for change. On the other hand, if the misunderstanding is eliminated, it is possible that the public will not be content with what it sees and thus will demand significant revision.

This book is dedicated to the premise that any change in the Social Security system during the years ahead should arise from a clearheaded understanding and appraisal of our existing system and not from our present state of bewilderment. This should permit Social Security to evolve over time, with minimal disruption, as it adjusts to the inevitable changes in our future social and economic environment.

Washington, DC   A. Haeworth Robertson
December 1991

Basis for Social Security Benefit Provisions and Financial Projections

The Social Security benefit provisions contained in this book are those in effect on January 1, 1990. These benefit provisions form the basis for the 1990 Annual Reports of the Boards of Trustees of the Old-Age and Survivors Insurance, Disability Insurance, Hospital Insurance, and Supplementary Medical Insurance Trust Funds, submitted to the Congress on April 18, 1990. Accordingly, the benefit provisions and the projections of future financial operations of the Social Security program do not include the effects of Public Law 101-508, the Omnibus Budget Reconciliation Act of 1990, which was enacted in November 1990. Appendix II presents a summary of the provisions of this legislation that might affect statements contained in this book.

For the OASDI program, the effects of this legislation are relatively minor. For HI and SMI (parts A and B of the Medicare program) the effects are more significant. In particular, the maximum amount of earnings on which HI taxes must be paid was increased by this legislation from $53,400 to $125,000 effective in January 1991. Despite these changes, the discussion in this book of the financial status of the HI program is still valid. Projected costs will far outstrip projected income, beginning in the near future, and major changes will be required to close this gap. The reader is referred to the most recent Trustees Reports, usually issued in April of each year, for the then-current benefit provisions and the latest specific income and expenditure projections for the Social Security program.

SOCIAL SECURITY
What Every Taxpayer
Should Know

Part One
Introduction

"What you don't know won't hurt you" may be an appropriate maxim in many situations, but Social Security is not one of them. There is widespread misunderstanding about Social Security, an institution having a pervasive effect on our lives and the lives of our children. Part One raises questions to heighten the awareness of the need to learn more about Social Security.

1
The Need to Know

Imagine, for the moment, that you live in a small community in the United States—a town or village, or a particular area of a larger city. Most of the people in the community work and support themselves in a variety of jobs. A few are retired, others are in school, some are unemployed from time to time. A few are rich, some are poor, and most are somewhere in between.

What if your family doctor, who was aged 62 and still in good health, came around one day and announced that he was tired of working; he wanted you and the rest of the townspeople to take up a collection and pay him a monthly pension so he could spend full time fishing and hunting. It is doubtful that you and the other citizens of the community would feel any obligation to honor this request. Would it be any different if it were the butcher or the baker? Probably not, if they were in good health and capable of working.

What if the cashier at the bank died suddenly, leaving behind a wife and two young children? Would the community have an obligation to support the survivors? Would it matter if the local life insurance agent had tried in vain to get the cashier to use part of his earnings to buy life insurance to protect his family, and the cashier had said, "Let them fend for themselves after I'm gone; I'd rather spend my money for a new motorcycle."?

What if a young fireman became totally and permanently disabled while fighting a fire that threatened to destroy the

3

town? What if the town librarian reached age 70, was unable to work any longer, and had lost all his or her savings in a stock market recession? Would the community have an obligation to support these individuals? If so, what level of support should be provided?

Questions such as these deserve careful thought, and they are not easy to answer. This is where the institution of Social Security comes to the rescue. Social Security boldly answers all these questions and many more. In thousands of pages of laws, regulations, and guidelines, Social Security defines the circumstances in which benefits will be paid, the amount of the benefits, and who will pay the taxes required to provide the benefits. It does all this on an impersonal basis not only for people in your community but also for people throughout the land. It is so impersonal, in fact, that we sometimes forget who pays for the benefits.

The Meaning of Government Sponsorship

Many of us have fallen into a bad habit of referring to "government sponsored" programs, "governmental responsibility," and having the "government pay" for things. Sometimes we behave as if the "government" not only *should* be ready to help us in time of financial need, but that the "government" *owes* us something—a retirement benefit, support for our dependents if we die, and so forth. When something in our lives goes wrong, the first place many people look for help is to the government.

Who is this "government" we keep looking to for help? Where does it get its money? We all know the answer: the government is simply a system we have established and a group of people we have hired or elected to carry out our wishes. Bureaucrats and politicians do not have any money to give us except what we ourselves have paid in taxes. When we demand a benefit from the government, we are demanding it from our friends and neighbors.

There is a basic truth of economics that people frequently overlook and that some people never even knew existed: Before the government can give one dollar to anyone, it must confiscate that dollar from some other person who has earned it. And to earn a dollar a person must produce something.

If the government sets up a program to give someone food stamps worth $100, the government must do two things:

> Find someone who is willing and able to perform work for which he or she will earn $100; and

> Convince this working person that he or she should give the government (by paying taxes) this $100 (plus governmental administrative expenses).

This reasoning is equally true whether we are considering food stamps, or disability benefits, or retirement benefits, or any other "income transfer" program the government uses to redistribute the production of America's workers.

It cannot be emphasized strongly enough that casual references to "governmental responsibility" or having the "government pay" for all or part of Social Security are extremely misleading. Stripped to its essentials, a governmental program like Social Security is just an agreement among the people of the nation that one segment of the population will receive certain benefits and that another segment of the population will pay for such benefits (with a certain amount of overlapping). The government may administer and enforce compliance with a program but, in the final analysis, any governmental program is paid for by and is for the benefit of the people of the nation. The government is simply the intermediary that carries out the wishes of the people.

The Need to Know

As we begin to think of Social Security as a program of benefits supported by taxpayers in order to meet the needs of our neighbors when they are in economic distress, it becomes obvious that we should take more of a personal interest in the program. Particularly in a democratic society where we have the power to influence the design of programs that our taxes support, it is incumbent on us to know a lot more about the institution of Social Security than we do.

Most of us do not understand what Social Security is all about. The general purposes of Social Security, the types and levels of benefits it provides, how it is financed, the relation between an individual's taxes and benefits—all of these areas are sources of confusion or uncertainty to many people.

Most of us do not realize how large Social Security has become or how rapidly it will grow in the future. In 1940 the Social Security program paid out less than $1 billion in benefits and administrative expenses; in 1989 it paid out $337 billion; in 2000 it will pay out an estimated $777 billion. During the next ten years, 1991 through 2000, it is estimated that about $5,665 billion will be paid out in benefits and administrative expenses.[1] In December 1989 Social Security monthly cash benefits were paid to some 40 million persons, one out of every seven Americans.

But what Social Security pays out in benefits it must first collect in taxes.

In 1989, 136 million workers paid about $180 billion in Social Security taxes, an average of roughly $1,340 per person. Ten years ago (1980) the average Social Security tax paid by each taxpayer was about $640; ten years from now (2000) it is estimated that it will be $2,370.[2]

In addition to these taxes paid directly by individuals, an approximately equal amount was paid by their employers.[3] Total income to the Social Security program in 1989, most of it from taxes of one kind or another, was some $411 billion ($410,502,562,779.04 to be precise). For three-fourths of working families, Social Security taxes (including the amount paid by their employers) now exceed personal income taxes.

Some Questions

What do we get for our money? What do you know about your own Social Security benefits? How much, if anything will you receive if today you become disabled and are unable to work any longer? Can you work part time and still collect disability benefits? Are your benefits higher if you are married? And have children? If Social Security benefits are not adequate to support you and your family, and if you or your spouse goes to work to supplement your income, will any of these benefits be forfeited?

If you die tomorrow will any benefits be paid to your spouse, children, parents? If so, how much? How long will the benefits be paid? Will this be enough to support your family? Will your spouse be able to work without forfeiting these benefits? Should you buy life insurance to supplement your Social Security benefits? If so, how much should you buy?

If you stay in good health and work until age 65, will you be eligible for a retirement benefit from Social Security? If so, how much will it be? Are there any strings attached to its payment? Can you continue working after age 65 and still receive your Social Security benefits? Can you collect the benefits if you move to another country when you retire? Will these benefits be enough to support you and your family? Should you have your own private savings program in order to supplement your Social Security benefits?

How much will you personally pay in Social Security taxes this year? Did you know that your employer will also pay this same amount? To get an idea of how much you and your employer pay in Social Security taxes, examine the following table which shows the amount of such taxes payable in 1990 for employees with different levels of pay. A person who is self-employed is considered to be his own employer and thus pays both the employee and employer taxes.[3]

| | Social Security Taxes | | |
Earnings in 1990	Paid by Employee	Paid by Employer	Total
$10,000	$ 765.00	$ 765.00	$1,530.00
$20,000	$1,530.00	$1,530.00	$3,060.00
$30,000	$2,295.00	$2,295.00	$4,590.00
$40,000	$3,060.00	$3,060.00	$6,120.00
$51,300 or more	$3,924.45	$3,924.45	$7,848.90

The maximum tax paid by the employee and employer combined is estimated by the Social Security Administration to rise from $7,848.90 in 1990 to $13,265 by the year 2000. This increase is due to a projected increase in the maximum amount of earnings subject to tax (an estimated $86,700 in 2000).

Do you spend this much money for anything else and know so little about what you get for your money? Whose fault is it that you do not know more about your Social Security benefits? Did you know that there are millions of people in the United States who do not participate in Social Security and thus do not pay its taxes and receive its benefits?

Is Social Security going bankrupt? Will there be enough money to pay your benefits when you retire? In 1950 the Social Security Trust Funds had enough money to pay benefits for twelve years (at the rate benefits were being paid in 1950); in 1960 there was enough money to pay benefits for about two years; at the beginning of 1990 there was enough money to pay benefits for only about ten months. What happened to all the money you and your employers paid into the Social Security Trust Funds?

On the other hand, many statements are currently made about how the Social Security trust funds will accumulate a total of $12 *trillion* over the next forty years to be used to help pay for the cost of retirement benefits to the "baby boom" generation. Is this true? If it is true, how will the money be used in the meantime?

If you don't know the answers to any or all of these questions, don't feel left out. Not many people know the answers. Social Security is one of the least understood, perhaps I should say most misunderstood, programs around.

The Problem

Social Security has been roundly criticized in recent years. Complaints are heard about its financial condition and whether it is overfinanced or underfinanced, the inadequacy of its benefits, the generosity of its benefits, the fact that some persons receive more in benefits than they pay in taxes, the fact that some people receive less in benefits than they pay in taxes, and so on. Although some of these criticisms are valid, many are not. And none of them poses a real threat to Social Security at this time.

The most serious threat to Social Security in the immediate future is the widespread misunderstanding of the program. Why is this misunderstanding a threat? Because the very survival of Social Security depends upon our continued ability and willingness to pay the taxes necessary to support the benefit payments. It is not reasonable to expect this support to continue if we do not understand and approve of the Social Security program.

The Social Security program is not what most people think it is. It is not what many critics, as well as many supporters, think it is. Because of this, it does not always behave the way we think it should. Therefore, it is natural for some to resent the program, the Congressmen who adopted it, the Social Security Administration and the Health Care Financing Administration which administer it, and most of all the tax collectors who take our hard-earned money and use it in ways that are different from the ways we thought it would be used.

The Social Security program does not have a chance of being successful in the future unless we understand it. Once we know what the program is and we decide what we believe our income security needs are, we can compare what we have with what we want. If they are the same, then we can be grateful to our leaders who designed Social Security over the years and be content. If they are different, we can set about to change the program to better suit our needs. Until then— until we really understand what the present Social Security program is—all discussions of the program will be chaotic and most of the proposed changes will be nonsensical.

The Solution—The First Step

Part Two of this book presents basic background information on Social Security and has one purpose: to help you understand the Social Security program in its present form. This is the first step toward accepting the program as it is or revising the program to make it what you want it to be.

In our complicated and technical society, there are undoubtedly issues that can be fully understood and evaluated only by a small group of informed experts. In these cases, the public must place substantial trust in its leaders.

For example, how is an average person to know for certain how much money should be spent for defense in order for America to remain a free and independent nation? What is the real threat to our freedom from other countries with different ideologies, food shortages, land shortages, or demagogic leaders? As we have seen from recent world events, these answers change as the international social, economic, and political environment changes.

How is an average person to know what our national energy policy should be if we are to avoid crippling shortages in the future? Should we have gasoline rationing, higher gasoline taxes, restrictions on oil imports, improved public transportation facilities, smaller cars, increased nuclear and solar energy capabilities, or should we take some other action?

What about the current debate over environmentalism? How do we balance the trade-off between continued industrial growth and a less healthful environment? How much is our increasingly crowded and polluted environment threatening our physical, emotional, and spiritual health?

In all these and many other areas we must rely heavily upon experts, people who study these matters full-time. But we ourselves should also be as fully informed as possible. We must not leave important decisions exclusively to the experts or to the politicians who act, sometimes solely, on their advice. This would seem obvious from revelations over the years concerning activities by the government and its various agencies where decisions were made by individuals and select groups of experts who did not think they were accountable to the public and who did not think the public knew what was best for it.

But what about the Social Security program? Is it so difficult a subject that only the experts can understand it? Is it so complex that we have no choice but to leave it to the experts and politicians to decide what is best for us without our being told the facts? I don't think so. Certainly, Social Security is complicated. Despite its complexity, it is possible to explain the program so that it can be understood.

This book is written for people who pay for and benefit from the Social Security program—people who want to understand how their Social Security program works. My sincere hope is that this book will help you gain the understanding of our Social Security program necessary to ensure that the Congress and the administration continue to revise the program from time to time so that it will meet our needs in a logical way and in accordance with our ability to pay for it.

Part Two
Basic Background
Information

For most of us, our knowledge of Social Security is based upon a hodgepodge of information we have gathered from radio, television, newspapers, magazines, employers, and friends. This is a difficult way to learn, especially when many of the fragments of information are misleading or even incorrect. It is no wonder that myths and misinformation abound.

Part Two is designed for the reader willing to discard all past information and misinformation received about Social Security and start with a clean slate. Chapters 2 through 7 present systematically the basic background information necessary to understand what Social Security is, how it works, and what it costs.

2
Social Security—
An Overview

Congress passed the Social Security Act in 1935 and it became effective on January 1, 1937. The original legislation has been amended many times since then and has become a complex maze of laws, rules, and regulations governing and influencing the lives of all Americans in one way or another. Some of these influences are obvious; others are not. Some of these influences are favorable; others may or may not be, depending upon your viewpoint. This chapter gives a brief overview of some but not all of the many aspects of Social Security.

What Is Social Security?

Mention Social Security to a dozen people and they will conjure up a dozen different ideas—and for good reason. The *Social Security Handbook*[1] published by the government contains 440 pages of explanation of the Social Security Act and then refers the reader to thousands of additional pages of explanation contained in other volumes. In describing Social Security, this handbook makes a general statement[2] which may be paraphrased fairly as follows:

> The Social Security Act and related laws establish a number of programs that have the basic objectives

13

of providing for the material needs of individuals and families, protecting aged and disabled persons against the expenses of illnesses that could otherwise exhaust their savings, keeping families together, and giving children the opportunity to grow up in health and security. These programs include:

Retirement Insurance (frequently referred to as
    Old-Age Insurance)
Survivors Insurance
Disability Insurance
Medicare for the aged and the disabled:
    Hospital Insurance
    Supplementary Medical Insurance
Black Lung Benefits
Supplemental Security Income
Unemployment Insurance
Public Assistance and Welfare Services:
    Aid to needy families with children
    Medical assistance
    Maternal and child-health services
    Child support enforcement
    Family and child welfare services
    Food stamps
    Energy assistance

The federal government operates the first six programs listed above. The remaining programs are operated by the states with the federal government cooperating and contributing funds.

This book limits itself to a discussion of the first four programs listed above and refers to them collectively as Social Security. This is partly for simplicity but largely because these four programs are financed primarily by the Social Security payroll taxes paid by employees, employers, and self-employed persons, and thus are usually thought of by the public as Social Security.[3] (The Supplementary Medical Insurance program, "Part B" of Medicare, is financed not by payroll taxes but rather by premiums paid by those electing to be covered and by general revenue.)

Who Participates in Social Security?

Who is covered by Social Security and is therefore eligible for Old-Age, Survivors, Disability, and Medicare benefits?

When Social Security took effect in 1937 it applied only to workers in industry and commerce and covered only about 60 percent of all working persons. Since then there has been a steady movement toward covering as many workers as possible under Social Security, and universal coverage has clearly been the ultimate goal. In the 1950s, coverage was extended to include most self-employed persons, most state and local government employees, household and farm employees, members of the armed forces, and members of the clergy. In 1983, coverage was further extended to include all federal employees hired after 1983; all employees of nonprofit charitable, educational, and religious organizations; members of Congress, judges, political appointees in the Executive Branch, and congressional employees not covered by the Civil Service Retirement System; and miscellaneous small groups of employees not formerly covered. Approximately 94 percent of all jobs in the United States are now covered by Social Security. This growth in coverage over the years is illustrated in Chart 2.A.[4]

Chart 2.A
Workers in Covered and Noncovered Employment, 1940 and 1989

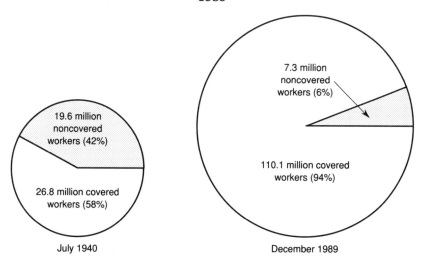

19.6 million noncovered workers (42%)

26.8 million covered workers (58%)

July 1940

7.3 million noncovered workers (6%)

110.1 million covered workers (94%)

December 1989

The principal groups that are not now covered automatically by Social Security are as follows:

    Civilian employees of the federal government hired prior to 1984

    Employees of state and local governments (although approximately 72 percent of such employees are covered on a voluntary basis)

    Farm and domestic workers with irregular employment

    Low-income, self-employed persons

Chart 2.B illustrates the number of persons in these categories whose jobs are not covered by Social Security.[5] A few words of background on some of these employee groups may help explain the rationale for their not being covered automatically by Social Security.

Federal Government Employees

In 1920 the Civil Service Retirement System was established to provide retirement and other benefits to civilian

Chart 2.B

**Principal Groups Not Covered by Social Security
as of December 1989 (estimates in thousands)**

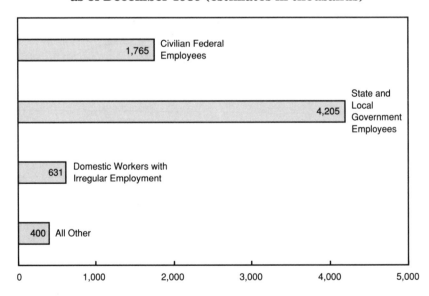

employees of the federal government. It was not particularly unusual, therefore, when Social Security began operation on January 1, 1937, that federal government employees were excluded from it. On the other hand, it would have been logical to include federal government employees in Social Security and to adjust the benefits under the Civil Service Retirement System accordingly. This is what most private employers did and still do; that is, they coordinate, or integrate, their private benefit systems with Social Security so that the two systems taken together provide the desired benefits.

Effective January 1, 1983, Social Security was amended to require all federal government employees to participate in the Hospital Insurance (HI) program; that is, to pay the HI portion of the Social Security taxes and thus become eligible for HI benefits. In 1983, a further amendment required all federal government employees hired after 1983 to participate in the Old-Age, Survivors, and Disability Insurance portions of Social Security. A revised system of civil service retirement benefits was designed for such employees to reflect their full participation in Social Security. Employees hired prior to 1984 were given the option of switching to the revised Civil Service Retirement System and participating in Social Security, but only about 4 percent of such employees made this election. With these changes, of course, all federal government employees will eventually participate fully in Social Security.

State and Local Government Employees

When Social Security was enacted in 1935 it was considered unconstitutional for the federal government to tax state governments. And since Social Security is financed from taxes paid by employees and employers, state and local government employees were not included.

In keeping with the steady movement to make Social Security coverage as universal as possible, legislation was enacted in 1950 and later to provide that employees of state and local governments could be covered under Social Security on a voluntary basis under certain conditions. For example,

Social Security coverage was made available on a group voluntary basis through agreements between the Secretary of Health and Human Services (formerly Health, Education, and Welfare) and the individual states.

Originally, state and local government employee groups that elected to participate in Social Security could change their mind—after meeting certain conditions—and terminate their coverage. But once such a termination became effective, it was irrevocable and the same group could not be covered again under Social Security.

In 1983, Social Security legislation changed this optional participation in two important respects. State and local government employee groups that had previously elected to participate in Social Security are no longer permitted to terminate their participation. And state and local government employee groups that had elected to participate but had subsequently terminated were given the right to again elect coverage.

Effective April 1, 1986, Social Security was amended to require all newly hired employees of state and local governments to participate in the Hospital Insurance program if they were not already covered by the full Social Security program. For state and local government employees in service on March 31, 1986, who were not covered by Social Security, participation in the Hospital Insurance segment of Social Security was made an option, subject to election by the government entity.

Approximately 11 million state and local employees, about 72 percent of the total, are covered by Social Security under voluntary participation arrangements. Compared with these 11 million participants, the number of employees who have voluntarily terminated is very small. A total of about 130,000 employees had terminated during the program's entire history through 1983.

As of mid-1990, state government employees in several states had never become covered by Social Security: Colorado, Maine, Massachusetts, Nevada, and Ohio. Three of these states—Colorado, Maine, and Nevada—include teachers in their general state retirement systems; hence their teachers are not covered by Social Security. In nine states with statewide teachers' retirement systems, teachers are not covered by Social Security: Alaska, California (except San Francisco), Connecticut, Illinois, Kentucky, Louisiana, Massachusetts, Missouri (with certain exceptions), and Ohio.

The states that have not elected to enter Social Security maintain programs of retirement and other benefits for their employees that are more liberal than Social Security in some respects and less liberal in others. A strict comparison of benefits is difficult because of the basic differences between Social Security and most public employee systems. For various reasons, some states prefer to continue their own employee benefit programs and to remain outside of Social Security.

Alaska is the only state that elected to cover its employees under Social Security and then terminated such coverage. The Alaska termination became effective December 31, 1979, and affected approximately 14,500 employees.

Employees of Nonprofit Organizations

Nonprofit organizations were not required to participate in Social Security when it was enacted, because of their tax-exempt status. Imposition of the employer Social Security tax on the organization would have violated this tax-exempt status.

Legislation was enacted over the years to permit nonprofit organizations to be covered by Social Security on a voluntary basis and by 1983, when coverage became mandatory, approximately 90 percent of the 4 million employees of nonprofit organizations had elected to be covered by Social Security.

Increased Possibility of Universal Coverage

As already indicated, during the entire history of the Social Security program the trend has been toward broader coverage. Increasing attention has been given in recent years to the question of Social Security coverage—how widespread it is and how widespread it "should be." It is probably only a question of time before virtually the entire work force is covered by the Social Security program.

Chart 2.C

Old-Age, Survivors, and Disability Insurance Program
Beneficiaries as of December 31, 1989 and
Amount of Benefits in Fiscal Year 1989, by Type of Beneficiary

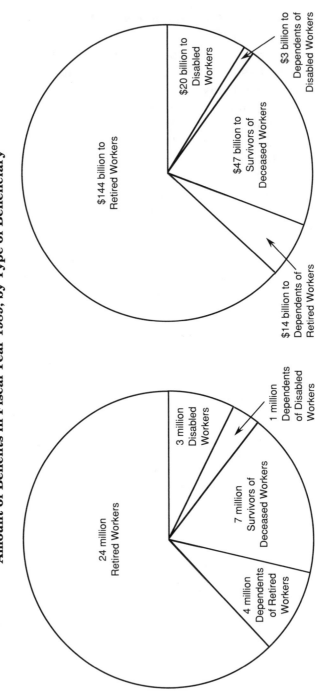

$20 billion to
Disabled
Workers

$3 billion to
Dependents of
Disabled Workers

$144 billion to
Retired Workers

$47 billion to
Survivors of
Deceased Workers

$14 billion to
Dependents of
Retired Workers

Amount of Benefits

3 million
Disabled
Workers

1 million
Dependents
of Disabled
Workers

24 million
Retired Workers

7 million
Survivors of
Deceased Workers

4 million
Dependents
of Retired
Workers

Beneficiaries

What Benefits Are Provided?

Because of the complexity of Social Security, this chapter will give only an overview of the benefits provided. More detail is included in Chapter 3. The idea at this point is to explain how Social Security works in general, not to enable you to determine the benefits you would receive in a particular case. If you need specific information concerning your own situation, it is normally best to contact your local Social Security Administration office.

In a nutshell: *Social Security replaces a portion of the earnings that are lost as a result of a person's old age, disability, or death, and pays a portion of the expenses resulting from the illness of aged and disabled persons.*

The benefits that are provided under the Old-Age, Survivors, and Disability Insurance programs (usually referred to as OASDI) are as follows:

> Monthly benefits for workers who are retired or partially retired and are at least 62 years old, and monthly benefits for their eligible spouses and children
>
> Monthly benefits for disabled workers and their eligible spouses and children
>
> Monthly benefits for the eligible survivors of deceased workers
>
> A nominal lump-sum death benefit payment for each worker who has a qualified survivor

To be eligible to receive these benefits at the time of retirement, disability, or death, a person must satisfy several conditions that are different for each type of benefit. In addition, a person's spouse and children or survivors must satisfy a variety of requirements to be eligible for benefits. These requirements, which are somewhat complex, are described in more detail in Chapter 3.

In mid-1990, approximately 40 million persons were receiving monthly Social Security benefit payments. That was more than one out of every seven persons since in mid-1990 there were approximately 259 million persons in the United States.[6] Total cash benefit payments in fiscal year 1989 amounted to $227 billion. Chart 2.C illustrates for 1989 the numbers of OASDI beneficiaries and the amount of their benefits in each of the various categories.

The Medicare program has two parts: Hospital Insurance (HI) and Supplementary Medical Insurance (SMI). The Hospital Insurance program, which is compulsory for those covered by Social Security, provides benefits for persons aged 65 or older and persons who have received Social Security disability benefits for more than twenty-four months. The program helps pay for inpatient hospital care and for certain follow-up care after leaving the hospital.

The Supplementary Medical Insurance program, which is voluntary, is offered to almost all persons aged 65 and over. In addition, the program is offered to all disabled Social Security beneficiaries who have received disability benefits for more than twenty-four months. The program helps pay for doctors' services, outpatient hospital services, and many other medical items and services not covered by the Hospital Insurance program.

During 1989, an average of 30 million persons aged 65 and over were covered under the Hospital Insurance program (that is, were eligible for hospital benefits in the event of illness). This represented about 95 percent of all persons aged 65 and over in the United States and its territories. Another 3 million disabled persons under age 65 were covered by Hospital Insurance.

Approximately 29 million persons aged 65 and over were covered under the Supplementary Medical Insurance program in 1989. Again, this represented about 95 percent of all persons aged 65 and over in the United States and its territories. Another 3 million disabled persons under age 65 were covered by Supplementary Medical Insurance.

It is estimated that Medicare benefit payments in 1987 on behalf of persons aged 65 and older covered approximately 45 percent of their total medical expenses.[7]

Who Pays for Social Security?

Social Security is financed primarily by "payroll taxes"— that is, by taxes based on the earnings of the active working population that participates in Social Security. These taxes, which are generally shared equally by employers[8] and their employees, currently account for about 83 percent of the total income to Social Security. General revenue, derived from taxpayers in general regardless of their participation in Social Security, accounts for another 9 percent of the income. Most of this general revenue is used to help finance the Supplementary Medical Insurance program. Premiums paid by individuals to obtain Supplementary Medical Insurance coverage account for about 3 percent of the total income to Social Security. The remaining 5 percent of income represents interest payments on Treasury securities held by the Social Security Trust Funds. Such interest payments are derived from general revenue, of course.

Who Administers Social Security?

Social Security is administered by the Social Security Administration and the Health Care Financing Administration. For fiscal year 1989, these agencies of the Department of Health and Human Services accounted for roughly 80 percent of the total expenditures of the Department. Of even more significance, they accounted for approximately 28 percent of total government expenditures.[9]

The Social Security Administration (SSA) administers the Old-Age, Survivors, and Disability Insurance program, along with several other programs not included in our present discussion of Social Security (the primary example being the Supplemental Security Income program). The determination of eligibility for disability benefits is handled by state agencies under contract to the Social Security Administration.

The Health Care Financing Administration (HCFA) administers the Medicare program, both Hospital Insurance and Supplementary Medical Insurance. It also oversees Medicaid, a program providing hospital and medical expense benefits for the needy—not considered part of Social Security in our present discussion. Prior to the formation of HCFA in March 1977, Medicare was administered by the Social Security Administration and Medicaid was administered by the Social and Rehabilitation Service.

Social Security taxes are collected for the Social Security Administration and the Health Care Financing Administration by the Internal Revenue Service. The Department of the Treasury issues the benefit checks, at the direction of the Managing Trustee of the Social Security Trust Funds, on the basis of benefit certifications by the Social Security Administration.

The Social Security Administration had 1,297 district and branch offices in operation around the country in 1989, facilities normally shared with the Health Care Financing Administration. Most administrative contact with the public is handled by these district and branch offices, which issue Social Security cards, process benefit claims, provide information about the program, and help resolve participants' problems. The local offices are supervised and assisted by ten regional offices. In addition, 37 "teleservice centers" around the country provide assistance to participants by telephone in order to give more prompt service and reduce the need for visits by the public to local offices.

The Social Security Administration's national headquarters, or central office as it is called, is located primarily in Baltimore, Maryland (with some offices in Washington, DC). The central office maintains the records of the millions of participants and oversees and directs the operation of the OASDI program and all its regional and local offices. The Health Care Financing Administration is also headquartered in Baltimore and Washington. To operate these offices and administer the Social Security program, these two agencies maintain (in 1990) a staff of some 65,000 full-time employees (down from about 80,000 ten years ago). This is not an unduly large administrative staff relative to the size and complexity of the program involved. Administrative expenses for the OASDI and Medicare programs combined were $4.7 billion in 1989, only 1.4 percent of total benefits paid during the year. With an appropriately increased budget, the Social Security Administration could provide better administrative service and do a more thorough job of explaining Social Security to the public, something that is certainly important at this critical time in the history of Social Security.

Conclusion

Any overview of Social Security reveals it to be almost overwhelming in size and complexity. Directly or indirectly,

Social Security touches the lives of virtually every resident of the U.S., and it can be startling to become more aware of its growing influence on our lives, individually and collectively as a nation. Social Security's significance to us and our children must not be underestimated.

3
Social Security Benefits

Social Security is simple in concept but complicated in actual operation. Essentially, Social Security replaces a portion of earned income that is lost as a result of a person's retirement, disability, or death; and it pays a portion of the hospital and medical expenses of aged and disabled persons. The complications arise in determining:

when a person is eligible to *begin* receiving benefits;

the amount of the benefits; and

when a person is no longer eligible to *continue* receiving benefits.

To explain all this in an efficient way requires that a few definitions and explanations be given at the start. This will also make the subsequent commentary on benefits easier to follow. You should probably not expect to learn how to calculate your exact benefits and the precise conditions under which they will be payable. The system, unfortunately, is just too complicated. On the other hand, you should understand Social Security well enough to know when you and your family members may be eligible for benefits and the approximate amounts of such benefits. This will enable you to obtain maximum advantage from Social Security and your tax dollar.

Eligibility for Benefits to Begin

Monthly benefits can be payable to a wide variety of persons, or beneficiaries as they are sometimes called. Benefits can be paid to you as a worker, as well as to your spouse, children, grandchildren, and parents. They can even be payable to a divorced spouse, a stepparent, a foster parent who adopted you before age 16, a stepchild, a legally adopted child, and an illegitimate child.

Various requirements must be met before benefits are payable to you or members of your family. An important underlying requirement for the payment of most benefits is that you have Social Security credit for certain minimum periods called "quarters of coverage." Normally, this credit is associated with the payment of Social Security taxes on "covered" wages, or earnings: that is, wages that are subject to Social Security taxation and that are used to determine benefits. During each year before 1978 a quarter of coverage was given for each calendar quarter in which you were paid at least $50 of wages for employment covered under the law. In 1978 one quarter of coverage was credited (up to a total of four) for each $250 of such wages. For each year after 1978 this $250 amount was increased automatically to reflect increases in average wages of the nation's workers. For 1990 the amount had risen to $520 and it will continue to rise in future years as average wages increase. For self-employed workers, quarters of coverage for 1978 and later are earned on the same basis as for employees. Prior to 1978, four quarters of coverage were earned for any year in which at least $400 of self-employment income was reported.

An individual has different levels of "insured status" depending upon the number of quarters of coverage that have been credited and the recency with which they have been earned. Different benefits require different levels of "insured status." There is a "currently insured" status, a "fully insured" status, and a "disability insured" status. All of this special terminology is the same as that used by the Social Security Administration.

Currently Insured Status

To be "currently insured" an individual must have at least six quarters of coverage in the thirteen-quarter period ending with the quarter in which death, disability, or entitlement to old-age benefits occurs. This level of insured status is easily maintained by a steady worker in employment covered by Social Security.

Fully Insured Status

To be "fully insured" an individual usually must have at least one quarter of coverage for each year after 1950 (or, if later, for each year after a person became 21) and before the year of death, disability, or reaching the age of 62, whichever occurs first. A minimum of six and a maximum of forty quarters of coverage is required. Once fully insured status for retirement benefits is acquired, it continues throughout life and no further work in covered employment is needed. The attainment of this permanent fully insured status relates only to *eligibility* for benefits and not to the *amount* of the benefits. The quarters of coverage do not have to be earned during the period used to define the required number of quarters. They can be earned also before or after that period.

Disability Insured Status

To be eligible for disability benefits, an individual must be both fully insured and:

> have earned at least twenty quarters of coverage during the forty-calendar-quarter period ending with the quarter in which disability begins; or

> if disability begins before age 31, have earned at least one-half the quarters of coverage possible during the period beginning with the quarter after reaching age 21 and ending with the quarter in which disability begins. (A minimum of six quarters of coverage earned during the preceding three years is required if disability begins before age 24.)

For an individual who meets the statutory definition of blindness, only the fully insured requirement need be met.

In addition to the insured status requirements, other conditions must be met before benefits will be payable to you or your dependents. These will be mentioned later when the various specific benefits are discussed.

Normal Retirement Age

When Social Security was adopted in 1935, the normal retirement age was set, rather arbitrarily, at age 65. If benefits commence prior to this age they are reduced; if benefits commence after this age they are increased.[1]

In 1983, Social Security was revised to provide a higher normal retirement age for persons born after 1937 and who, therefore, reach age 65 after the year 2002. An individual's normal retirement age now depends upon his year of birth, as shown in the following table. The normal retirement age applies not only to the primary beneficiary but also to a spouse who may be eligible for benefits. (The normal retirement age schedule is slightly different for widows.)

Year of Birth	Normal Retirement Age
1937 or earlier	65
1938	65 years, 2 months
1939	65 years, 4 months
1940	65 years, 6 months
1941	65 years, 8 months
1942	65 years, 10 months
1943–1954	66
1955	66 years, 2 months
1956	66 years, 4 months
1957	66 years, 6 months
1958	66 years, 8 months
1959	66 years, 10 months
1960 or later	67

Amount of Benefits

The amount of monthly cash benefits paid by Social Security is based principally upon the following factors:

Your average covered earnings, excluding earnings for certain years and adjusted for changes over the years in the average earnings of the nation's workers

The number and kind of your family members

Consumer Price Index changes that occur after you become eligible for benefits

Furthermore, the amount of monthly cash benefits may be reduced, or even completely withheld, as a result of earnings by you and your family members after becoming eligible for benefits.

Medicare benefits, on the other hand, are the same for everyone who is eligible for them and are not affected by average earning or earnings after becoming eligible for benefits.

For the time being, let us concentrate on the amount of monthly cash benefits initially payable to a given beneficiary, ignoring subsequent upward adjustments because of changes in the Consumer Price Index and downward adjustments because of an individual's earned income.

The key factor in determining monthly cash benefits initially payable is the Primary Insurance Amount (PIA). All monthly cash benefits are based upon the Primary Insurance Amount. The Primary Insurance Amount is the monthly benefit payable to a disabled worker or to a worker at his normal retirement age. For those who reach age 62, first become disabled, or die before age 62 in 1979 or later, the PIA is determined by a formula applied to the individual's Average Indexed Monthly Earnings.[2] Determination of the Average Indexed Monthly Earnings is somewhat complicated; it is computed for retirement and disability benefits approximately as follows:

Only earnings covered under Social Security are used. Thus, earnings in excess of the maximum taxable earnings in each year are not included. Table 6.2 in Chapter 6 lists the maximum taxable earnings for each year in the past. The amount has increased from $3,000 prior to 1951 to $51,300 in 1990, and will continue to increase in the future as average wages of the nation's workers increase.

Only earnings after 1950 are used.

Earnings are "indexed" by applying a ratio to the individual's earnings for each year. The ratio is the average wages of all the nation's employees in the second year before the year of the individual's eligibility for benefits, divided by the average wages of all the nation's employees in the year being indexed. For example, an individual with $3,600 of taxable earnings in 1951 who reached age 62 in 1990 would have these earnings indexed to become $24,865.51, thus adjusting the old earnings approximately to their equivalent value today.

The average of these indexed earnings is then computed using the highest 35 years of indexed earnings (a shorter averaging period is allowed for workers reaching age 62 prior to 1991).

This is a rather complicated process intended to produce average earnings that are representative of the value of today's dollar and today's earnings. It is important to note that average earnings are based on virtually an entire working career; accordingly, years of no earnings or low earnings can result in reduced average earnings and thus in reduced benefits. People sometimes erroneously assume that if they are *fully insured* they are eligible for *maximum benefits*.

When considering the amount of Social Security benefits payable, it is important to note that they are increased automatically to reflect increases in the Consumer Price Index. Generally speaking, benefit increases are made annually, beginning with the payment for December (which is received about January 3rd).

Also important is the fact that Social Security benefits are subject to relatively little income tax. Prior to 1984, benefits were not subject to *any* federal, state, or local income tax. Beginning in 1984, however, as much as 50 percent of an individual's Old-Age, Survivors, and Disability Insurance benefit can be subject to federal income tax and, in some cases, to state and local income tax. In 1989 roughly 15 percent of all beneficiaries paid at least some federal income tax on their Social Security benefits. This tax provision is a little complicated, but it may be summarized as follows:

If the sum of (1) income from earnings, pensions, dividends, interest, and other sources; (2) interest on tax-exempt bonds; and (3) 50 percent of Old-Age, Survivors, and Disability Insurance benefits exceeds the threshold amount ($25,000 for single persons and $32,000 for married persons filing a joint return), then 50 percent of the excess—but not more than 50 percent of the benefit—is included in the Adjusted Gross Income in computing the federal income tax liability.

Since these threshold amounts are not indexed for future years, an increasing proportion of Social Security benefits (reaching a maximum of 50 percent) will eventually be subject to tax unless the law is changed.

Eligibility for Benefits to Continue

Once benefits begin, their continuation hinges upon a variety of conditions being satisfied, depending upon the particular benefit. In every case benefits to an individual stop upon his or her death. A disability benefit normally terminates shortly after the disability ends (at normal retirement age it is converted to an old-age benefit). Benefits payable to children generally stop at age 18, but not if the child was disabled before age 22; children's benefits also generally stop if the child marries. Benefits to widows and widowers who are caring for young children terminate when the children reach 16 (unless they are disabled) or upon remarriage. Benefits payable to older widows and widowers (that is, persons over 60 or over 50 and disabled) do not cease upon remarriage.

Benefits usually stop or are reduced if the individual receiving the benefits has earnings in excess of specified amounts. This is because of the provision in the law usually referred to as the earnings test or earnings limitation. Only earned income can result in a loss of benefits; unearned income (such as investment income, rental income, pensions, and retirement pay) is not taken into account.[3] The amount of the earnings limitation is different for beneficiaries under age 65 than for those aged 65 or older. An individual aged 70 or older can have unlimited earned income and continue to receive full Social Security benefits.

An individual aged 65 to 69 can have an earned income of $9,360 in 1990 without affecting the receipt of Social Security benefits; however, benefits will be reduced by $1 for every $3 of earned income in excess of $9,360. This earnings limitation will increase each year in the future to keep up with increases in average earnings of all the nation's employees.

An individual who is under age 65 can have an earned income of $6,840 in 1990 without affecting the receipt of Social Security benefits. Benefits will be reduced by $1 for every $2 of earned income in excess of $6,840. This earnings limitation will increase each year to keep up with increases in average earnings of all the nation's employees.

In the case of a worker and dependents receiving Social Security benefits based on the earnings record of the worker, earnings of the worker in excess of the earnings limitation will reduce the benefits of both the worker and the dependents. On the other hand, earnings of a dependent in excess of the earnings limitation will reduce only the dependent's benefits.

This earnings limitation applies to the earnings of dependent beneficiaries of a disabled worker but not to the earnings of the disabled worker. Different criteria than this earnings limitation are used to determine continued eligibility for disability benefits.

Retirement Benefits

An individual must be "fully insured" to be eligible for retirement benefits under Social Security (sometimes referred to as old-age benefits since that terminology is used in the law). Monthly retirement benefits can begin as early as age 62 and are payable for life. The starting date depends upon the individual's election and the individual's earned income after the starting date selected.

For retirement at the normal retirement age, a fully insured individual would receive benefits equal to his Primary Insurance Amount. This amount is subject to a special minimum benefit designed for individuals with low earnings but many years of employment. For an individual retiring at age 65 in January 1990, the retirement benefit ranges from a minimum of only a few dollars to a maximum (in normal circumstances) of $975 per month. The higher the worker's average earnings, the higher the benefit. The monthly benefit for an otherwise similar individual whose career earnings had always equaled the average wage for all U.S. employees would be approximately $720. After the retirement benefit begins, it increases with the benefit escalator provisions of the law.

If retirement is delayed beyond the normal retirement age or if benefits are completely withheld under the earnings test, the benefit otherwise determined at the actual retirement date is increased for each month that retirement is delayed. For individuals reaching age 65 between 1982 and 1989, this delayed retirement credit amounts to an increase of 1/4 of 1 percent for each month (3 percent for each year) that benefits are not received between ages 65 and 69. The increase applies only to old-age benefits and to the benefits of widows and widowers of workers who earned the credit, and not to benefits to other family members. This delayed retirement credit is scheduled to increase gradually, for persons reaching their normal retirement age between 1990 and 2009, from 3 to 8 percent per year.

Retirement may be elected as early as age 62 with the Primary Insurance Amount reduced by 5/9 of 1 percent for each of the first 36 months (and, beginning in the year 2000 when the normal retirement age starts to increase, 5/12 of 1 percent for each month in excess of 36) that retirement precedes the normal retirement age.

Benefits are subject to reduction or complete withholding before age 70 if the individual's earned income exceeds the earnings limitation mentioned previously.

Disability Benefits

An individual must be "disability insured" to be eligible for disability benefits under Social Security. Disability means the inability to engage in any substantial gainful activity because of a medically determinable physical or mental impairment that can be expected to result in death or has lasted, or can be expected to last, for a continuous period of not less then twelve months; or, for an individual who has attained age 55, blindness that prohibits such individual from engaging in substantial gainful activity requiring skills or abilities comparable to those of any gainful activity in which he previously engaged with some regularity over a substantial period of time.

The disability benefit is payable following a waiting period of five consecutive calendar months throughout which the individual has been disabled. The disability benefit is equal to the Primary Insurance Amount, computed as though the individual had reached age 62 in the first month of his waiting period. Accordingly, the amount of the disability benefit is the same as the retirement benefit at normal retirement age, if the average earnings on which benefits are based are the same. Since average earnings vary with the age at disability, however, so does the amount of the disability benefit. For an individual who became disabled in July 1989 and who was therefore eligible for benefits in January 1990, the maximum benefit would be $1,178 per month. The disability benefit increases with the benefit escalator provisions in the law.

The total disability benefits paid to a worker and his dependents may be reduced if he is receiving certain other disability benefits. Social Security disability benefits plus workers' compensation benefits and certain other publicly provided benefits under federal, state and local laws cannot exceed 80 percent of "average current earnings" prior to disability. Average current earnings for this purpose means actual earnings, not merely amounts covered under Social Security, and is usually defined as the individual's best year in the period consisting of the calendar year in which disability started and the five years immediately preceding that year. If applicable state law as of February 18, 1981 provided that workers' compensation benefits are reduced by Social Security disability benefits, there will be no reduction in Social Security disability benefits because of the workers' compensation benefits.

An individual's disability benefits end with the month preceding the earlier of (a) the month in which he dies, (b) the month in which he attains normal retirement age, and

(c) the third month following the month in which disability ceases. Benefits may be continued while the disabled individual participates in a "trial work period." The retirement benefit at normal retirement age, for an individual entitled to a disability benefit until then, generally will be equal to the Primary Insurance Amount on which the disability benefit is based.

An individual who applies for disability benefits, whether he receives monthly benefits or not, is considered for rehabilitation services by his state vocational rehabilitation agency. These services include counseling, teaching of new employment skills, training in the use of prostheses, and job placement. Benefits may be withheld for any month in which the worker refuses—without good cause—to accept such rehabilitation services.

The earnings limitation that applies to retirement benefits does not apply to the payment of disability benefits. Instead, special limitations are used which are intended to measure the continuation of disability on an all-or-none basis.

Husband's or Wife's Benefits

At his or her normal retirement age a husband or wife will receive 50 percent of the spouse's Primary Insurance Amount, a benefit which is payable, of course, only if the spouse was fully insured or disability insured and is receiving benefits. Payments may commence before normal retirement age (as early as age 62), but in that event will be reduced by 25/36 of 1 percent for each of the first 36 months (and, beginning in the year 2000 when the normal retirement age starts to increase, 5/12 of 1 percent for each month in excess of 36) in the reduction period. Payments will cease with the month before the month in which (a) either spouse dies, (b) they are divorced (except if the duration of the marriage was at least ten years), (c) the primary insured individual is no longer entitled to disability benefits and is not entitled to retirement benefits, or (d) the spouse becomes entitled to a larger benefit as a worker.

This same benefit that is payable to a spouse is also payable to a divorced spouse with at least ten years of marriage, even though the primary insured individual has not retired or claimed benefits (as long as the divorce has been in effect for at least two years and the primary insured individual is at least age 62). If the benefit commences prior to the divorced spouse's normal retirement age, it is subject to the same reductions as specified above for a spouse. Payment will cease with the month before the month in which (a) either spouse dies, (b) the primary insured individual is no longer entitled to disability benefits and is not entitled to retirement benefits, (c) the divorced spouse remarries, unless the marriage is to a person receiving Social Security benefits as a spouse, widow, widower, parent, or disabled child, or (d) the divorced spouse becomes entitled to a larger benefit as a worker.

A wife or husband who has not yet reached normal retirement age may also be eligible for spouse's benefits if she or he is caring for the worker's child who is under age 16 (or disabled) and entitled to a child's benefit. The spouse's benefit in this case is 50 percent of the worker's Primary Insurance Amount. Benefit payments will cease with the month before the month in which (a) either spouse dies, (b) the primary insured individual is no longer entitled to disability benefits and is not entitled to retirement benefits, (c) there is no longer a child who is under age 16 (or disabled) and entitled to benefits, or (d) the spouse becomes entitled to a larger benefit as a worker. If benefit payments cease as a result of the death of the worker, the surviving spouse may be entitled to widow's or widower's benefits, or mother's or father's benefits as described below.

Widow's or Widower's Benefits

At or after normal retirement age, a widow or widower will receive 100 percent of the Primary Insurance Amount of the deceased spouse, provided that the spouse was fully insured and had not received a reduced old-age benefit before death. Payments may begin before normal retirement age (as early as age 60), but in that event they will be reduced by 28.5 percent if the benefits start at age 60 and by a proportionately smaller reduction as the age of benefit commencement approaches the normal retirement age. If the deceased spouse was receiving a reduced old-age benefit at the time of death, the widow's or widower's benefit may not exceed the greater of (a) the amount of the reduced old-age benefit of the spouse, and (b) 82.5 percent of the spouse's Primary Insurance Amount. On the other hand, the widow's or widower's benefit is increased by any delayed-retirement increment for which the deceased spouse was eligible. Also, an alternate method of computing benefits may be available (using a different indexing point) and could result in a higher benefit.

Severely disabled widows or widowers are entitled to a percentage of the spouse's Primary Insurance Amount at or over age 50 (71.5 percent if the benefit is awarded between ages 50 and 59, grading up to 100 percent as the age at the time of the award increases from age 60 to the normal retirement age). The disability must have occurred within seven years after the death of the spouse (or, if later, within seven years after the last eligible child attains age 16 or ceases to be disabled).

These same benefits are payable to a surviving divorced spouse with at least ten years of marriage. Benefit payments cease with the month before the month in which the surviving spouse dies or becomes entitled to a larger retirement benefit based on his or her own earnings. Remarriage prior to age 60 (for nondisabled persons) or age 50 (for disabled persons) will disqualify you for these benefits. Remarriage after these ages will not disqualify you.

Child's Benefits

Every child of an individual entitled to old-age or disability insurance benefits, or of an individual who dies while fully or currently insured, is entitled to a monthly benefit equal to 50 percent of the individual's Primary Insurance Amount if the individual is living, or 75 percent of his Primary Insurance Amount if he is deceased.

Payments stop with the month preceding the earliest of (a) the month in which such a child dies or (with certain exceptions) marries, (b) the month in which this child reaches age 18 and is not disabled (benefits will be continued through the end of the school period, for elementary or secondary school, in which age 19 is attained), and (c) if the child's entitlement was based solely on his being disabled, the third month following the month in which he ceases to be disabled.

A grandchild can qualify as a "child" of a grandparent if both parents are disabled or dead and if the grandchild is living with and being supported by the grandparent.

Mother's or Father's Benefits

A mother's or father's benefit is payable to the surviving spouse of an individual who dies while fully or currently insured, provided the surviving spouse (a) with certain exceptions, is not remarried, (b) is not entitled to a widow's or widower's benefit, and (c) at the time of filing an application is caring for a child of the deceased spouse entitled to a child's benefit, provided the child has not reached age 16 (unless the child is disabled). This same benefit is payable to a divorced spouse even though the marriage did not endure ten years, provided that she or he has not remarried. The mother's or father's benefit is equal to 75 percent of the Primary Insurance Amount of the deceased individual. Benefit payments will cease with the month before the recipient remarries, dies, becomes entitled to a widow's or widower's benefit, or has no child of the deceased individual who is entitled to a child's benefit and is under age 16 (unless the child is disabled).

Parent's Benefits

A parent of an individual who dies while fully insured is entitled to monthly benefits if this parent (a) has reached age 62, (b) was receiving at least one half of his support from the deceased individual, (c) with certain exceptions, has not married since the individual's death, (d) has filed an application for parent's benefits, and (e) is not entitled to a larger benefit as a worker. Generally, the parent's benefit is equal to 82.5 percent of the Primary Insurance Amount of the deceased individual. For any month for which more than one parent is entitled to parent's benefits, the benefit for each parent is equal to 75 percent of the Primary Insurance Amount. The parent's benefits cease upon death or, in certain circumstances, remarriage.

Maximum Limit on Family Benefits

The law limits the total of monthly benefits payable to a family entitled to benefits on the basis of wages of an insured individual. In retirement and survivor cases this maximum is about 175 percent of the individual's Primary Insurance Amount for high-wage earners; for low-wage earners and average-wage earners, the percentage varies between 150 and 188 percent. In disability cases, the percentage varies from 100 percent at very low wage levels to 150 percent at higher wage levels.

Generally, when benefits are subject to reduction because they exceed the limits on maximum family benefits, each monthly benefit except the old-age or disability benefit is decreased proportionately.

Lump Sum Death Payments

If an individual dies while fully or currently insured, an amount equal to $255 is payable, under certain circumstances, to a surviving spouse or children. Application for the payment must generally be filed within two years after the death of the insured individual.

Nonduplication of Benefits

An individual entitled to benefits based on both his own earnings record and as a dependent or survivor of another worker may (in effect) receive only the larger of the two benefits.

Medicare Benefits

The Medicare program consists of Hospital Insurance (HI) and Supplementary Medical Insurance (SMI), frequently referred to as Part A and Part B, respectively. Hospital Insurance provides partial protection against the cost of inpatient hospital services as well as a number of other services such as those provided by a skilled nursing facility or a home health agency. Supplementary Medical Insurance helps pay for the cost of physician services plus certain other expenses such as outpatient hospital care and home health agency visits. Not all medical services are covered by Medicare, the major exceptions being routine care, outpatient drugs, eyeglasses, and dental care.

HI benefits are payable automatically once you reach age 65 if you are entitled to a Social Security benefit as a retired worker, spouse, widow(er), or other beneficiary. HI benefits are available even if your monthly cash benefit is withheld completely because of earnings in excess of the earnings limitation. If you are not receiving monthly cash benefits at age 65, however, you may have to apply specifically for HI benefits.

The SMI program is voluntary and at the present time (1990) requires payments of $28.60 per month. (These premiums are subject to increase in the future as the cost of medical care increases.) If you are receiving a Social Security monthly benefit, the SMI premium will be deducted automatically from your benefit unless you specifically elect *not* to participate in the SMI program.

If you have been receiving Social Security benefits as a disabled beneficiary for at least twenty-four months you are eligible for Medicare benefits, even if you are under age 65. Medicare benefits are also available if you (or one of your dependents) have chronic kidney disease requiring dialysis or a kidney transplant.

The HI program pays for a hospital stay after certain deductible and coinsurance requirements are met. Hospital services (in semi-private accommodations) for up to ninety days in a "spell of illness" are covered; furthermore, you have a "lifetime reserve" of an additional sixty days that can be drawn on if you stay in a hospital for more than a total of ninety days in one spell of illness. (A "spell of illness" ends once you have remained out of the hospital or skilled nursing facility for sixty days.) The hospital is usually paid directly for the cost of your care over and above the amount you are required to pay. You must pay the first $592 of expenses (the HI deductible for 1990, subject to future increases) and you must pay $148 per day if your hospital stay lasts longer than sixty days and $296 per day if you use any of your "lifetime reserve" days. These "coinsurance" amounts of $148 and $296 are also subject to increase in future years.

If you have been hospitalized for at least three days and then enter a skilled nursing facility for follow-up care within thirty days after leaving the hospital, the services provided by the facility will be covered in part by the HI program for up to 100 days in a spell of illness. For days 21 through 100 you must pay a daily coinsurance amount of $74 in 1990 (subject to future increase). Home health services benefits (including visiting-nurse services and various types of therapy treatment) are provided, under certain conditions, without limit and without coinsurance or a deductible.

The SMI program helps pay for the costs of physician services, outpatient services by hospitals and clinics, and home health agency visits. Reimbursement is on the basis of "reasonable charges" for such services: that is, maximum amounts that Medicare can, according to the law and regulations, pay for services covered under SMI. You pay the first $75 of reasonable charges each calendar year (a deductible that is *not* subject to automatic increase) and coinsurance of 20 percent of reasonable charges in excess of the deductible. You also pay all amounts in excess of Medicare's reasonable charges. In some cases the physician or other person or organization who provides covered services may agree to bill Medicare directly and accept as payment in full the amounts determined to be reasonable charges, in which event there will be no excess charges.

Conclusion

This relatively brief description makes it obvious that Social Security is so incredibly complicated that it is not possible to explain in detail in just a few pages all the benefits and all the conditions for receiving these benefits. It is possible, however, to give a general idea of the kinds of benefits payable, how they are determined, and who is eligible to receive them. With this information you should be able to work more effectively with your local Social Security office in making sure that you get maximum advantage from the program and receive all the benefits to which you are entitled.

4

How Much Do Social Security Benefits Cost?

There are several ways to state the money cost of Social Security. For the purpose of this chapter let us use a simple definition: The cost of the Social Security program in any given year is the amount paid in benefits and administrative expenses for that year—a simple but valid definition.

For many years after a social insurance program is adopted, costs can be expected to rise. This is true for several reasons. During the first year of a new program very few retired persons receive benefits (persons who are already past the retirement age when a program is adopted are not usually eligible for benefits). During the second year of a program there are a few more retired persons receiving benefits, the third year a few more, and so on. Eventually the retired persons begin to die, but there is still a net increase in the number of retired persons receiving benefits for many years after a new program is adopted. The same is true of benefits paid to survivors of deceased workers: the number of survivors receiving benefits increases steadily for many years after a program is adopted.

Costs also increase as new benefits are added. For example, disability benefits were added to the Social Security program in 1956. The predictable result was a steady increase in the number of disabled persons receiving benefits for many

Table 4.1

Number of Social Security Beneficiaries in Selected Calendar Years

	Average Number of Persons during Year (in thousands) Who Were:			
	Receiving. . .		Eligible for Benefits under. . .	
Calendar Year	Old-Age and Survivors Insurance Benefits	Disability Insurance Benefits[a]	Hospital Insurance Program[b]	Supplementary Medical Insurance Program[b]
(1)	(2)	(3)	(4)	(5)
1940	97	—	—	—
1950	2,930	—	—	—
1960	13,740	522	—	—
1970	22,618	2,568	20,361	19,584
1980	30,385	4,734	25,104	24,680
1989	34,754	4,105	33,000	32,000

[a] The Disability Insurance program was enacted in 1956 and began operation in 1957.

[b] The Medicare program was enacted in 1965 and began operation in 1966.

years to come. Medicare benefits, paying part of the hospital and other medical expenses of retired persons, were added in 1965. As a result, the number of persons receiving Medicare benefits should increase along with the increase in the number of persons receiving retirement benefits.

Social Security costs can be expected to increase for other reasons, such as an increased number of persons covered by the program and increased benefits (as a result of inflation as well as benefit liberalizations). Accordingly, it is predictable and not at all unusual for the total cost of a new social insurance program to increase steadily for many years after it is adopted.

How does this theory hold up in light of past experience? Table 4.1 shows the number of persons who were receiving various types of Social Security benefits during selected calendar years. As was to be expected, the number of beneficiaries generally has increased steadily since Social Security was enacted. The total number of beneficiaries is not meaningful and is not shown since some persons receive more than one type of benefit (for example, both Old-Age and Medicare benefits).

Table 4.2

**Amount of Benefits and Administrative Expenses Paid
during Selected Calendar Years
(in millions of dollars)**

Calendar Year	Old-Age and Survivors Insurance Program	Disability Insurance Program[a]	Hospital Insurance Program[b]	Supplementary Medical Insurance Program[b]	Total
(1)	(2)	(3)	(4)	(5)	(6)
1940	$ 62	—	—	—	$ 62
1950	1,022	—	—	—	1,022
1960	11,198	$ 600	—	—	11,798
1970	29,848	3,259	$ 5,281	$ 2,212	40,600
1980	107,678	15,872	25,577	11,245	160,372
1989	212,489	23,753	60,803	39,783	336,828

[a] The Disability Insurance program was enacted in 1956 and began operation in 1957.

[b] The Medicare program was enacted in 1965 and began operation in 1966.

Just as an increase in the number of beneficiaries was to be expected, so was an increase in the amount of benefits paid. Table 4.2 shows the amounts that were paid in benefits and administrative expenses for the four separate parts of the Social Security program during selected calendar years. There has been a spectacular increase in costs since Social Security began: from $62 million in 1940 to $336,828 million in 1989. These figures are almost meaningless, however, taken by themselves. It is more appropriate to view them in relation to the size of the U.S. population, or the Gross National Product (the total amount of goods and services produced by the population), or some other measure of the population affected by Social Security.

As we will see in a later chapter, our Social Security program is financed primarily by taxes based on the earnings of the active working population that participates in Social Security. Therefore, it is convenient and meaningful to compare the cost of Social Security with the total earnings of persons covered by Social Security, excluding that portion of earnings exempt from the Social Security tax.

This procedure may be illustrated with the following statistics for calendar year 1989. Approximately 132 million

Table 4.3

Amount of Benefits and Administrative Expenses as a Percentage of Taxable Payroll[a] during Past Calendar Years

Calendar Year	Old-Age and Survivors Insurance Program	Disability Insurance Program[b]	Hospital Insurance Program[c]	Total for OASDHI	Supplementary Medical Insurance Program[c]	Total for OASDHI & SMI
(1)	(2)	(3)	(4)	(5)	(6)	(7)
1940	0.19%	—	—	0.19%	—	0.19%
1945	0.48	—	—	0.48	—	0.48
1950	1.17	—	—	1.17	—	1.17
1955	3.34	—	—	3.34	—	3.34
1960	5.59	0.30%	—	5.89	—	5.89
1965	7.23	0.70	—	7.93	—	7.93
1970	7.32	0.81	1.20%	9.33	0.50%	9.83
1975	9.29	1.36	1.69	12.34	0.69	13.03
1980	9.32	1.37	2.19	12.88	0.96	13.84
1985	9.96	1.13	2.64	13.73	1.30	15.03
1989	9.42	1.05	2.60	13.07	1.70	14.77

[a] "Taxable payroll" consists of the total earnings subject to Social Security taxes, after adjustments in applicable years to reflect (i) deemed wages based on military service, and (ii) the lower tax rates on self-employment income, tips, and multiple-employer "excess wages." This adjustment is made to facilitate both the calculation of tax income (which is thereby the product of the tax rate and the payroll) and the comparison of expenditure percentages with tax rates. This taxable payroll is slightly different for OASDI and HI because of past differences in the tax treatment of self-employed persons and current differences in coverage of employment; however, these differences do not materially affect the comparisons.

[b] The Disability Insurance program was enacted in 1956 and began operation in 1957.

[c] The Medicare program was enacted in 1965 and began operation in 1966. Although the SMI program is not financed by payroll taxes, its cost is shown for comparative purposes as a percentage of payroll that is taxable for HI purposes. Participation in SMI is optional and is financed by premiums paid by the enrollees and by general revenue.

persons worked in employment that was covered by the Old-Age, Survivors, and Disability Insurance programs. Their total earnings in such employment were about $2,610 billion. But the portion of an individual's earnings in excess of $48,000 per year did not count for Social Security purposes; that is, it did not count for computing benefits and it was not subject to tax. Only about 87 percent of total earnings, or $2,260 billion, was subject to Social Security tax. Total expenditures in 1989 for benefits and administrative expenses amounted to about $236.2 billion under the Old-Age,

Survivors, and Disability Insurance programs. This was 10.5 percent of the total taxable payroll of $2,260 billion.

Table 4.3 shows the cost as a percentage of taxable payroll for the four separate parts of the Social Security program during selected calendar years in the past. It is important to note that the Supplementary Medical Insurance program is not financed by a payroll tax; nevertheless, this method of expressing costs is used in order to have a convenient method of comparing the cost of this program and its growth with the other parts of the Social Security program. In reviewing Table 4.3 it may be useful to note that the percentage of the total earnings subject to tax has not always been 87 percent. Table 4.4 indicates what these percentages have been for selected years in the past as well as what they are projected to be in the future. It should also be noted that in 1986 (the most recent year for which data are available), the total amount of covered earnings of persons participating in Social Security represented about 85 percent of the total earnings of all workers in the United States.

Table 4.4

Percentage of Total Earnings in Employment Covered by the OASDI Program That Is Subject to the OASDI Payroll Tax

Calendar Year	*Percentage*
(1)	(2)
1940	92
1945	88
1950	80
1955	80
1960	78
1965	71
1970	78
1975	84
1980	88
1985	90[a]
1990	87[a]
1995	86[a]
2000 and later	86[a]

[a] Estimated.

A review of Tables 4.2 and 4.3 substantiates the obvious. The cost of Social Security has grown significantly, not only in dollar amounts but also in relation to the earnings of those who are covered by Social Security. This increase in cost, relative to taxable payroll, abated somewhat during the 1980s as the active work force, swollen by the baby boom generation, grew more rapidly than the retired population. As will be noted later, these costs will resume their upward spiral when the baby boom generation begins retiring, early in the next century.

How long will the cost of Social Security continue to rise? As a matter of fact, barring major legislative changes, costs will continue to rise until the population of active workers and beneficiaries (retired workers, disabled workers, surviving spouses, etc.) reaches a mature stage—that is, at least seventy-five to one hundred years after the program was adopted. Another way to think about it: the program and the population covered by the program reach a mature stage when the program has existed unchanged for the entire adult lifetime of every person who is covered by the program, and when the characteristics of the population (birth rates, death rates, retirement ages, etc.) have remained unchanged for the entire lifetime of the existing population. A further requirement for the maturity of the program is that there have been no large fluctuations in the economic experience (wage increases, Consumer Price Index changes, unemployment, etc.) during the working lifetime of every person who is covered by the program.

These conditions make it seem as if our Social Security program will never mature, and it probably will not; but for all practical purposes we can assume that it will mature approximately seventy-five years from now. In the year 2065 most of the active workers and the retired workers and other beneficiaries will have participated in the program throughout their entire working lifetime. Of course, we have no assurance that population characteristics, economic conditions, and the program itself will remain stable throughout this period, but if they should do so, then we could expect program costs to level off around the middle of the next century.

It is possible to obtain a more specific idea of future Social Security costs. Every year the Board of Trustees of the Social

Table 4.5

Projected Expenditures for Benefits and Administration as a Percentage of Taxable Payroll[a] during Future Calendar Years

Calendar Year	Old-Age and Survivors Insurance Program	Disability Insurance Program	Hospital Insurance Program	Total for OASDHI	Supplementary Medical Insurance Program[b]	Total for OASDHI & SMI
(1)	(2)	(3)	(4)	(5)	(6)	(7)
1990	9.54%	1.06%	2.56%	13.16%	1.80%	14.96%
1995	9.57	1.10	3.13	13.80	2.46	16.26
2000	9.36	1.20	3.69	14.25	3.33	17.58
2010	9.52	1.56	4.67	15.75	4.87	20.62
2020	12.09	1.77	6.18	20.04	6.15	26.19
2030	14.43	1.85	7.69	23.97	7.64	31.61
2040	14.73	1.82	8.32	24.87	8.17	33.04
2050	14.77	1.93	8.52	25.22	8.35	33.57
2060	15.31	1.92	8.75	25.98	8.82	34.80

[a] "Taxable payroll" consists of the total earnings subject to Social Security taxes, after adjustments in applicable years to reflect (i) deemed wages based on military service, and (ii) the lower tax rates on self-employment income, tips, and multiple-employer "excess wages." This adjustment is made to facilitate both the calculation of tax income (which is thereby the product of the tax rate and the payroll) and the comparison of expenditure percentages with tax rates. This taxable payroll is slightly different for OASDI and HI because of past differences in the tax treatment of self-employed persons and current differences in coverage of employment; however, these differences do not materially affect the comparisons. Projections are based on the intermediate "II-B" set of assumptions from the 1990 Annual Report of the Board of Trustees.

[b] Although the SMI program is not financed by payroll taxes, its cost is shown for comparative purposes as a percentage of payroll that is taxable for HI purposes. Participation in SMI is optional and is financed by premiums paid by the enrollees and by general revenue.

Security program issues reports based on studies made by the actuaries of the Social Security Administration and the Health Care Financing Administration. These reports include projected future costs of the program for as long as seventy-five years in the future. The projected costs, based on the 1990 Trustees Reports and on a limited number of unpublished studies, are summarized in Table 4.5. Total expenditures for benefits and administration are projected to increase from about 15 percent of taxable payroll in 1990 to approximately 18 percent by the year 2000, to 32 percent by the year 2030, and to grow somewhat more slowly thereafter.

Do these figures surprise you? Do you believe them? It is difficult not to believe the figures that are shown in Table 4.3 for the fifty years from 1940 through 1989, because that is past history. What about the future—is it possible for the total cost of the Social Security program to be as high as 30 percent to 35 percent of taxable payroll? Yes, it is not only possible, it is quite likely the cost will reach these or higher levels if there are no significant changes in the present program.

These figures are no surprise to an actuary who is familiar with the Social Security program. It is no surprise that they increased rapidly in the past, and it is no surprise that they are expected to increase in the future. It may be of interest to note that the early actuarial studies in 1938 indicated that the cost of retirement benefits under Social Security would rise steadily from 0.2 percent of taxable payroll in 1940 to 9.35 percent of taxable payroll by 1980.[1] These figures are quoted not to prove the accuracy of long-range projections, but rather to illustrate that from the very start of Social Security, actuaries have been providing information about the trend and level of future costs.

What Is an Actuary?

A short digression about actuaries may be in order. What is an actuary? I have heard that somewhere in the Congressional Record there is a statement that an actuary is a person who is always taking the pessimistic view by looking many years into the future. It is true that the actuary's job is to look into the future; however, whether or not this is a pessimistic exercise is in the eye of the beholder. If you like the result that is projected, you would probably consider it optimistic; if you don't like the result, you would probably consider it pessimistic.

The most widely accepted standard of professional qualification in the United States for actuaries who work with life insurance, health insurance, pensions, and social insurance is membership in the Society of Actuaries. There are other actuarial organizations designed to serve the specialized needs of their membership: American Academy of Actuaries,

Conference of Consulting Actuaries, Casualty Actuarial Society, and American Society of Pension Actuaries.

The Society of Actuaries is a professional organization of actuaries whose purpose is to advance the knowledge of actuarial science and to maintain high standards of competence within the actuarial profession. At the end of 1989, there were 11,784 members of the Society of Actuaries, of whom 6,241 were Fellows (the ultimate membership designation). In early 1990 the Social Security Administration employed fifteen members of the Society of Actuaries, and the Health Care Financing Administration employed sixteen members.

In its publication describing the actuarial profession, the Society of Actuaries states:

> An actuary is an executive professionally trained in the science of mathematical probabilities. He uses mathematical skills to define, analyze, and solve complex business and social problems. He designs insurance and pension programs which meet the public's needs and desires, and which are financially sound. He forecasts probabilities and he commits his company or his client to long-range financial obligations for a generation or more.

One of the principal jobs of the actuaries of the Social Security Administration and the Health Care Financing Administration is to make long-range forecasts of the cost of the present Social Security program, as well as any proposed changes, and thus provide the information that will enable the program to be financed on a sound basis both now and in the future.

Long-Range Forecasts

In making long-range forecasts of the amounts that will be paid out in benefits under the Social Security program, actuaries must make assumptions regarding a host of factors, including:

mortality
disability

immigration and emigration
birth rates
wages and salaries
Consumer Price Index changes
unemployment rates
age at retirement
participation in the work force by males and by females
marriage rates

For a given set of assumptions, projections of future costs can be made with a reasonably high degree of accuracy. But it is obvious that no one can accurately select these assumptions, particularly those concerning wages, the Consumer Price Index, and birth rates, all of which are important determinants of future costs. By expressing future costs as a percentage of future taxable payroll, rather than in dollar amounts, the predictability of future costs is greatly improved. Nevertheless, the overall level of certainty of long-range cost projections for a program like Social Security is still less than we might hope for.

The trustees of Social Security, as well as the government actuaries, recognize that it is impossible to predict the future accurately. They also recognize, however, that it is essential to adopt one or more sets of assumptions about the possible future social and economic environment and then to project future income and outgo under Social Security to determine whether or not it would be financially sound under those conditions.

In recent years the trustees have employed four alternative sets of assumptions about the future, two of which are usually labeled "optimistic" and "pessimistic," respectively, and two of which are termed "intermediate." Projections of future expenditures under the optimistic and pessimistic assumptions indicate a broad range within which it might reasonably be expected that expenditures will fall during the coming years. Projected expenditures based upon the less favorable of the two intermediate sets of assumptions (labelled the "II-B" assumptions) are normally used for planning purposes since it is too cumbersome to deal in every instance with a range of future costs. The projected expenditures, as well as the projected income, shown throughout this book

Table 4.6

Projected Expenditures for Benefits and Administration of the Social Security Program[a] under Alternative Demographic and Economic Assumptions,[b] Expressed as a Percentage of Taxable Payroll[c]

Calendar Year	Optimistic Assumptions	Intermediate Assumptions	Pessimistic Assumptions
(1)	(2)	(3)	(4)
1990	14.86%	14.96%	15.27%
1995	14.74	16.26	17.96
2000	14.80	17.58	20.07
2010	15.76	20.62	24.80
2020	18.60	26.19	34.11
2030	20.81	31.61	44.52
2040	20.65	33.04	49.08
2050	20.36	33.57	51.45
2060	20.47	34.80	54.46

[a] Amounts shown include expenditures for OASDI, HI, and SMI combined.

[b] See Chapter 10 and Appendix I for discussion of alternative sets of assumptions.

[c] "Taxable payroll" consists of the total earnings subject to Social Security taxes, after adjustments in applicable years to reflect (i) deemed wages based on military service, and (ii) the lower tax rates on self-employment income, tips, and multiple-employer excess wages. This adjustment is made to facilitate both the calculation of tax income (which is thereby the product of the tax rate and the payroll) and the comparison of expenditure percentages with tax rates. This taxable payroll is slightly different for OASDI and HI because of past differences in the tax treatment of self-employed persons and current differences in coverage of employment; however, these differences do not materially affect the comparisons. Although the SMI program is not financed by payroll taxes, its cost is shown for comparative purposes as a percentage of payroll that is taxable for HI purposes. Participation in SMI is optional and is financed by premiums paid by the enrollees and by general revenue.

are based upon the intermediate "II-B" assumptions used in the 1990 Trustees Reports, unless indicated otherwise.[2] Appendix I contains a summary of the more important of these assumptions, and Chapter 10 discusses the nature and significance of these assumptions in more detail.

Table 4.6 and Chart 4.A illustrate the range of projected expenditures for Social Security under the optimistic, pessimistic and intermediate sets of assumptions. Expenditures include both benefits and administrative costs for all elements of the Social Security program that are under consideration here: Old-Age, Survivors, and Disability Insurance and Medicare (Hospital Insurance and Supplementary Medical Insurance). While it may be reasonable to assume

Chart 4.A

Projected Expenditures for Benefits and Administration of the Social Security Program[a] under Alternative Demographic and Economic Assumptions,[b] Expressed as a Percentage of Taxable Payroll[c]

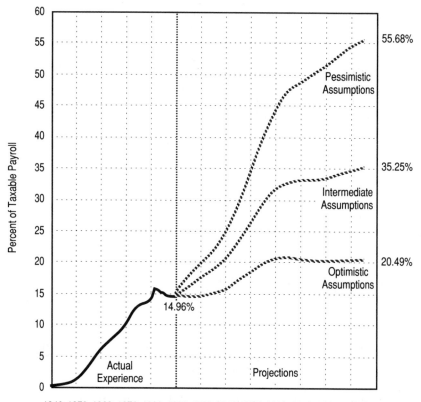

[a] Amounts shown include expenditures for OASDI, HI, and SMI combined.

[b] See Chapter 10 and Appendix I for discussion of alternative sets of assumptions.

[c] "Taxable payroll" consists of the total earnings subject to Social Security taxes, after adjustments in applicable years to reflect (i) deemed wages based on military service, and (ii) the lower tax rates on self-employment income, tips, and multiple-employer "excess wages." This adjustment is made to facilitate both the calculation of tax income (which is thereby the product of the tax rate and the payroll) and the comparison of expenditure percentages with tax rates. This taxable payroll is slightly different for OASDI and HI because of past differences in the tax treatment of self-employed persons and current differences in coverage of employment; however, these differences do not materially affect the comparisons. Although the SMI program is not financed by payroll taxes, its cost is shown for comparative purposes as a percentage of payroll that is taxable for HI purposes. Participation in SMI is optional and is financed by premiums paid by the enrollees and by general revenue.

that actual experience will fall within the range defined by these alternative projections, particularly during the first twenty-five years of the projection, there can be no assurance that this will be the case because of the high degree of uncertainty in the selection of assumptions for long-range forecasting.

Accordingly, the future costs shown in Table 4.6, particularly the costs after the turn of the century, should not be viewed as absolute amounts but rather as trends based upon assumptions that seem reasonable to us at the present time. By updating the cost projections on a regular basis and by revising the assumptions in the light of emerging trends, actuaries can provide extremely important information for making sound future financial plans for the Social Security program. We should not ignore these future cost estimates just because they will affect *future* generations and not us, or just because we know that actual future costs will not be exactly the same as projected future costs.

As Table 4.6 and Chart 4.A indicate, under all three sets of assumptions, expenditures are projected to rise somewhat until about the year 2010 and to grow much more rapidly thereafter. Most of the projected increase in costs between now and the year 2010 is attributable to the Hospital Insurance and Supplementary Medical Insurance programs.[3]

The much larger increases during the twenty-year period following the year 2010 are attributable primarily to the large number of persons then attaining age 65 (from among the children born during the post-World War II "baby boom" period from 1946 to the mid-1960s). The birth rate among these baby boom generations has been and is expected to continue to be lower than that of their parents, resulting in an eventual increase in the size of the older benefit-collecting population relative to the younger tax-paying population. Chart 4.B compares the size of these two segments of the population at three points in time: 1950, 1990, and 2030. The figures for 2030 are estimates based upon the optimistic, intermediate, and pessimistic sets of birth rate and mortality assumptions.

As indicated in Table 4.6, the costs under the intermediate assumptions are projected to rise rapidly after the turn of the

Chart 4.B
Past, Present, and Projected Covered Workers, Retired Workers, and Other Social Security Beneficiaries

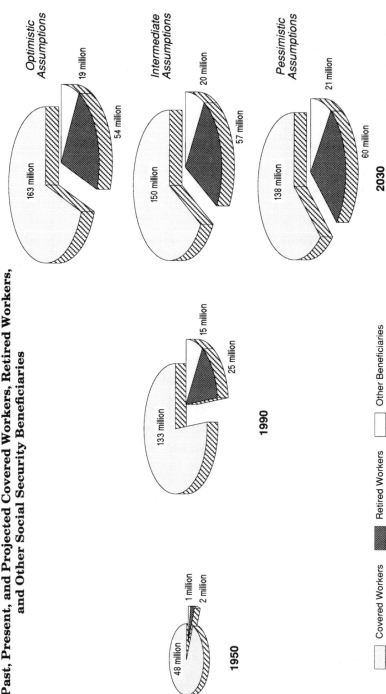

Optimistic Assumptions

19 million
54 million
163 million

Intermediate Assumptions

20 million
57 million
150 million

Pessimistic Assumptions

21 million
60 million
138 million

2030

15 million
25 million
133 million

1990

1 million
2 million
48 million

1950

Covered Workers   Retired Workers   Other Beneficiaries

century to about 32 percent of taxable payroll in the year 2030, at which time the rate of growth begins to slow. The projected costs reach 35 percent of taxable payroll at the end of the 75-year projection period. This is more than twice the current expenditures of some 15 percent of taxable payroll. Under the more optimistic assumptions, costs would still rise substantially above current levels but to an ultimate level of only about 20 to 21 percent of taxable payroll. Under the more pessimistic assumptions, projected expenditures would rise to over 44 percent of taxable payroll by the year 2030 and would continue increasing to some 54 percent by the year 2060. We may be deluding ourselves by relying unduly on just the intermediate assumptions and by failing to emphasize that future costs can be predicted only within a broad range. Also, although it is a matter of judgment, I believe that future Social Security costs are much more likely to be higher than the intermediate cost projections than they are to be lower than such projections.

The so-called pessimistic assumptions selected by the Board of Trustees do not represent the most pessimistic view that it would be reasonable to take in determining whether Social Security will be viable in the future. For example, it can be argued that improvements in life expectancy will continue at a faster rate than has been assumed; or it is possible that average wages will not increase much, if any, faster than the cost of living, reflecting a marked slowdown in the steady improvement in the standard of living to which we have become accustomed—and which has been assumed for the future. Either of these events would result in much higher future Social Security costs (expressed as a percentage of taxable payroll).

Furthermore, none of the customary projections takes into account a variety of significant events that are conceivable, but that would not ordinarily be expected. Unfortunately, there is no obvious way to prepare in advance to cope with some of these events. A significant improvement in health at the older ages is one of the easiest to comprehend of such possible events. People who were aged 60 in 1990 could expect to live another twenty-one years, on average, or until about age 81. It should be emphasized that 81 is the average age; some people will live to age 100, others will die soon after age 60. About 90 percent of persons aged 60 in 1990 will die before reaching age 94. Sixty years ago in 1930, persons aged 60 could expect to live to age 75, on average. Sixty years from now in the year 2050, the projections assume that persons who are then aged 60 can expect to live to age 84, on average (according to the intermediate set of assumptions). It is entirely possible, however, that the average life span for persons aged 60 could be somewhat higher in the future, say 85 or 90; and with major breakthroughs in health care or improved understanding of the aging process, it could even be 95 or 100. Some analysts predict that life-extending techniques will become so developed in the 21st century that we may live well beyond 100 years. Even if there are no remarkable increases in our average life span, we can expect generally improved health during our old age. Major improvements in the health of the elderly or significant increases in life span would make our present Social Security system totally inappropriate.

Another example of a possible event that is difficult to comprehend, much less assess the impact of, is cataclysmic change in the earth resulting from volcanic eruptions, earthquakes, or polar shifts. These would lift large areas of land, submerge others in the sea, change underwater currents and tides, revise weather patterns, and generally transform the nation's coastal areas and mountain regions. Such changes would undoubtedly have a dramatic effect on human life— not only on the size of the population initially surviving these disasters but also on the population's ability for continued survival.

A still different type of development that is almost impossible to understand or predict the consequences of is the social evolution going on in this country and throughout the world. If this evolution should turn into a revolution, we could easily find our present Social Security system as well as most other institutions to be completely obsolete and all of our projections about future costs to have been of no avail. And, of course, there is continued potential for atomic catastrophe on a worldwide scale, whether accidental or the result of deliberate aggression by a desperate nation.

None of this is to say that we should ignore the future because it is not predictable with certainty or because it may be calamitous. We must make every effort to design our institutions, including Social Security, so that they:

appear to be appropriate in a future environment that we can postulate and comprehend; and

are adaptable to noncalamitous future change.

Conclusion

Long-term projections such as those presented in this chapter provide information that is vital to our long-range planning and to our assessment of whether the present Social Security program is appropriate for the future. The projections indicate that future costs will continue to rise in the future no matter what assumptions are employed; it is just a question of how much they will rise. It is clearly inappropriate, therefore, to rely upon some undefined good fortune to enable us to continue our present Social Security program without paying substantially higher costs. Unfortunately these long-term projections and their significance do not appear to be widely known and understood by the public or the Congress or the administration. Continued failure to heed these indications of the future is, at best, extremely shortsighted and it could prove to be disastrous.

5

How Is the Money Obtained to Pay for Social Security Benefits?

In the last chapter we saw how the cost of any social insurance program can be expected to rise steadily as it matures. And we saw, in particular, how the cost of our Social Security program has grown in the past and how it is likely to grow in the future.

The question we turn to now is how we obtain the money necessary to pay these costs in order to fulfill the promise of the Social Security program to pay the various benefits outlined in Chapter 3. Obviously, we must levy some kind of tax against some segment of the population.

Sources of Federal Government Income

There are numerous ways taxes can be assessed. Chart 5.A illustrates the major sources of federal government income in fiscal year 1989 used to operate all our government programs (not just Social Security).

Federal Income Tax

The federal income tax is the tax we are most familiar with. It is paid by most individuals and businesses. In fiscal

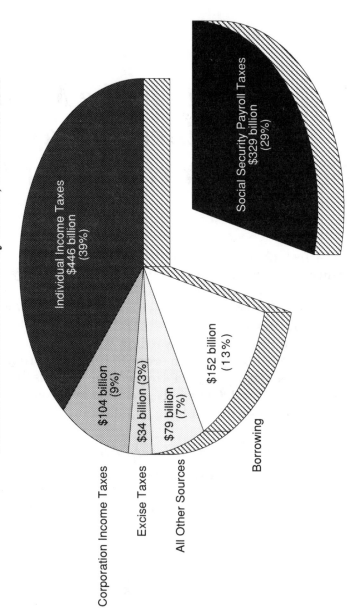

Chart 5.A

Federal Government Income by Source, Fiscal Year 1989

Individual Income Taxes
$446 billion
(39%)

Social Security Payroll Taxes
$329 billion
(29%)

Corporation Income Taxes

$104 billion
(9%)

Excise Taxes

$34 billion (3%)

All Other Sources

$79 billion
(7%)

$152 billion
(13%)

Borrowing

Fiscal Year 1989 Total: $1,143 billion

year 1989 the federal government received $446 billion in personal income taxes paid by individuals, and $104 billion in income taxes paid by corporations. This was 48 percent of all income received by the government.

Miscellaneous Taxes

A variety of special taxes of one kind or another is collected by the federal government: excise taxes (on alcohol, tobacco, gasoline, and entertainment, for example), gift taxes, estate taxes, licensing fees, customs taxes, and so on. In fiscal year 1989, the total of these miscellaneous taxes amounted to $113 billion, or 10 percent of all income received by the government.

Borrowing

The money to pay for federal programs does not necessarily have to be collected immediately in the form of taxes. Any excess of appropriations for expenditures over tax income constitutes a "budget deficit" and is made up by borrowing additional money from the general public, both here and abroad. This borrowing is carried out by the sale of U.S. government securities, with the repayment of principal and interest to be made from future income (from taxes or further borrowing). In fiscal year 1989, an additional $152 billion was borrowed. This represented about 13 percent of total federal government income.

General Revenue

The total of the federal income taxes, the miscellaneous taxes mentioned above (excluding amounts specified by law for a particular purpose, such as the Highway Trust Fund), and newly borrowed amounts is sometimes called "general revenue." General revenue is available to the government to spend for general purposes; that is, there is not usually a direct connection between the source of the tax and how it is spent. Last year, general revenue was spent for national security, interest on the public debt, veterans' services and benefits, welfare (Supplemental Security Income, Medicaid, Food Stamps, Aid to Families with Dependent Children, etc.), operating the federal government, and other purposes. Approximately 66 percent of total income to the federal government in fiscal year 1989 (including the amounts borrowed from the public to finance the budget deficit) represented "unallocated" income or general revenue.

General revenue is used to pay for a relatively small part of the total Social Security program. In 1989 about 9 percent of the total income for Social Security ($36.6 billion out of total income of $410.5 billion) was accounted for by general revenue. Thus, general revenue can be considered to have financed about 9 percent of Social Security's total expenditures.[1] This excludes interest payments on Treasury securities held by the Social Security Trust Funds, although such payments are made from general revenue. About 5 percent of Social Security income in 1989 came from interest payments.

General revenue is used in cases where special benefits are granted a person even though he has not paid the normal Social Security taxes to be eligible for such benefits: for example, for gratuitous wage credits for military service and for Japanese internees during World War II. Also, since 1984, up to half of Old-Age, Survivors, and Disability Insurance benefits for high-income persons has been subjected to income tax. The resulting tax revenue is then transferred to the particular trust fund that paid the benefits. This constitutes a form of earmarked general revenue. In 1989, general revenue arising from benefit taxation amounted to 0.6 percent of total Social Security income. It is projected to represent 1.3 percent of such income by the year 2000 and to continue increasing thereafter to an ultimate level of about 3.2 percent of Social Security income under present law.

General revenue is used to pay a relatively large portion of the cost of the Supplementary Medical Insurance part of the Medicare program. In 1989 approximately 72 percent of the income for Supplementary Medical Insurance was accounted for by general revenue (excluding the short-lived effects of the Medicare Catastrophic Coverage Act of 1988). The remainder came from contributions, or "premiums," paid by those who elected to have this benefit, together with interest earnings on the trust fund. If Supplementary Medical Insurance is excluded, in 1989 less than 2 percent of the cost of Social Security was financed by general revenue.

Payroll Tax

Sometimes special taxes are assessed based on a worker's gross earnings without any exemptions or deductions. They are referred to as payroll taxes and are usually earmarked for special purposes.

This is the way the money is raised to pay for most (83 percent) of the cost of the present Social Security program. In 1990 an employee paid taxes of 7.65 percent of his earnings; his employer also paid taxes equal to 7.65 percent of the employee's earnings (but this amount was not deducted from the employee's earnings); and a self-employed person paid taxes of 15.3 percent of his earnings.[2] In each case, no tax was payable on earnings in excess of $51,300 in 1990. Table 5.1 shows examples of the Social Security taxes payable in 1990 by several individual workers and their employers, as well as by self-employed persons.

Payroll taxes such as these, which are collected by the Internal Revenue Service, and the relatively small amounts

Table 5.1

Social Security Taxes Payable in 1990 with Respect to Selected Individuals

If Your Earnings in 1990 Were	Your Social Security Taxes Were . . .			If You Are Self-Employed Your Social Security Taxes Were[a]
	Paid by Employee	Paid by Employer	Total	
(1)	(2)	(3)	(4)	(5)
$10,000	$ 765.00	$ 765.00	$1,530.00	$1,530.00
20,000	1,530.00	1,530.00	3,060.00	3,060.00
30,000	2,295.00	2,295.00	4,590.00	4,590.00
40,000	3,060.00	3,060.00	6,120.00	6,120.00
51,300 or more	3,924.45	3,924.45	7,848.90	7,848.90

a Assumes that column (1) represents net self-employment earnings for Social Security tax purposes.

of general revenue referred to earlier are placed in special trust funds that are invested in U.S. government securities until they are used to pay Social Security benefits. These taxes can be used only to pay Social Security benefits (and related administrative expenses) and cannot be used for any other purposes. Furthermore, general revenue cannot be used to pay Social Security benefits except to the extent outlined above.

It is important to note, however, that since payroll taxes that are not required for current benefit payments are invested in U.S. government securities, they are—in effect—loaned to the government to spend for general purposes and are thus available, at least temporarily, for non-Social Security purposes. On the other hand, when the trust fund's U.S. government securities are redeemed in the future to pay benefits, the government must collect general revenue (or borrow) to redeem the bonds. This crossover in the use of payroll taxes and general revenue at various points in time can become a significant issue (as it is in 1990) when a large Social Security trust fund buildup is anticipated. This question will be discussed further in Chapter 6.

Why Do We Pay for Social Security the Way We Do?

When Social Security was adopted, only about 60 percent of the working population was eligible to participate. There was apparent justification, therefore, in assessing a payroll tax on the segment of the population eligible for its direct benefits rather than using general revenue paid by a broader segment of the population. The use of a payroll tax was also consistent with the notion, mistaken though it was, that there was a strong relationship between taxes paid and benefits received for an individual under the Social Security program. Now, even more than when Social Security was enacted, this logic is questionable, to say the least. Approximately 94 percent of the working population is currently covered by Social Security. Furthermore, the relationship between taxes and benefits for an individual is so tenuous as to be virtually nonexistent.

There is no particular reason that an employee and his employer should share equally the cost of Social Security;

that is, there is no reason that the worker and his employer should pay the same amount in Social Security payroll taxes—except that it happens to be the law.[3] Also, there is no particular reason why the tax rate should be the same for all levels of earnings. The Social Security tax rate could be variable rather than constant. It could increase or decrease as the level of earnings increases. In fact, Social Security could be financed by general revenue or some other form of tax instead of by the present payroll tax.

If there is no particular theoretical reason why we should pay for most of our Social Security benefits with a tax that is a constant percentage of payroll and that is paid in equal amounts by an employee and his employer, why do we do it this way? Why do we use a payroll tax instead of general revenue? Many justifications can be given and many theoretical arguments can be constructed; but, in fact, the reasons seem to be rather arbitrary.

It may be interesting to note the recollections of J. Douglas Brown, a member of the staff of President Roosevelt's Committee on Economic Security. This committee made the recommendations in 1934–35 leading to the adoption of the Social Security Act on August 14, 1935.

> Departing from European tradition, we proposed the use of a uniform percentage of wages in determining the amount of contribution rather than a flat dollar amount or a series of amounts by wage classes.[4]

> From the first, we assumed that contributions to old age insurance should be "in equal shares by employer and insured employee" as stated in the September 13th draft. A "fifty-fifty" ratio seemed to us to be justified by an "esthetic" logic difficult to controvert. I remember proposing this ratio to William Green, then President of the American Federation of Labor, as we were going to the White House for the President's reception on November 14th. He agreed that labor should go along with an equal sharing of the cost of old age insurance. . . . There never was any objection from the labor movement against equal contributions to old age insurance.[5]

The above memoirs are not quoted to suggest that the decisions made in 1934–35 were anything less than well thought out and sound. Undoubtedly there were other considerations than those reflected in the memoirs. One of those considerations is suggested by an observation made by President Franklin D. Roosevelt in response to a visitor who complained about the economic effect of the tax:

> I guess you're right on the economics, but those taxes were never a problem of economics. They are politics all the way through. We put those payroll contributions there so as to give the contributors a legal, moral, and political right to collect their pensions. . . . With those taxes in there, no damn politician can ever scrap my social security program.[6]

How High Will Future Tax Rates Be?

As indicated in Chapter 4, projections have been made of the future cost of Social Security. It is fairly easy to review these projected costs and determine what the corresponding payroll tax rates would have to be to finance the promised benefits. If the benefits are not changed and if Social Security is financed the way it generally has been in the past (primarily by payroll taxes and on a pay-as-you-go basis with a nominal trust fund buildup intended to serve as a contingency reserve), then the required future tax rates are projected to be approximately as indicated in Table 5.2. The rates shown are for the Old-Age, Survivors, and Disability Insurance program and the Hospital Insurance portion of the Medicare program (i.e., the part of Social Security that is currently financed by the payroll tax) and are based on the intermediate "II-B" assumptions in the 1990 Trustees Reports.

It should be noted that the tax rates scheduled in present law do not match those shown in Table 5.2. The principal differences are as follows:

> Tax rates scheduled in present law (15.30 percent for employee and employer combined) exceed those needed to pay benefits and administrative expenses from 1990 through 2009, but are increasingly deficient after 2009, based on the intermediate assumptions.

Table 5.2

Projected Tax Rates Necessary to Finance Present Social Security Program, under "Intermediate" Demographic and Economic Assumptions[a]

Calendar Year	Tax Rates for Employed Persons			Tax Rates for Self-Employed Persons
	Paid by Employee	Paid by Employer	Total	
(1)	(2)	(3)	(4)	(5)
1990	6.50%	6.50%	13.00%	13.00%
1995	6.80	6.80	13.60	13.60
2000	7.00	7.00	14.00	14.00
2010	7.70	7.70	15.40	15.40
2020	9.75	9.75	19.50	19.50
2030	11.65	11.65	23.30	23.30
2040	12.10	12.10	24.20	24.20
2050	12.25	12.25	24.50	24.50
2060	12.60	12.60	25.20	25.20

[a] Figures represent the tax rates necessary, based on the intermediate "II-B" assumptions in the 1990 Trustees Reports, to finance benefits and administrative expenses assuming no change is made in present law and assuming no further buildup in the trust funds. This does not include the taxes necessary to support the Supplementary Medical Insurance program, which is not financed by payroll taxes.

Note: The tax rates shown above are rounded, following the procedures generally used by Congress.

During the period from 1990 through 2009 the scheduled tax rate must be reallocated among the three segments of the program (OASI, DI, and HI) if each segment is to be financed adequately. Currently, the OASI program is "overfinanced" (a fact that is widely publicized), the DI program is about right, and the HI program is vastly underfinanced (a fact that is rarely publicized).

After 2009, the OASDI and HI programs could continue to operate for roughly another 10 years (based on present law tax rates but assuming that tax rates were reallocated) but only by drawing on interest earnings and, subsequently, the principal of invested assets. The theoretical tax rates necessary to finance the programs, as shown in Table 5.2, are designed to match each year's payroll tax income closely to that year's expenditures and assume that

Table 5.3

Projected Tax Rates Necessary to Finance Present Social Security Program, under "Pessimistic" Demographic and Economic Assumptions[a]

Calendar Year	Tax Rates for Employed Persons			Tax Rates for Self-Employed Persons
	Paid by Employee	Paid by Employer	Total	
(1)	(2)	(3)	(4)	(5)
1990	6.65%	6.65%	13.30%	13.30%
1995	7.65	7.65	15.30	15.30
2000	8.25	8.25	16.50	16.50
2010	9.60	9.60	19.20	19.20
2020	13.20	13.20	26.40	26.40
2030	17.00	17.00	34.00	34.00
2040	18.65	18.65	37.30	37.30
2050	19.65	19.65	39.30	39.30
2060	20.95	20.95	41.90	41.90

[a] Figures represent the tax rates necessary, based on the pessimistic (alternative III) assumptions in the 1990 Trustees Reports, to finance benefits and administrative expenses assuming no change is made in present law and assuming no further buildup in the trust funds. This does not include the taxes necessary to support the Supplementary Medical Insurance program, which is not financed by payroll taxes.

Note: The tax rates shown above are rounded, following the procedures generally used by Congress.

trust fund assets are maintained at a relatively low level, for contingency purposes only.

The tax rates in present law are scheduled to remain at their present level in the future. If benefits are to be paid after 2020 or so, however, the payroll tax rates must eventually rise significantly, as indicated in Table 5.2, to a level of some 24 to 25 percent of taxable payroll (for employee and employer combined) when all the baby boomers have reached age 65.

The figures in Table 5.2 and the related discussion are based on the intermediate "II-B" assumptions in the 1990 Trustees Reports. Table 5.3 indicates the required future tax rates that would be necessary based on the so-called pessimistic set of assumptions. These tax rates are much higher than those in Table 5.2, and the discrepancy from the scheduled tax rates is correspondingly greater.

The "financial deficits" for the next century (the difference between the tax rates that are scheduled in law and the tax rates that will be required to pay benefits) are given remarkably little attention. Yet just as costs have risen in the past, they will rise in the future. Ignoring the projected high future costs will not change them. These deficits are explored in more detail in Chapter 7.

The tax rate is applied to a worker's earnings subject to an upper limit called the "maximum contribution and benefit base." For 1990 the maximum was $51,300; thus the portion of an individual's earnings in excess of $51,300 in 1990 does not count for computing benefits and was not subjected to tax. This maximum is scheduled to increase in the future at the same rate as the average wages and salaries of the nation's workers increase.

Supplementary Medical Insurance Financing

The Supplementary Medical Insurance portion of Medicare is an optional program available to most persons aged 65 and over and to certain disabled persons. About 95 percent of those eligible for this program have elected to participate. The cost of SMI benefits is not financed by payroll taxes as is the rest of Social Security. The cost of SMI benefits was met originally by premiums paid by the participants and approximately matching payments from general revenue. In most past years, premiums were prevented by law from rising as rapidly as the total cost of benefits, hence over time an increasing proportion of the cost has been borne by general revenue. In recent years, Congress has acted to prevent the proportion from exceeding 75 percent (and, in fact, the ratio has stayed at 75 percent for several years). Under present law, however, the proportion drawn from general revenue will continue to increase.

The SMI Trustees Report normally shows projected expenditures only for a 3-year period;[7] nonetheless, the same demographic changes in the population that will cause the projected OASDI and HI program costs to increase rapidly after the turn of the century will also cause the SMI program costs to grow rapidly. Table 5.4 illustrates the projected expenditures under the SMI program for the next

Table 5.4

**Projected Supplementary Medical Insurance Expenditures
and Proportion Financed by General Revenue**

Calendar Year	Supplementary Medical Insurance Expenditures in Dollars (in billions)	Supplementary Medical Insurance Expenditures as a Percentage of Hospital Insurance Taxable Payroll[a]	Percentage of Income (Other Than Interest) Drawn From General Revenue
(1)	(2)	(3)	(4)
1990	$ 45.1	1.80%	75%
1995	83.1	2.46	83
2000	150.9	3.33	88
2010	—[b]	4.87	93
2020	—[b]	6.15	94
2030	—[b]	7.64	94
2040	—[b]	8.17	95
2050	—[b]	8.35	96
2060	—[b]	8.82	96

[a] Although the SMI program is not financed by payroll taxes, its cost is shown for comparative purposes as a percentage of payroll that is taxable for HI purposes.

[b] Dollar amounts are not shown in the distant future since they tend to lose their meaning except when related to an index such as taxable payroll.

Note: Estimates are based on the intermediate "II-B" set of assumptions in the 1990 Trustees Reports.

seventy-five years.[8] Although the SMI program is not financed by payroll taxes, its cost for comparative purposes has been computed as a percentage of the payroll that is taxable for HI purposes. On this basis, as shown in column (3) of Table 5.4, the expenditures under the SMI program are projected to increase from the equivalent of 1.80 percent of taxable payroll in 1990 to 8.82 percent in the year 2060. It is unfortunate that these projected long-range costs of the SMI program are not presented in the SMI Trustees Report so that there would be more awareness and concern about our ability to keep these promises. It is difficult to devise a solution to a problem when the magnitude of the problem is unknown.

General Revenue versus Payroll Tax Financing

As indicated previously, more than 98 percent of the cost of the Old-Age, Survivors, and Disability Insurance and

Hospital Insurance programs is financed by income sources other than general revenue; less than 2 percent is financed by general revenue. With respect to the Supplementary Medical Insurance program, approximately 25 percent is currently financed by premiums paid by the participants and the remaining 75 percent is financed by general revenue. (As mentioned previously, the latter percentage will increase over time without further congressional action.) These figures exclude the interest received on the Treasury securities held by the Social Security Trust Funds.

There is an ongoing debate about whether these financing methods are proper and whether we should rely less on payroll taxes and more on general revenue or some other form of taxes. It is not the purpose of this section to discuss the relative advantages of general revenue and payroll tax financing or other forms of taxation. A few general statements, however, may be helpful in establishing a perspective on financing.

It is important to note that if more general revenue and less payroll tax were used it would not change the total cost of Social Security or the total amount of taxes collected—it would simply change the way the tax is spread among the taxpayers, and some people would pay more and some would pay less than they do now.

To the extent that payroll taxes are used to finance Social Security, the taxes are paid by the same groups of persons who receive benefits. That is not to say that each person receives the exact benefits that can be "purchased" by his taxes. The relationship between the value of taxes paid and benefits received is discussed in Chapter 11.

To the extent that general revenue is used to finance Social Security, the taxes are paid by the entire population without regard to whether they participate in Social Security. Consider, for example, an employee who never works in employment covered by Social Security. Such a person will never pay Social Security taxes and will never be eligible for Social Security benefits (unless he voluntarily enrolls in the HI and SMI programs at age 65 and pays the required premiums). Nevertheless, the federal income taxes he pays contribute to general revenue which is used to pay for 9 percent of total Social Security benefits.

One of the most important drawbacks of general revenue financing as currently practiced is that it seems to facilitate ignoring the future. The Supplementary Medical Insurance program provides a good example. The government does not make long-range plans to finance the Supplementary Medical Insurance program. Provision is made only two years in advance. There seems to be a feeling that, since the program is financed primarily by general revenue, there is no need to be aware of the future cost or to make any advance plans to finance future benefits. The theory apparently is: "We can always increase general taxes enough to pay for SMI, so why worry about it."

This viewpoint is clearly inappropriate in a program like Social Security, under which it is entirely possible to promise more in future benefits than the nation will be able and willing to pay for when they fall due.

Conclusion

In summary, Social Security benefits must be financed by taxes of one kind or another. The particular tax that is selected is important because of the way in which it spreads the burden among the various segments of the population. It is important psychologically because the taxpayer may be more willing to pay one form of tax than another. Finally, it is important because of the degree of fiscal responsibility it encourages—or discourages—among the Congress and other policymakers, as well as the taxpayers.

6

When Do We Pay for Social Security Benefits?

In Chapter 4 we saw how expenditures for benefits and administration under a social insurance program can be expected to grow steadily until the program matures—that is, for at least fifty to seventy-five years after it begins. In particular, we saw how expenditures under our Social Security program have grown in the past and how they are likely to grow in the future. For convenient reference this pattern of expenditures is shown in Table 6.1 for the Old-Age, Survivors, Disability, and Hospital Insurance parts of the Social Security program (i.e., everything except Supplementary Medical Insurance, which is optional and is financed principally by general revenue). The dollar amounts in column (2) are shown only through the year 2000 since the figures in the later years tend to lose their meaning except when related to an index such as taxable payroll. The projected future costs are based upon the intermediate set of assumptions as discussed in Chapter 4, and actual future costs may be higher or lower than those indicated in Table 6.1.

In Chapter 5 we discussed the various kinds of taxes that could be collected to pay for these benefits and saw that traditionally a payroll tax, shared equally by the worker and his employer, has been used as the principal means of financing our Social Security program.

Table 6.1

Expenditures for Benefits and Administration under the Old-Age, Survivors, Disability, and Hospital Insurance Program for Selected Years

| | Expenditures Expressed as a . . . | |
Calendar Year	Dollar Amount (in millions)	Percentage of Taxable Payroll[a]
(1)	(2)	(3)
1940	$ 62	0.19%
1945	304	0.48
1950	1,022	1.17
1955	5,079	3.34
1960	11,798	5.89
1965	19,187	7.93
1970	38,389	9.33
1975	80,765	12.34
1980	149,127	12.88
1985	239,042	13.73
1990	317,500[b]	13.16[b]
1995	450,800[b]	13.80[b]
2000	626,000[b]	14.25[b]
2010	—[c]	15.75[b]
2020	—[c]	20.04[b]
2030	—[c]	23.97[b]
2040	—[c]	24.87[b]
2050	—[c]	25.22[b]
2060	—[c]	25.98[b]

[a] "Taxable payroll" consists of the total earnings subject to Social Security taxes, after adjustments in applicable years to reflect (i) deemed wages based on military service, and (ii) the lower tax rates on self-employment income, tips, and multiple-employer "excess wages." This adjustment is made to facilitate both the calculation of tax income (which is thereby the product of the tax rate and the payroll) and the comparison of expenditure percentages with tax rates. This taxable payroll is slightly different for OASDI and HI because of past differences in the tax treatment of self-employed persons and current differences in coverage of employment; however, these differences do not materially affect the comparisons.

[b] Estimated based on intermediate "II-B" set of assumptions in the 1990 Trustees Reports.

[c] Dollar amounts are not shown in the distant future since they tend to lose their meaning except when related to an index such as taxable payroll.

In this chapter we will discuss the question of how the amount of payroll tax to be paid at any given time by employees and employers is determined. In 1940 a worker paid taxes of 1 percent of the first $3,000 of his earnings, a maximum of $30.00; in 1990 a worker paid 7.65 percent of the first $51,300 of his earnings, a maximum of $3,924.45. How was it decided that the tax rate would be 1 percent in 1940 and 7.65 percent in 1990? How was it decided that a worker would pay tax on $3,000 of his earnings in 1940 and on $51,300 in 1990? What will those amounts be in the future?

Current-Cost Financing Method

There is a variety of "financing methods" available to pay for a social insurance program just as there is a variety of financing methods available to pay for automobiles, houses, life insurance policies, and almost everything else we buy.

The most obvious financing method for a social insurance program is what is sometimes called the pay-as-you-go method, or the "current-cost method." Under this method, just enough taxes are collected each year to pay the benefits and administrative expenses that fall due that year—the "current costs." Since it is difficult to estimate the exact amount of expenditures for a given year, it is usual to plan to collect slightly more in taxes than is likely to be needed. This excess amount of taxes is set aside in a reserve fund, or "trust fund," to be used in years when benefit payments are higher than expected or tax collections are lower than expected or a combination of both. Under current-cost financing the trust fund never becomes very large since it serves merely as a contingency fund.

What is the pattern of tax collections that can be expected under a current-cost financing method? Basically, it is about the same as the pattern of program expenditures illustrated in column (2) of Table 6.1. The current cost of benefits and administration started very low at $62 million in 1940 and rose steadily to an estimated $317,500 million by 1990. Column (3) of Table 6.1 expresses these costs as a percentage of taxable payroll and permits a more meaningful comparison from year to year.

A few words of review about the "taxable payroll" may be of help in interpreting the figures in Table 6.1. The taxable payroll in a given year is the total earnings subject to Social Security tax for persons who pay Social Security taxes during that year, but it does not include earnings for any

Table 6.2

History of Increases in the Maximum Taxable Earnings Base

Calendar Year	Maximum Taxable Earnings Base
(1)	(2)
1937–50	$ 3,000
1951–54	3,600
1955–58	4,200
1959–65	4,800
1966–67	6,600
1968–71	7,800
1972	9,000
1973	10,800
1974	13,200
1975	14,100
1976	15,300
1977	16,500
1978	17,700
1979	22,900
1980	25,900
1981	29,700
1982	32,400
1983	35,700
1984	37,800
1985	39,600
1986	42,000
1987	43,800
1988	45,000
1989	48,000
1990	51,300

individual in excess of the "maximum contribution and benefit base," sometimes loosely referred to as the "maximum taxable earnings base." In 1990, for example, this maximum was $51,300; thus the taxable payroll was the total earnings subject to Social Security tax for all persons who paid Social Security taxes in 1990, but it did not include earnings in excess of $51,300 for any individual. Reference was made to "earnings subject to Social Security tax" to recognize that some earnings are not taxable: earnings in jobs not covered by Social Security and investment earnings, for example.

From 1937 through 1950 the maximum earnings subject to Social Security tax was $3,000. It is estimated that 97 percent of the persons covered by Social Security earned less than $3,000 in 1937, and 71 percent earned less than $3,000 in 1950. Table 6.2 illustrates how this maximum taxable earnings base has increased from time to time. Under present law, the maximum taxable earnings base will increase automatically after 1990 to keep up with increases in the average wages and salaries of American workers.

In 1990 an estimated 94 percent of those covered by Social Security earned less than the maximum taxable earnings base and thus had all of their earnings taxed under the Social Security program. It is estimated that this percentage will remain at about that level unless the law is amended to provide otherwise. It is estimated that 86 to 87 percent of total earnings in covered employment in 1990 and later will be subjected to Social Security tax.

Table 6.3 shows the total amount of expenditures for benefits and administration compared with the actual tax income from 1937 to 1990 under our Social Security program. The table covers the Old-Age, Survivors, Disability and Hospital Insurance parts of the Social Security program; the Supplementary Medical Insurance program is discussed later. Although tax collections began in 1937, no benefits were paid from 1937 through 1939 except for the return of the workers' taxes in the event of death. Through 1983, the tax income indicated in column (3) equals the combined worker and employer tax rates. For example, in 1937 the workers' tax rate was 1 percent and the employers' tax rate was 1 percent, or a combined tax rate of 2 percent. Beginning in 1984, the tax income shown in column (3) equals the combined worker and employer tax rates plus the relatively small amount of income taxes paid on OASDI benefits and transferred to the trust funds.

Self-employed persons first became covered in 1951 and paid Social Security taxes in amounts larger than the workers' tax and smaller than the combined worker and employer tax until 1989, after which they pay the combined worker and employer tax. For convenience of presentation, the figures in Table 6.3 have taken these different tax rates into

Table 6.3

Comparison of Cost Rates and Income Rates, and Trust Fund Levels, under the Old-Age, Survivors, Disability, and Hospital Insurance Program for Selected Years

Calendar Year	Cost Rates: Expenditures as Percentage of Taxable Payroll[a]	Income Rates: Tax Income[b] as Percentage of Taxable Payroll	Amount in Trust Funds at Beginning of Year[c]	
			Dollar Amount (in millions)	Multiple of Expenditures during Year
(1)	(2)	(3)	(4)	(5)
1937	—[d]	2.00%	$ 0	—
1940	0.19%	2.00	1,724	27.81
1945	0.48	2.00	6,005	19.75
1950	1.17	3.00	11,816	11.56
1955	3.34	4.00	20,576	4.05
1960	5.89	6.00	21,966	1.86
1965	7.93	7.25	21,172	1.10
1970	9.33	9.60	36,687	0.96
1975	12.34	11.70	55,005	0.68
1980	12.88	12.26	43,519	0.29
1981	13.74	13.30	40,202	0.23
1982	14.58	13.40	43,287	0.22
1983	14.16	13.84	32,942	0.16
1984	13.88	14.19	51,524	0.23
1985	13.73	14.49	62,090	0.26
1986	13.53	14.50	79,021	0.31
1987	13.17	14.46	105,194	0.41
1988	13.09	15.18	144,228	0.52
1989	13.07	15.13	204,062	0.69
1990[e]	13.16	15.51	274,411	0.86

[a] "Taxable payroll" consists of the total earnings subject to Social Security taxes, after adjustments in applicable years to reflect (i) deemed wages based on military service, and (ii) the lower tax rates on self-employment income, tips, and multiple-employer "excess wages." This adjustment is made to facilitate both the calculation of tax income (which is thereby the product of the tax rate and the payroll) and the comparison of expenditure percentages with tax rates. This taxable payroll is slightly different for OASDI and HI because of past differences in the tax treatment of self-employed persons and current differences in coverage of employment; however, these differences do not materially affect the comparisons.

[b] Includes OASDI and HI payroll tax income, and revenue from the taxation of OASDI benefit payments.

[c] In 1984 and later, includes advance tax transfers to OASI and DI Trust Funds for month of January.

[d] During 1937–39 no benefit payments were made except a return of employee taxes in the event of death.

[e] Figures for 1990 are estimated, with the exception of the amount in the trust funds at the beginning of the year (which is based on actual data).

account by expressing the current costs in column (2) as a percentage of a "hypothetical taxable payroll." This payroll was constructed so that the application of the worker and employer tax rates to such payroll would yield the same total taxes as would the application of the actual different tax rates to the actual taxable payroll in each category of employment. This procedure also adjusts for other minor deviations in the financing.

A study of the figures in Table 6.3 indicates that during its first twenty years of operation Social Security collected considerably more in taxes than it paid out in benefits but that during the past thirty years or so the taxes have been approximately equal to the current expenditures. The years from 1975 through 1982 were an important exception, and expenditures for benefits and administration exceeded tax collections, thus requiring previously accumulated funds to pay a portion of the benefits. Beginning in 1983, provision was made for increased taxes that will exceed projected expenditures and result in a significant trust fund buildup during the next decade or two, depending on the assumptions employed. This development will be discussed later in the chapter.

The Supplementary Medical Insurance program has always been financed on a current-cost basis, so far as is practical. Participants pay premiums specified by law, and Congress appropriates whatever amount of general revenue is necessary to pay the balance of the cost each year. In practice, this is done on an estimated basis and income and outgo do not always come out even; therefore, a small trust fund balance is maintained. Also, provision is made for medical expense claims that begin in one year but carry over into the next year.

For all practical purposes, therefore, Social Security has been financed on a current-cost basis, and the trust funds have been intended only to reflect all financial transactions and to serve as contingency funds in absorbing temporary differences between income and expenditures. At the beginning of 1990 the trust funds were adequate to pay only about 6 percent of the program costs during the next ten years and thus will play a relatively minor role in ensuring the payment of future benefits. If there is a significant trust fund buildup over the next twenty years or so (as is currently anticipated for the Old-Age, Survivors, and Disability Insurance parts of the Social Security program), the role of the trust funds could change. For the time being, however, it is the ongoing collection of Social Security taxes that is the most important factor in providing benefits under the program.

Although the trust funds are relatively small at the present time, some background information on how they are invested may be useful in understanding certain aspects of the financing questions to be discussed later. The portion of each trust fund that, in the judgment of the Secretary of the Treasury (the Managing Trustee of the trust funds), is not required to meet current expenditures for benefits and administration is invested on a daily basis in one of the following types of security:

> Interest-bearing obligations of the U.S. government, including special public-debt obligations utilized only by the trust funds
>
> Obligations guaranteed as to both principal and interest by the United States
>
> Certain federally sponsored agency obligations designated as lawful investments for fiduciary and trust funds under the control and authority of the United States or any officer of the United States

The trust funds earned interest amounting to $21.2 billion during 1989, equivalent to an effective annual rate of about 9.8 percent on the total assets of the trust funds.

Alternatives to Current-Cost Financing

There are alternatives to the current-cost financing method. Instead of collecting just enough in taxes each year to pay the benefits for the year, we could collect more in taxes than needed to pay current benefits and place the excess contributions in a reserve fund or a trust fund. The higher the taxes, the larger the trust fund. This procedure is usually termed "advance funding." There are different levels at which advance funding can take place, depending upon the theory being followed as well as certain practicalities. Columns (4) and (5) of Table 6.3 indicate the extent to which Social Security was advance funded during its early history.

Why would we want to collect more in taxes than we need to pay current benefits? Why would we want to accumulate sizable trust funds? There are advantages and disadvantages to both the current-cost and the advance-funding methods, some of which are obvious but many of which are not.

Current-cost financing is easy to understand. Simply collect enough taxes each year to pay the benefits falling due that year. Most governmental programs are financed in this way. The taxes are low in the early years of the program and increase gradually as the public "gets used to paying the taxes." There is no sizable fund to invest, thus numerous investment problems are avoided. If a large fund were to exist, the public might misunderstand the purpose of the fund and believe that benefits could be expanded more than was in fact economically sound.

On the other hand, current-cost financing may mislead the public. The public may think that the low cost in the early years will continue indefinitely and thus may demand or be enticed into accepting a Social Security program that is more generous than will be affordable at some time in the future. Steadily increasing tax rates, which is an integral part of the current-cost method, may not be desirable. The public may prefer to have tax rates that are more predictable and that remain the same for many years at a time.

Advance Funding of Private Employee Benefit Systems

If the Social Security program were a private system, under normal circumstances it would be considered desirable to collect more income than is necessary for current benefit payments and to accumulate a substantial fund. This is in fact the normal procedure for a private employee benefit system for reasons that include the following:

> *Security of benefits.* The existence of a large fund gives the employees some assurance that if the system terminates and no future income to the system is available, the benefits accrued to date can in fact be paid, at least

to the extent that the accumulated fund is adequate. (The Employee Retirement Income Security Act of 1974 requires that most private pension plans accumulate a fund in order to give employees this added security.)

Reduction of future contributions. The amount of investment earnings on the trust fund can be used to pay a portion of future benefits and thus permit a reduction in the amount of future contributions otherwise required to finance the benefits.

Allocation of costs to the period during which they are incurred. Even though benefits may not be paid until some future date, the cost of these benefits can be considered as having been incurred gradually over an employee's working lifetime as he earns the benefits. The recognition of this principle through payment of sufficient contributions to fund the benefit obligations as they accrue will generally lead to the accumulation of a substantial fund.

When a private system is advance funded, it is not anticipated that the assets will be used except to earn interest and thus reduce future costs. In particular it is not anticipated that the assets will be liquidated and used to pay benefits, except to smooth out minor fluctuations in income and outgo or in the event of the plan's termination.

It is important to note that this rationale for the advance funding of a privately sponsored system (as distinguished from a government-sponsored system) assumes that the assets of the trust fund are invested "outside" the sponsoring organization. For example, if Company A establishes a pension system and makes contributions to a trust fund to advance fund the system, the assets of the trust fund are not used to buy bonds and stock of Company A (in fact, strict limitations are placed on such investments in a system that meets federal government requirements).

If the assets *were* so invested in Company A, the pensioners would be dependent for their future benefits solely upon the fortunes of Company A and would have little, if any, more security than if there were not a trust fund and no advance funding. The only advantages of such a procedure would relate to "allocation of costs" (as mentioned above), and a nominal earmarking of Company A assets for pension purposes. In order to provide the "security of benefits" (as mentioned above) the assets must be invested outside of Company A: for example, in Companies B, C, and D, or in securities issued by federal, state, and local governments, not necessarily confined to the United States. Of course, it can be argued that by investing the assets of the trust fund in Company A (or not even bothering to set aside money to advance fund the pension benefits), Company A will utilize these funds so as to be financially stronger in the future and thus be better able to pay the benefits as they become due.

The point, however, is that the concept of advance funding of private systems is based on investing the assets of the trust fund *outside* the sponsoring organization. If the assets are reinvested in the sponsoring organization, then advance funding takes on an entirely different meaning; and at worst, advance funding means no funding at all—even though the parties involved may *think* that traditional advance funding, with its attendant advantages, has taken place.

Advance Funding of a National Social Insurance System

The above-stated rationale for the advance funding of a private pension system is less valid for national compulsory social insurance—such as the Social Security program which covers substantially the entire population and which has investment limitations and consequences that do not apply to private pension systems. To understand this requires a thoughtful analysis of what happens when Social Security is advance funded, a process that, for convenience, may be described in simple terms as follows:

Social Security taxes are collected from employees and employers and deposited in trust funds.

Benefits are paid from the trust funds and any money not required for current benefit payments is loaned to the federal government, which issues interest-bearing bonds to the trust funds.

The government pays interest on the bonds and redeems the bonds when they mature. Interest earnings, as well as proceeds from maturing bonds, that are not required for benefit payments are invested in additional bonds.

In future years when then-current Social Security taxes are inadequate to pay benefits, interest earnings and the proceeds from the maturing bonds are used to make benefit payments.

While this process of accumulating assets in the trust funds, earning interest on the assets, and then selling the assets as necessary to make future benefits payments may seem simple and straightforward, it immediately becomes quite complicated when the following unique characteristics of the transactions are considered:

When the trust funds initially loan Social Security taxes (not then needed for benefit payments) to the government in exchange for bonds, the government has disposable funds and the consequences will be one or more of the following:

The government can collect less in general revenue than would have been necessary otherwise.

The government can borrow less from the public than would have been necessary otherwise.

The government can levy general revenue and borrow in the same amounts as if there had been no loans from the trust funds, and the government will have additional funds— equal to the loans from the trust funds—to spend or invest at the government's discretion.

The economic effect on the nation and its taxpayers, now and in the future, including the effect on the operating deficit and the amount of national debt held by the public and by the government, will depend upon how the government utilizes these funds borrowed from the trust funds. But it is probably impossible to determine with certainty exactly how the government's actions are influenced by the availability of these Social Security loans.

When the government pays interest each year on the bonds, and redeems them at or before maturity, the consequences will be one or more of the following:

The government can collect more in general revenue than would have been necessary otherwise.

The government can borrow more from the public than would have been necessary otherwise.

The government can levy general revenue and borrow in the same amounts as if the interest payments and redemption payments were not due, and the government can correspondingly reduce its spending on other programs or sell some of its assets.

Here, again, the economic effect on the nation and its taxpayers will depend upon where the government obtains the funds necessary to redeem the bonds and to pay interest on them before they mature.

In summary, then, the particular actions taken by the government at the time it acquires the loans from the trust funds, as well as when it repays the loans together with interest thereon, will have some effect (not always determinable either in advance or retrospectively) on:

the government's current operating deficit or surplus,

the national debt, held by government agencies as well as by the public,

the amount of saving and investment by the government,

the amount of saving and investment by the public, individually and collectively, the economic strength of the national economy currently and in the future, and the ability of that economy to produce goods and services desired by the public and to generate a tax base that will support Social Security as well as other government-mandated programs, and

the psychology of the Congress, the administration, and the public.

Is it any wonder that discussions about the consequences of advance funding versus current-cost financing are confused and confusing? Consider, however, the following comments about the advantages and disadvantages of advance funding for a social insurance system whose assets must be invested in government bonds, summarized under the same three headings used earlier to discuss the advantages of the advance funding of a private employee benefit system.

Security of benefits. Whether or not the accumulation of bonds in the trust funds makes the future payment of benefits more secure depends upon what the government does with its newfound money. If it spends it in such a way that the future economy is no stronger than it would otherwise have been, then the benefits will be no more secure than if there were no advance funding. On the other hand, if the government invests its newfound money so as to strengthen the future economy, then benefit security will be enhanced because it will be easier to collect the future taxes required to pay interest and to redeem the bonds as needed to pay future benefits. The only source of money to pay future benefits is future taxes or future borrowing, regardless of whether or not the trust funds hold government bonds as assets. Therefore, it can be argued that the added security of benefits, if any, will not be the result of the nominal assets in the trust funds but it will be the result of how the future economy is affected by implementing the advance-funding process.

The question of using advance funding to protect the participants in the event of the system's termination is not relevant. First, the trust fund assets have no tangible value and represent only a claim on future federal revenue. Second, it is usually assumed that the Social Security program will continue indefinitely and that the taxing power of the federal government is adequate assurance that the benefits will be provided. This is probably a justifiable assumption provided that the Social Security benefits, together with all the other benefits and services supplied through the government, that have been promised for the future are not unreasonable and can in fact be provided. (It should be noted that there have been several benefit reductions since 1977, some of which applied to past benefit accruals, that are tantamount to a partial termination of the Social Security system.)

Reduction of future contributions. The accumulation of a fund for Social Security would have a paradoxical effect. Higher Social Security taxes would be required from today's generation of taxpayers (perhaps offset by concurrently lower general taxes or reduced borrowing), but tomorrow's generations of taxpayers, considered as a whole, would pay the same total amount of taxes to support Social Security—Social Security taxes and general taxes—as if there were no fund. This is true because Social Security trust funds are invested in government securities, the interest on which and the redemption of which is paid from general revenue; therefore, the accumulation of a fund would result in lower future Social Security taxes but higher future general taxes. In other words, the total future cost of Social Security would be the same but would be distributed differently within each generation and would be paid not only by persons who pay Social Security taxes but also by those who do not pay such taxes.

On the other hand, the accumulation of a trust fund that is invested in government securities could serve to reduce the amount of government securities issued to other parties to finance government activities. Accordingly, the total outstanding government securities, including those issued to the trust fund, could be the same as if there were no trust fund. In this event, total general revenue collected in the future by the government for all purposes would be unaffected by the accumulation of a trust fund, Social Security payroll taxes would eventually be lower, and the nation's total tax burden would be reduced (by an amount equivalent to the higher Social Security taxes levied in the past to accumulate a trust fund, together with interest thereon).

Allocation of costs to the period during which they are incurred. An argument can be made (under a national social insurance system as well as under a private employee benefit system) for recognizing that a liability is accruing during a person's active working lifetime, even though the benefits and the costs thereof may not be paid until a later date. Recognition of this liability does not necessarily take the form of accumulating a fund that is related to the value of the benefits being accrued.

An argument is being made in some quarters these days for advance funding of the Social Security program for a reason that does not apply to an individual private pension plan. It goes something like this: Since a large part of a person's retirement needs are met by the Social Security program, his private saving for retirement is reduced; the result is that the nation's capital accumulation needs are partially unmet; to offset this reduced saving by the individual, the Social Security program should collect more in taxes than is needed for current benefits payments and thus accumulate a sizable trust fund; the assets of the trust fund would be invested in government securities; thus the amount of government securities held privately would be reduced and more private savings would be freed for use in developing the economy. Elaboration of this argument will not be made here; however, many of the points covered in the preceding pages have a bearing on the subject. In addition to these considerations, it should be noted that it is difficult for various experts to reach agreement on the extent, if any, to which the Social Security program has resulted in a reduction in private saving.

The question of whether or not to fund Social Security in advance would be completely different if it were possible to invest the assets of the trust funds other than in government bonds—for example, to invest in the stocks and bonds of private corporations, foreign as well as domestic, or in bonds issued by foreign governments. If this were possible—requiring, of course, a change in our laws—then the advance funding of Social Security would be more nearly comparable to the advance funding of private pension systems. As far-fetched as these investment ideas may sound now, it is probably only a question of time before such ideas become accepted as the norm.

With respect to the general question of funding, whatever the rationale, it is important to note the difficulty of assessing the effect on the economy, particularly over the longer term, of collecting higher Social Security taxes from today's generation of taxpayers (possibly accompanied by lower general revenue taxation and/or reduced government borrowing from the public) and the same or lower total taxes from tomorrow's generations. The effect would depend in part upon how the government utilized the additional funds, if any, placed at its disposal as well as the ways in which private saving would in fact be affected. These matters are extremely difficult to evaluate retrospectively; they are even more difficult to evaluate in advance.[1]

In discussing the advance funding of a private system, it was noted that the assets are intended only to earn interest and thus reduce future costs. It is not anticipated that the assets will be liquidated to pay benefits so long as the private system continues to operate. On the other hand, current discussions (in 1990) about the advance funding of Social Security frequently contemplate the buildup of a large fund that will eventually be liquidated to pay benefits as the baby boom generation retires. There are important consequences of such a procedure that are seldom mentioned.

First, if traditional financing practices are followed, when all the assets have been liquidated, the Social Security payroll tax rate must increase abruptly to make up the portion of the total benefit cost that was theretofore paid by the liquidation of the trust fund assets. For the Old-Age, Survivors, and

Chart 6.A

Projected Expenditures and Tax Income for Old-Age, Survivors, and Disability Insurance Program under Intermediate Assumptions,[a] Expressed as a Percentage of Taxable Payroll[b]

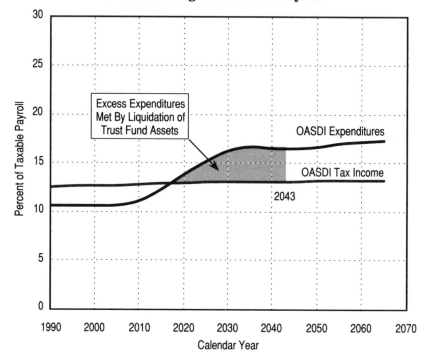

[a] See Chapter 10 and Appendix I for discussion of alternative sets of assumptions. Tax income includes OASDI payroll taxes and revenue from the income taxation of OASDI benefit payments.

[b] "Taxable payroll" in 1990 and later consists of the total earnings subject to Social Security taxes, after adjustments to reflect (i) deemed wages based on military service and (ii) the lower tax rates on multiple-employer "excess wages." This adjustment is made to facilitate both the calculation of tax income (which is thereby the product of the tax rate and the payroll) and the comparison of expenditure percentages with tax rates.

Disability Insurance part of Social Security, this would entail a combined employee-employer payroll tax rate increase in 2043 from 12.4 percent (as currently scheduled in present law) to about 16 percent under the intermediate assumptions.

This phenomenon is illustrated in Chart 6.A, which shows the expenditures (for benefits and administration) and the

Chart 6.B

**Projected Expenditures and Tax Income for Old-
Age, Survivors, and Disability Insurance Program
under Pessimistic Assumptions,[a] Expressed
as a Percentage of Taxable Payroll[b]**

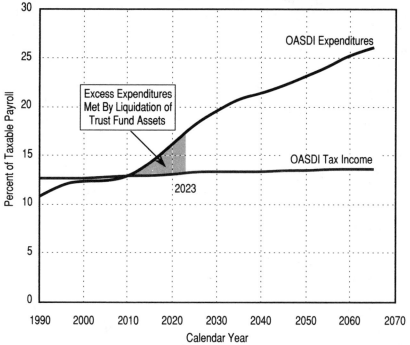

[a] See Chapter 10 and Appendix I for discussion of alternative sets of assumptions. Tax income includes OASDI payroll taxes and revenue from the income taxation of OASDI benefit payments.

[b] "Taxable payroll" in 1990 and later consists of the total earnings subject to Social Security taxes, after adjustments to reflect (i) deemed wages based on military service and (ii) the lower tax rates on multiple-employer "excess wages." This adjustment is made to facilitate both the calculation of tax income (which is thereby the product of the tax rate and the payroll) and the comparison of expenditure percentages with tax rates.

tax income for the Old-Age, Survivors, and Disability Insurance part of Social Security according to the intermediate
assumptions. The shaded area in the chart represents the
excess of expenditures over payroll tax income that would
be met by liquidating the trust fund assets—a procedure
that would take place during the years from 2017 through
2043. In the year 2042, the final year before asset depletion,

79 percent of expenditures would be met by Social Security payroll taxes (and income taxes on benefits), and 21 percent would be met by interest and liquidating the trust fund assets (i.e., with general revenue collected to pay interest and to redeem the Treasury bonds held by the trust fund). In 2043, there would be no further assets to liquidate, and the payroll tax would have to be abruptly increased to make benefit payments.

Of course it is unlikely that it would be feasible to increase the Social Security payroll tax abruptly in a single year and to decrease general revenue by a like amount. As illustrated in the chart, a procedure would have been put in place to collect general revenue in steadily increasing amounts during the asset liquidation period from 2017 to 2043 and it would be awkward to dismantle that procedure. It would be much less disruptive to increase general revenue and/or payroll taxes gradually in the years following asset depletion as necessary to make benefit payments. If payroll taxes are unchanged and if increases in general revenue are used to meet the rising costs, approximately 21 percent of the total cost of the OASDI program will be met from general revenue by the mid-21st century. If the deficits under the Hospital Insurance program are also met by general revenue, fully 36 percent of the cost of the OASDI and HI programs combined will be met from general revenue by the mid-21st century. Paradoxically, if all of this happens, by converting Social Security in 1983 to what was publicized as a "partially advance-funded system," Congress will have laid the foundation for a smooth transition to a "partially general-revenue financed system" by the middle of the 21st century. It is not clear whether this was a deliberate plan or just the unintended and unforeseen consequence of an incomplete analysis of the revised financing procedure.

Chart 6.B is the counterpart of Chart 6.A, but it is based upon the pessimistic assumptions of the 1990 trustees reports. Under these assumptions, liquidation of the trust fund assets would begin earlier and the assets would be depleted earlier (in 2023).

Conclusion

In assessing the financial stability of Social Security, much more is involved than the question of whether to use current-cost or advance-funding methods. The most important test of financial soundness for Social Security is whether future benefits and administrative expenses can reasonably be expected to be met by future income (Social Security payroll taxes plus general revenue needed to pay interest on the trust fund's bonds, as well as to redeem such bonds as necessary).

This condition does not prevail uniformly for the various segments of the Social Security program. Under the Old-Age, Survivors, and Disability Insurance program, projected future income is approximately equal to future outgo for the next thirty-five to fifty-five years, according to the pessimistic and intermediate assumptions, respectively, described in Appendix I. Thereafter, substantial deficits are expected during the second half of the next century (after all the children of the post-World War II baby boom have retired) and no provision has been made to collect the necessary taxes. Under the Hospital Insurance program, deficits are projected to begin to occur in the mid-1990s and to continue in rapidly increasing amounts each year thereafter. Under the Supplementary Medical Insurance program, there are no earmarked taxes scheduled beyond the next three years; hence it is difficult to define the deficit. Nonetheless, substantial increases in expenditures are projected for the next fifty years or so.

The matter of future financial deficits in the Social Security program is extremely important and is discussed in more detail in Chapter 7.

7
Trillion Dollar "Actuarial Deficits" and "Accrued Liabilities"

Actuarial Deficits

As discussed in Chapter 6, Social Security has generally operated on a pay-as-you-go financing basis, sometimes called a current-cost basis. The trust funds have not been large, relative to expenditures, and have served only as contingency funds, not as guaranty funds. The financial stability of Social Security has depended, therefore, and will continue to depend on the ability and willingness of the nation's workers and employers to continue to pay the taxes necessary to support the benefit payments.[1] Accordingly, it is essential that we constantly monitor estimated future income and expenditures to determine whether they are in "actuarial balance" and whether our Social Security program is still viable. When projected future income (including income attributable to the trust funds) and expenditures are not in balance, an "actuarial deficit" or an "actuarial surplus" exists—depending on whether projected expenditures are greater than income, or vice versa. Actuarial projections made during the past several years, including the most recent projections, indicate that Social Security has a significant actuarial deficit. This deficit is discussed in the following sections for each of the major portions of the Social Security program.

OASDI Deficit

In determining the actuarial balance of the Old-Age, Survivors, and Disability Insurance program, projections have customarily been made during a 75-year future period. This covers the remaining lifetime of most current participants in Social Security.

Chart 7.A shows graphically the projected expenditures and tax income under the OASDI program based on the 1990 Annual Report of the Board of Trustees.[2] Expenditures are shown based on the intermediate assumptions contained in this report and would, of course, have been lower or higher if the optimistic or pessimistic assumptions had been depicted.[3] Table 7.1 gives the corresponding numerical comparison of the projected expenditures and tax income, and the resulting differences, over various periods. For convenience of presentation, the year-by-year figures in both the chart and the table ignore the trust fund balances and the interest earnings thereon; however, this will be discussed in due course throughout the text.[4]

As indicated in Chart 7.A, tax income is projected to rise very gradually in future years. This tax income is comprised of a level Social Security tax rate and a slightly increasing general revenue component. Expenditures remain relatively level for the next twenty years, reflecting the combined effect of a projected rise in Disability Insurance expenditures and an expected temporary decline in Old-Age Insurance expenditures as the small birth cohorts of the Depression years reach retirement age. Expenditures start rising rapidly early in the 21st century as the children of the post-World War II "baby boom" begin reaching retirement age. Around the year 2035, after all the children of this baby boom period (which ended in the 1960s) have reached retirement age, expenditures roughly level off.

Under the intermediate assumptions, OASDI tax income is projected to exceed expenditures during the period from

Chart 7.A

Projected Expenditures and Tax Income[a] for Old-Age, Survivors, and Disability Insurance Program Expressed as a Percentage of Taxable Payroll[b]

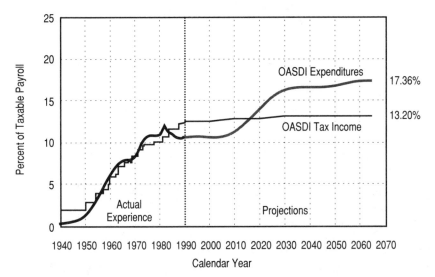

[a] Projected under intermediate II-B set of demographic and economic assumptions in 1990 Trustees Report. Tax income includes OASDI payroll taxes and revenue from the income taxation of OASDI benefit payments.

[b] "Taxable payroll" consists of the total earnings subject to Social Security taxes, after adjustments in applicable years to reflect (i) deemed wages based on military service, and (ii) the lower tax rates on self-employment income, tips, and multiple-employer "excess wages." This adjustment is made to facilitate both the calculation of tax income (which is thereby the product of the tax rate and the payroll) and the comparison of expenditure percentages with tax rates.

1990 until the year 2017. At this time the combined OASDI trust funds are projected to be equal to nearly five years' outgo. Thereafter outgo will exceed tax income, requiring that the interest earnings on the trust funds, and later the principal of the trust funds, be used to make benefit payments. By the year 2038, the trust funds are projected to fall to the level of one year's outgo, thus requiring an increase in taxes at that time in order to continue payment of benefits and to preserve the trust funds' ability to act as contingency reserves.

It is important to note that when the trust fund assets must be liquidated to close the gap between outgo and tax income, general revenue taxes must be levied to redeem the

BASIC BACKGROUND INFORMATION

Table 7.1

Projected Expenditures and Tax Income for Old-Age, Survivors, and Disability Insurance Program[a] Expressed as a Percentage of Taxable Payroll[b]

Calendar Year	OASDI Expenditures	OASDI Tax Income[c]	Difference[d]
(1)	(2)	(3)	(4)
1990	10.60%	12.61%	2.01%
1995	10.67	12.62	1.95
2000	10.56	12.65	2.09
2010	11.08	12.82	1.74
2020	13.86	12.98	-0.88
2030	16.28	13.12	-3.16
2040	16.55	13.15	-3.40
2050	16.70	13.16	-3.54
2060	17.23	13.19	-4.04
25-year averages			
1990–2014	10.83	12.67	1.84
2015–2039	15.20	13.02	-2.18
2040–2064	16.89	13.14	-3.75
75-year average[e]	13.95	13.04	-0.91

[a] Projected under intermediate II-B set of demographic and economic assumptions in 1990 Trustees Report.

[b] "Taxable payroll" consists of the total earnings subject to Social Security taxes, after adjustments in applicable years to reflect (i) deemed wages based on military service, and (ii) the lower tax rates on self-employment income, tips, and multiple-employer "excess wages." This adjustment is made to facilitate both the calculation of tax income (which is thereby the product of the tax rate and the payroll) and the comparison of expenditure percentages with tax rates.

[c] Includes OASDI payroll taxes and revenue from the income taxation of OASDI benefit payments, expressed as a percentage of taxable payroll.

[d] Negative figures represent deficits.

[e] Tax income for 75-year period includes trust fund assets on hand at beginning of period.

bonds held by the trust fund (unless money is borrowed and its repayment by the collection of taxes is deferred further). The economic significance of the trust funds is discussed in Chapter 6.

The actuarial balance of the OASDI program during the next seventy-five years may be summarized as follows: an actuarial surplus during the first twenty-five years of the 75-

year projection period, an approximately offsetting actuarial deficit during the second 25-year period, and a substantial actuarial deficit during the latter third of the 75-year period.

The average annual amount by which expenditures are projected to exceed tax income over the entire 75-year projection period is 0.91 percent of taxable payroll. This actuarial deficit represents about 7 percent of the average expenditures of 13.95 percent of taxable payroll.

Another way to express the actuarial deficit is as a single-sum amount—$1,200 billion (or $1.2 trillion) as of January 1, 1990—determined by computing the excess of expenditures over tax income (sometimes positive and sometimes negative) in each of the next seventy-five years and discounting these amounts at interest[5] to the present time, and then reducing the sum of these amounts by the value of the trust fund at the present time.

If the OASDI actuarial deficit determined in 1990 is to be eliminated by the payment of additional taxes, it could be achieved, at least in theory, in one of two ways. A single-sum amount of $1,200 billion could be placed in the trust funds immediately, and the resulting trust funds together with interest thereon, supplemented by the currently scheduled Social Security taxes, would be sufficient to pay all benefits falling due in the next seventy-five years. At the end of that period, the trust funds would be exhausted.

As an alternative to this obviously impossible solution, additional taxes could be collected over the next seventy-five years. The average additional taxes would have to be equivalent to 0.91 percent of taxable payroll (approximately 7 percent of the average scheduled taxes). If it is desired that the trust fund be maintained at a relatively low level to serve as a contingency fund—as in recent years—the additional taxes would not be constant throughout the next seventy-five years but would be variable so as to approximately match emerging expenditures. In this event, average taxes (paid by the employee and employer combined) would be about 2 percent of taxable payroll less than already scheduled until 2015, about 2 percent more than already scheduled during the next twenty-five years, and about 4 percent more than already scheduled thereafter.

In summary, the actuarial deficit is simply the amount by which projected future expenditures for benefits and administration exceed the projected income and the value of the trust funds. The actuarial deficit can be stated in various ways, some of which make it appear more formidable than others. There should be no question, however, about the necessity of eliminating any significant actuarial deficit that may appear from time to time. Otherwise, scheduled benefits cannot be paid.

Chart 7.B

Projected Expenditures and Tax Income[a] for Hospital Insurance Program Expressed as a Percentage of Taxable Payroll[b]

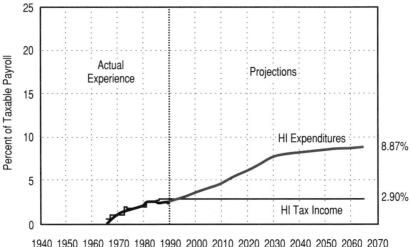

[a] Projected under intermediate II-B set of demographic and economic assumptions in 1990 Trustees Report. Tax income includes HI payroll taxes only.

[b] "Taxable payroll" consists of the total earnings subject to Social Security taxes, after adjustments in applicable years to reflect (i) deemed wages based on military service, and (ii) the lower tax rates on self-employment income, tips, and multiple-employer "excess wages." This adjustment is made to facilitate both the calculation of tax income (which is thereby the product of the tax rate and the payroll) and the comparison of expenditure percentages with tax rates. This taxable payroll is slightly different for OASDI and HI because of past differences in the tax treatment of self-employed persons and current differences in coverage of employment; however, these differences do not materially affect the comparisons.

Table 7.2

Projected Expenditures and Tax Income for Hospital Insurance Program,[a] Expressed as a Percentage of Taxable Payroll[b]

Calendar Year	HI Expenditures	HI Tax Income[c]	Difference[d]
(1)	(2)	(3)	(4)
1990	2.56%	2.90%	0.34%
1995	3.13	2.90	-0.23
2000	3.69	2.90	-0.79
2010	4.68	2.90	-1.78
2020	6.18	2.90	-3.28
2030	7.69	2.90	-4.79
2040	8.32	2.90	-5.42
2050	8.52	2.90	-5.62
2060	8.75	2.90	-5.85
25-year averages			
1990–2014	3.83	2.90	-0.93
2015–2039	7.08	2.90	-4.18
2040–2064	8.56	2.90	-5.66
75-year average[e]	6.22	2.97	-3.25

[a] Projected under intermediate II-B set of demographic and economic assumptions in 1990 Trustees Report.

[b] "Taxable payroll" consists of the total earnings subject to Social Security taxes, after adjustments in applicable years to reflect (i) deemed wages based on military service, and (ii) the lower tax rates on self-employment income, tips, and multiple-employer "excess wages." This adjustment is made to facilitate both the calculation of tax income (which is thereby the product of the tax rate and the payroll) and the comparison of expenditure percentages with tax rates. This taxable payroll is slightly different for OASDI and HI because of past differences in the tax treatment of self-employed persons and current differences in coverage of employment; however, these differences do not materially affect the comparisons.

[c] Represents HI payroll taxes, expressed as a percentage of taxable payroll.

[d] Negative figures represent deficits.

[e] Tax income for 75-year period includes trust fund assets on hand at beginning of period.

HI Deficit

In determining the actuarial balance of the Hospital Insurance program, projections are now made during a 75-year future period. Prior to 1985, projections were made for only twenty-five years. It is only reasonable that the same 75-year period be used to determine the actuarial balance of both the HI and the OASDI programs. Hospital Insurance is, in effect, a deferred retirement benefit commencing at age 65 (or after the receipt of twenty-four months of disability benefits). It is similar to an old-age retirement benefit except it is not paid in cash but in the form of partial provision of hospital services. The demographic changes in the population that will cause the OASDI program costs to increase rapidly after the turn of the century will also cause the HI program costs to increase rapidly.

Chart 7.B shows graphically the projected expenditures and tax income under the HI program based upon the 1990 Annual Report of the Board of Trustees.[6] Expenditures are shown based upon the intermediate assumptions contained in this report and would have been lower or higher if the optimistic or pessimistic assumptions had been depicted.[3] Table 7.2 gives the corresponding numerical comparison of the projected expenditures and tax income, and the resulting differences, over various periods. As was the case with OASDI, the year-by-year figures in both the chart and the table ignore the trust fund balances and the interest earnings thereon.

Tax income is scheduled to be level throughout the projection period. Expenditures are projected to rise throughout the period before approximately leveling off somewhat after the children of the post-World War II baby boom have reached retirement age. An actuarial deficit first occurs in the mid-1990s when expenditures begin to exceed tax income. Thereafter, an actuarial deficit is projected to occur each year in the future.

The average annual amount by which expenditures are projected to exceed tax income over the entire 75-year projection period is 3.25 percent of taxable payroll, or about 52 percent of the average expenditures of 6.22 percent of taxable payroll. Expressed as a single-sum amount, this actuarial deficit is about $4,400 billion (or $4.4 trillion) as of January 1, 1990.

Accordingly, if the HI actuarial deficit is to be eliminated by the payment of additional taxes it could be achieved by:

   placing a single-sum amount of $4,400 billion in the trust fund; or

   paying additional taxes that would average about 3.25 percent of taxable payroll over the next seventy-five years (an increase of approximately 112 percent over the average scheduled taxes of 2.90 percent).

Assuming that the trust fund is to be maintained at a relatively low level to serve only as a contingency fund, the additional taxes would not be constant throughout the next seventy-five years but would be variable so as to approximately match emerging expenditures. In this event, average taxes (paid by the employee and employer combined) would be almost 1 percent of taxable payroll more than already scheduled until about 2015, about 4 percent more than already scheduled during the next twenty-five years, and about 6 percent more than already scheduled thereafter.

This is a formidable deficit no matter how it is presented: a lump sum of $4,400 billion, or increased taxes averaging more than 3 percent of taxable payroll. This HI actuarial deficit is nearly four times the size of the OASDI actuarial deficit, yet it is given relatively little attention, while disproportionate attention is focused on the OASDI surplus during the next twenty-five years or so.

OASDI and HI Combined Deficit

The preceding discussions of actuarial deficits for OASDI and HI were based upon the intermediate set of demographic and economic assumptions used by the Social Security actuaries in making projections for the 1990 Trustees Reports. The actual situation could be better—or it could be worse. Chart 7.C depicts the projected expenditures for OASDI and HI combined under the optimistic and pessimistic assumptions as well as the intermediate assumptions used in the 1990 Trustees Reports. It also depicts actual past expenditures and tax income for easy comparison. Tax income expressed as a percentage of taxable payroll remains approximately the same under all sets of assumptions. Table 7.3 gives the corresponding numerical comparison of the average expenditures and tax income, and the resulting deficits, over various future periods for each of the three sets of assumptions. Table 6.3 in the previous chapter gives the corresponding numerical comparison of actual past expenditures and tax income.

Table 7.3

Projected Expenditures, Tax Income, and Deficits for Old-Age, Survivors, Disability, and Hospital Insurance Programs Combined, under Alternative Demographic and Economic Assumptions,[a] Expressed as a Percentage of Taxable Payroll[b]

	OASDHI Expenditures under...				Tax Income Less Expenditures under... [d]		
Calendar Year	Optimistic Assumptions	Intermediate Assumptions	Pessimistic Assumptions	Tax Income[c]	Optimistic Assumptions	Intermediate Assumptions	Pessimistic Assumptions
(1)	(2)	(3)	(4)	(5)	(6)	(7)	(8)
1990	13.06%	13.16%	13.47%	15.51%	2.42%	2.35%	2.07%
1995	12.55	13.80	15.50	15.52	2.95	1.72	0.05
2000	12.22	14.25	16.74	15.55	3.29	1.30	-1.16
2010	12.62	15.75	19.69	15.72	3.02	-0.03	-3.90
2020	15.13	20.04	27.00	15.88	0.64	-4.16	-11.02
2030	16.96	23.97	34.81	16.02	-1.11	-7.95	-18.64
2040	16.61	24.87	38.24	16.05	-0.76	-8.82	-21.97
2050	16.21	25.22	40.35	16.06	-0.37	-9.15	-24.00
2060	16.21	25.98	43.03	16.09	-0.37	-9.89	-26.56
25-year averages							
1990-2014	12.57	14.66	17.24	15.57	2.97	0.92	-1.63
2015-2039	16.07	22.28	31.58	15.93	-0.28	-6.35	-15.52
2040-2064	16.30	25.45	40.87	16.04	-0.48	-9.41	-24.53
75-year average[e]	14.84	20.17	27.89	16.01	1.04	-4.16	-11.73

[a] See Chapter 10 and Appendix I for discussion of alternative sets of assumptions.

[b] "Taxable payroll" in 1990 and later consists of the total earnings subject to Social Security taxes, after adjustments to reflect (i) deemed wages based on military service and (ii) the lower tax rates on multiple-employer "excess wages." This adjustment is made to facilitate both the calculation of tax income (which is thereby the product of the tax rate and the payroll) and the comparison of expenditure percentages with tax rates. This taxable payroll is slightly different for OASDI and HI because of differences in coverage of employment; however, these differences do not materially affect the comparisons.

[c] Includes OASDI and HI payroll taxes, and revenue from the income taxation of OASDI benefit payments, expressed as a percentage of taxable payroll. Figures shown are based on the intermediate assumptions. Estimates under the alternative assumptions differ slightly.

[d] For intermediate assumptions, difference is based on figures shown in columns (3) and (5). Differences for optimistic and pessimistic assumptions are based on costs shown in columns (2) and (4), less tax income under corresponding sets of assumptions (not shown). Negative figures represent deficits.

[e] Tax income for 75-year period includes trust fund assets on hand at beginning of period.

Chart 7.C

Projected Expenditures for Old-Age, Survivors, Disability, and Hospital Insurance Programs Combined under Alternative Demographic and Economic Assumptions,[a] and Tax Income[b] Expressed as a Percentage of Taxable Payroll[c]

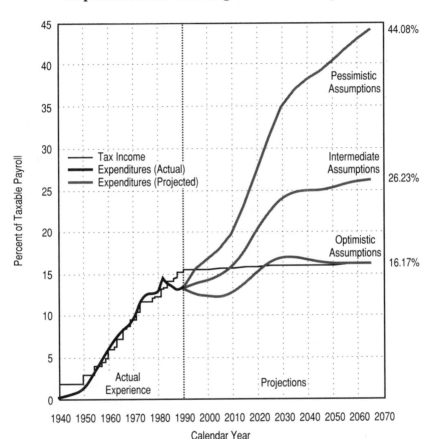

[a] See Chapter 10 and Appendix I for discussion of alternative sets of assumptions.

[b] Tax income includes OASDI and HI payroll taxes and revenue from the income taxation of OASDI benefit payments. Figures shown are based on the intermediate II-B assumptions. Estimates under the alternative assumptions differ slightly.

[c] "Taxable payroll" consists of the total earnings subject to Social Security taxes, after adjustments in applicable years to reflect (i) deemed wages based on military service, and (ii) the lower tax rates on self-employment income, tips, and multiple-employer "excess wages." This adjustment is made to facilitate both the calculation of tax income (which is thereby the product of the tax rate and the payroll) and the comparison of expenditure percentages with tax rates. This taxable payroll is slightly different for OASDI and HI because of past differences in the tax treatment of self-employed persons and current differences in coverage of employment; however, these differences do not materially affect the comparisons.

Based upon the intermediate assumptions, the actuarial deficit for the OASDI and HI programs combined is 4.16 percent of taxable payroll on the average over the next seventy-five years (equivalent to $5,600 billion as of January 1, 1990). The optimistic assumptions produce an actuarial surplus of 1.04 percent of taxable payroll on the average over the next seventy-five years (equivalent to $1,500 billion as of January 1, 1990). The pessimistic assumptions produce an actuarial deficit of 11.73 percent of taxable payroll on the average over the next seventy-five years (equivalent to $13,200 billion as of January 1, 1990).

The taxes that are scheduled under present law (a tax rate for employees and employers combined of 15.30 percent of taxable payroll plus small amounts of general revenue arising primarily from the income taxation of Social Security benefits) will not be adequate to provide future benefits except under the optimistic assumptions. Under the pessimistic assumptions, scheduled future tax rates are woefully inadequate; that is, they are sufficient to provide only about three-fifths of the benefits that will become payable during the coming seventy-five years.

At least one thing seems clear from examining these actuarial deficits. Only the foolhardy would continue to ignore the longer range financial problems projected for the Social Security program. It is not a question of whether future costs will be higher; it is a question of whether they will be so much higher as to be unaffordable. It is a question of whether we are making promises we will not be able to keep.

SMI Deficit

The question of the actuarial balance of the Supplementary Medical Insurance program is a difficult one because of the way in which the program is financed and the way in which future costs are presented (or not presented). Participants in SMI pay monthly premiums that currently account for about 25 percent of the cost of the program. Under present law this percentage will decrease in the future (so long as medical cost inflation continues to exceed general inflation), and it is expected to be about 12 percent by the year 2000. The amount of these premiums is determined for

Chart 7.D

**Projected Expenditures and Premium Income[a] for
Supplementary Medical Insurance Program
Expressed as a Percentage of Taxable Payroll[b]**

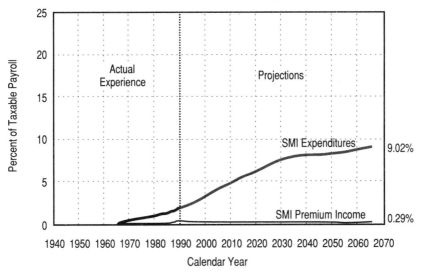

[a] Projected under intermediate II-B set of demographic and economic assumptions in 1990 Trustees Report.

[b] Although the SMI program is not financed by payroll taxes, its cost is shown for comparative purposes as a percentage of payroll that is taxable for HI purposes. Participation in SMI is optional and is financed by premiums paid by the enrollees, and by general revenues.

one year at a time, approximately one year in advance. The balance of SMI costs is paid with general revenue.

The 1990 Annual Report of the Board of Trustees[7] on the financial condition of SMI includes projections of income and expenditures for only three years.[8] This limits any formal statement about the actuarial balance of the SMI program to a three-year period. SMI costs (relative to the payroll of active workers) may be expected to continue their rise indefinitely, reaching five times their current level by the middle of the next century, yet no formal provision has been made to collect the taxes necessary to pay for these benefits.

Chart 7.D shows graphically the projected expenditures for the SMI program under the intermediate set of assumptions consistent with those used for the OASDI and HI programs. Also shown is the projected income from participants'

Table 7.4

Projected Expenditures, Premium Income, and General Revenue Requirements for Supplementary Medical Insurance Program,[a] Expressed as a Percentage of Taxable Payroll[b]

Calendar Year	SMI Expenditures	SMI Premium Income	Amount to Be Drawn from General Revenue
(1)	(2)	(3)	(4)
1990	1.80%	0.45%	1.35%
1995	2.46	0.42	2.04
2000	3.33	0.40	2.93
2010	4.87	0.35	4.52
2020	6.15	0.39	5.76
2030	7.64	0.42	7.22
2040	8.17	0.39	7.78
2050	8.35	0.35	8.00
2060	8.82	0.31	8.51
25-year averages			
1990–2014	3.59	0.39	3.20
2015–2039	7.04	0.40	6.64
2040–2064	8.48	0.34	8.14
75-year average[c]	6.11	0.37	5.74

[a] Projected under intermediate II-B set of demographic and economic assumptions in 1990 Trustees Report.

[b] Although the SMI program is not financed by payroll taxes, its cost is shown for comparative purposes as a percentage of payroll that is taxable for HI purposes. Participation in SMI is optional and is financed by premiums paid by the enrollees, and by general revenues.

[c] Premium income for 75-year period includes trust fund assets on hand at beginning of period.

premiums. Table 7.4 gives the corresponding numerical comparison of the expenditures and premium income, as well as the differences that must be drawn from general revenue during selected time periods. These amounts are expressed as a percentage of the payroll that is taxable for HI purposes even though the SMI program is not financed by payroll taxes. This is done to facilitate comparison with the other parts of the Social Security program. For convenience of presentation, the year-by-year figures in both the chart and the table ignore the trust fund balances since they play a relatively small role in the financing of the SMI program.

Chart 7.E

Projected Expenditures for Supplementary Medical Insurance Program under Alternative Demographic and Economic Assumptions[a] Expressed as a Percentage of Taxable Payroll[b]

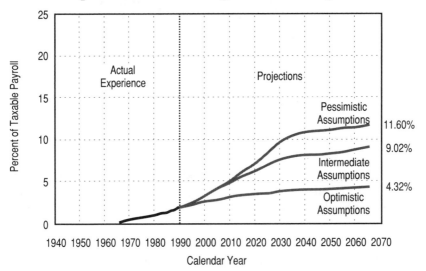

[a] See Chapter 10 and Appendix I for discussion of alternative sets of assumptions.

[b] Although the SMI program is not financed by payroll taxes, its cost is shown for comparative purposes as a percentage of payroll that is taxable for HI purposes. Participation in SMI is optional and is financed by premiums paid by the enrollees, and by general revenues.

In contrast to the procedures for the OASDI and HI programs, a long-range actuarial balance for the SMI program is not officially calculated or even defined. The SMI actuarial deficit could well be considered to be the amount by which projected future expenditures for benefits and administration exceed the projected income from premiums paid by the participants. Under this theory, future general revenue would not be taken into account since it has not been earmarked in any way to ensure its availability. Using such a definition, the actuarial deficit over the next seventy-five years would average approximately 5.74 percent of the payroll taxable for HI purposes. Expressed as a single-sum amount, this actuarial deficit is about $7,600 billion as of January 1, 1990.[9]

A range of possible future SMI costs is illustrated by Chart 7.E which shows projected expenditures under the three alternative sets of assumptions consistent with those used for the OASDI and HI programs. These projections imply an SMI actuarial deficit as of January 1, 1990, of $4,100 billion under the optimistic assumptions and $9,600 billion under the pessimistic assumptions. There is no assurance, of course, that actual future costs will fall within this range.

The most important conclusions to be drawn from these statements about the actuarial deficit of the SMI program are that:

significantly larger costs can be expected for the future; and

these costs should be estimated, acknowledged, and some formal procedure adopted to assure their payment.

The present procedure of not formally acknowledging these future costs is unfair to present and future taxpayers and beneficiaries. It makes it too easy for us to make promises of future benefits that we may not be able and willing to finance.

The Need to Eliminate Actuarial Deficits

Substantial actuarial deficits exist for all segments of the Social Security program. The OASDI deficit has been determined and acknowledged; but since it will not become significant until all the children of the post-World War II baby boom have retired, some forty years from now, it has not yet been taken seriously. The HI deficit during the next seventy-five years has been determined but not very well acknowledged. SMI deficits—or high future costs, if you will—are not officially computed, they are not communicated to Congress, and it appears they are not even worried about by anyone except a few knowledgeable and concerned individuals.

The total amount of these actuarial deficits for the Social Security program (OASDI, HI, and SMI combined) is a staggering sum: $13,200 billion, or $13.2 trillion, under the intermediate assumptions. This combined actuarial deficit is $22.8 trillion under the pessimistic assumptions and $5.6

trillion under the optimistic assumptions. These actuarial deficits must be eliminated. Indeed, they *will* be eliminated sooner or later. *It should be obvious that gaps between income and outgo (actuarial deficits) will be closed eventually by either raising taxes or lowering benefits.* It is simply a question of whether we plan in advance the best way to close these future gaps or wait until it is so late that we have no desirable options available to us.

The only prudent action is to eliminate the actuarial deficits now: to revise the benefits or the financing procedures, or both, so that anticipated future expenditures will equal anticipated future income on the basis of the best information available at this time. To do otherwise is irresponsible in the extreme.

Accrued Liabilities

Once the actuarial deficits have been eliminated and Social Security is in actuarial balance—with anticipated future income equal to anticipated future expenditures—there is still the question of the "accrued liability." This is a completely separate issue from the "actuarial deficit." The existence and the amount of the accrued liability has no relation whatsoever to the actuarial deficit, although these two terms are frequently confused.

The accrued liability can be defined as the present value of benefits that have been earned or accrued as of a given date but will not actually be paid until a later date. This concept is discussed in the following sections for each major portion of the Social Security program.

OASDI Accrued Liability

At the beginning of 1990 there were 39 million persons receiving monthly Social Security benefits of about $250 billion per year under the OASDI program. All conditions had been met for these benefits to be payable in the future, thus the benefits may be considered to have been fully earned or accrued. The present value of these future benefits is estimated to be about $2,700 billion; that is, a fund of $2,700 billion invested at interest would be just enough to pay all the future benefits to these persons and the fund would be exhausted at the time the last benefit payment fell due. Accordingly, the accrued liability for benefits payable to these 39 million persons may be said to be $2,700 billion.

It is more difficult to define the accrued liability for the more than 130 million persons who have participated in the Social Security program at some time in the past and who are potential recipients of benefits at some time in the future. Because of their earlier participation, these persons may be considered to have earned or accrued a certain portion of the benefits that will be paid to them at some time in the future. A variety of methods can be used to calculate the amount of benefits and the value thereof that should be assigned to this earlier participation. According to recent unpublished studies made by the Office of the Actuary of the Social Security Administration, it is reasonable to consider this accrued liability as of January 1, 1990, to be approximately $4,000 billion.

When that amount is added to the accrued liability of $2,700 billion for those persons already receiving benefits, the result is a total accrued liability of some $6,700 billion. Since the OASDI trust funds had assets of about $189 billion on January 1, 1990, the "unfunded accrued liability" could be considered to be about $6,511 billion, or $6.5 trillion. The unfunded accrued liability as of any given date may be viewed as the amount by which benefits, paid or promised with respect to earlier years of participation in the system, exceed the amount of taxes paid during those years by employees and their employers (appropriately adjusted for assumed interest earnings).

It should be emphasized, however, that these accrued benefits—even those currently being paid—are not vested from a legal point of view because, in theory at least, the entire program could be substantially modified (or even terminated) by Congress at any time. Section 1104 of the Social Security Act provides that "the right to alter, amend, or repeal any provision of this Act is hereby reserved to the Congress." As a practical matter, however, it is more reasonable to assume that Social Security will continue without abrupt change.

HI Accrued Liability

There has been little, if any, concern expressed about the accrued liability under the HI program. Yet, the HI program is similar to the OASDI program in most respects that are relevant to an accrued liability. Hospital Insurance is, in effect, a deferred benefit commencing at age 65 (or, if earlier, after the receipt of twenty-four months of disability benefits). The benefit is not paid in cash but rather "in kind" in the form of partial provision of hospital services. An individual may not be hospitalized and thus may not appear to receive tangible benefits; nevertheless, benefits are received just as surely as if cash benefits were paid to the individual in the amounts necessary to purchase the Hospital Insurance benefits. The program is financed by a portion of the Social Security taxes paid by active workers. To be eligible for HI benefits, a retired worker must be eligible for monthly old-age benefits, which in turn requires a certain minimum period of tax-paying participation in Social Security.

At the beginning of 1990, there were roughly 33 million persons eligible to receive partial reimbursement for hospital costs in the event of their illness. All conditions had been met for these benefits to be payable in the future, thus the benefits may be considered to have been fully earned or accrued without further payment of Social Security taxes by the individuals eligible for benefits. The present value of these future benefits is estimated to be about $800 billion; that is, a fund of $800 billion invested at interest would be just enough to pay all the future benefits to these persons, and the fund would be exhausted at the time the last benefit payment fell due. Accordingly, the accrued liability for benefits payable to these 33 million persons may be said to be $800 billion.

Similarly, it is reasonable to assume that an accrued liability exists for the more than 130 million persons who have participated in the Social Security program at some time in the past and who are potential recipients of benefits at some time in the future. Because of their earlier participation, these persons may be considered to have earned or accrued a certain portion of the HI benefits that will be paid to them in the future, although these benefits are not vested from a legal point of view. No formal estimates have been made of this accrued liability by the actuaries of the Health Care Financing Administration; however, it is probably of the magnitude of $2,900 billion. When that amount is added to the accrued liability of $800 billion for those persons already eligible for HI benefits, the result is a total accrued liability of about $3,700 billion. Since the HI trust fund had assets of $86 billion as of January 1, 1990, this would still leave an unfunded accrued liability of $3,614 billion, or about $3.6 trillion. Just as with the OASDI program, the unfunded accrued liability as of any given date may be viewed as the amount by which benefits, paid or promised with respect to earlier years of participation in the system, exceed the amount of taxes paid during those years by employees and their employers (appropriately adjusted for assumed interest earnings).

SMI Accrued Liability

The accrued liability for the SMI program is somewhat more elusive and difficult to define because of two features that distinguish it from the OASDI and HI programs:

> Participation is voluntary, although some 95 percent of those eligible are in fact participants.

> Eligibility does not depend upon whether past Social Security taxes have been paid; rather, it depends upon whether "premiums" are paid after eligibility for benefits commences. Anyone eligible for the HI program is eligible for SMI, but anyone aged 65 and over with at least five years' residence in the United States is also eligible.

These differences are more of form than substance, however. Virtually everyone who becomes eligible will undoubtedly elect to participate in SMI, and participation will continue throughout his remaining lifetime. Furthermore, although eligibility does not depend upon the payment of Social Security taxes, the premiums required for eligibility are so insignificant it seems reasonable to assume that the right to receive SMI benefits after age 65 accrues ratably during a person's working lifetime prior to age 65.

At the beginning of 1990 there were approximately 32 million persons eligible to receive partial reimbursement for medical costs covered under the SMI program. All conditions had been met for these benefits to be payable in the future provided only that the participants continue to pay nominal premiums. For this group of participants, the premiums are projected to represent less than 20 percent of the total cost of future benefits; therefore, it is virtually certain that present participants will continue their eligibility by paying premiums.

The present value of the portion of these future benefits that will not be financed by the participants' premiums and thus will be paid from general revenue is estimated to be about $400 billion. This may be termed the accrued liability for these 32 million participants.

Similarly, it seems reasonable to assume that an accrued liability exists for the more than 130 million persons who are in the active work force paying taxes (personal income taxes, not payroll taxes) to support the SMI program and who will be eligible for SMI benefits when they reach age 65. Just as with the other parts of Social Security, from a strictly legal point of view there are no vested benefits or accrued liabilities because the entire program can be changed or terminated at any time. It seems more reasonable, however, to assume that the SMI program will continue without abrupt change.

Although no formal estimates have been made of this accrued liability by the actuaries of the Health Care Financing Administration, it is probably of the magnitude of $1,400 billion. When that amount is added to the accrued liability of $400 billion for those persons already eligible for SMI benefits, the result is a total accrued liability of about $1,800 billion. Since the SMI trust fund had assets of $14 billion as of January 1, 1990, this would leave an unfunded accrued liability of $1,786 billion, or about $1.8 trillion. The unfunded accrued liability as of any given date may be viewed as the amount by which benefits, paid or promised with respect to earlier years of participation in the system, exceed the amount of premiums paid by participants and general taxes paid by all taxpayers and allocated to the SMI program during those years (appropriately adjusted for assumed interest earnings).

The Significance of the Accrued Liability

The total accrued liability as of January 1, 1990, under Social Security (OASDI, HI, and SMI combined) is some $12,200 billion, or about $12 trillion. The total assets of the Social Security trust funds are only $288 billion, thus the *unfunded* accrued liability is also approximately $12 trillion.[10]

This unfunded accrued liability is based upon the intermediate set of demographic and economic assumptions used by the Social Security actuaries in making projections for the 1990 Trustees Reports. It would not be markedly different based upon the optimistic or pessimistic assumptions referred to previously. Compared with the actuarial deficit, there is relatively little variation in the unfunded accrued liability based upon the alternative assumptions. This is true, in part, because the unfunded accrued liability is related to a closed group of existing participants in Social Security and is thus independent of future birth rates.

As indicated in Chapter 6, if the Social Security program were a private system, it would be considered desirable to begin to collect more income than is necessary for current benefit payments and to accumulate a substantial fund in order to transform this *unfunded* accrued liability into a *funded* accrued liability. But, as also discussed in Chapter 6, it is not necessary to fund the Social Security accrued liability if it is assumed that Social Security will exist forever and that its promised benefits, together with other national commitments for the future, are consistent with the nation's ability to produce in the future. In other words, an unfunded accrued liability is not necessarily unacceptable for the Social Security program.

The existence of an unfunded accrued liability is significant, however, and should not be dismissed lightly—as some observers are wont to do. As already noted, an accrued liability represents the value of benefits that have been earned or accrued as of today but that will not be paid until a later date. A small part of the accrued liability is funded but most of it is unfunded. The unfunded accrued liability represents the value of benefits that have been promised as a result of service to date but have not yet been paid for.

In other words, persons who have participated in Social Security during the past fifty years or so have received benefits (some of which will not be paid until later) of considerably greater value than the taxes they have paid. This excess value is equal to the unfunded accrued liability or approximately $12 trillion. Is it any wonder that we heard so few complaints about Social Security during its first fifty years of existence? If taxpayers had paid the full cost of benefits accruing during the past fifty years, their taxes would have been more than twice as much as were actually paid.

Some critics advocate terminating Social Security, part of their reasoning being that such a termination would resolve its financial problems. If Social Security were terminated today and if we satisfied the promises made to date, we would have to pay benefits to millions of people currently receiving benefits or expecting to receive benefits in the future (only the benefits earned because of past service and excluding benefits that would have been earned in the future). This would require a lump sum amount today of $12 trillion (the unfunded accrued liability) or an equivalent amount spread over future years. The nation thus has a "hidden liability" of approximately $78,000 for every adult now between ages 20 and 65, or more than $46,000 for every living man, woman, and child regardless of age. This is four times the estimated national debt of $2,953 billion as of January 1, 1990, the government's officially acknowledged liability.

The fact we must face is that we have made promises worth $12 trillion more than we have collected in taxes in the past. The choices are not many. We can make good on the promises by collecting higher future taxes than would have been required otherwise, or we can renounce some of the promises already made. Some would favor continuing to hide this unfunded accrued liability; but, whether hidden or explicitly acknowledged, it represents a significant lien on the nation's goods and services to be produced in the future.

Conclusion

We have seen that the existence of an unfunded accrued liability is not necessarily a sign of financial weakness in our Social Security system, provided we have arranged for future tax collections that are adequate to pay future benefits. In the final analysis, the future financial stability of Social Security depends upon the ability and willingness of the nation's workers and employers to continue to pay the taxes necessary to support the benefit payments.

The combined tax rate in 1990 was 15.30 percent of taxable payroll (7.65 percent from the worker and 7.65 percent from the employer). It is scheduled by law to remain at that level for all future years.

The actuarial deficits under our present Social Security program imply *tax increases above and beyond currently scheduled rates*. To eliminate these substantial actuarial deficits, it seems likely that the combined tax rates under the OASDI and HI programs must rise to at least 24 percent within the next forty or fifty years; that is, more than 50 percent above present tax rates. Under more pessimistic assumptions, these tax rates must eventually be almost triple the present rates. In addition, substantial but as yet unrecognized future taxes will be required to support the SMI program.

Painful as it may be to communicate this information to the taxpayer, it must be done. Since the financial stability of Social Security is based upon the taxpayer's *ability and willingness* to pay future taxes, we have a compelling obligation to keep the taxpayer informed about how high those taxes may be. If we are not willing to so advise the taxpayer, we have no right to use a current-cost financing method whose very foundation is the taxpayer's *ability and willingness* to make future tax payments.

Part Three
Commentary on
Selected Topics

Part Two contained basic descriptions of the Social Security program and the way it works. It gave the background information to permit a more informed discussion of Social Security—the way it is now and the way the reader may wish it to be in the future.

Part Three is designed to answer in a more direct way some of the questions that are frequently raised about Social Security. Also, it presents a commentary on aspects of Social Security that are ignored too frequently. In some cases the commentary will stand on its own; however, in others it will be more meaningful if Part Two has been read previously. To the extent the commentary on a topic is self-contained, it may duplicate other sections of the book.

8
Public Understanding of Social Security

The most important problem confronting Social Security in the immediate future is not high cost, mismanagement, inappropriate benefits, unfair treatment of participants, or any of the other charges sometimes directed at it by critics. The major problem facing Social Security is the widespread lack of understanding of the program—its basic rationale, the type and level of benefits it provides, the method of financing, the significance of its high future cost, and the tenuous relationship between taxes paid and benefits received by an individual. The average individual does not know what Social Security is really all about. He does not know what to expect from Social Security. Should he expect it to meet all of his needs (and those of his dependents) in the event of old age, disability, death, or sickness? Or should he expect it to be merely a floor of protection in meeting these needs, a floor upon which he and his employer should build through supplemental private saving and insurance and some form of retirement program? Apart from his expectations, what type and level of benefits does Social Security actually provide in meeting these various needs? Most people don't know.

Social Security was enacted on August 14, 1935, some fifty-five years ago. It is not a new program and no sudden and dramatic revisions have been made. The Social Security Administration and, since 1977, the Health Care Financing Administration have published millions of pamphlets explaining Social Security. The news media—radio, television, magazines, and newspapers—have issued billions of words and pictures on the subject. Hundreds of books have been written about every aspect of Social Security. So how did this public misunderstanding come about? It is probably a result of the following combination of factors.

First, in explaining Social Security over the years the government has employed certain rhetoric that has contributed to the confusion. The use of words and phrases such as "insurance," "trust fund," "account," "contributions," and "earned right," while not necessarily wrong, has sometimes conveyed the wrong impression. Although the government may not have deliberately misled the public, it certainly has not been in the forefront of a movement to explain to the public the rationale and basic nature of the Social Security program.

Moreover, during the first forty years of the program, the public did not devote very much effort to finding out what Social Security was all about. Taxes (euphemistically called "contributions") were fairly low; benefits to a retiring individual were high in relation to the taxes that had been paid; it almost seemed like something for nothing. That should have been reason enough to provoke a few more penetrating questions by the public than were actually asked. Over the past fifteen years, however, this public apathy has evaporated just as rapidly as Social Security taxes have risen. A substantial number of people pay more in Social Security taxes than they do in federal income taxes. In 1980 an employee who earned $25,900 or more paid $1,587.67 in Social Security taxes. This was matched by his employer, resulting in total tax payments of $3,175.34. In 1990 this tax for a high-wage earner has more than doubled to $3,924.45 for the employee and another $3,924.45 for the employer, or a total of $7,848.90. This combined employee-employer Social Security tax is projected to exceed $13,000 by the year 2000. No longer will the public be indifferent to Social Security—the taxes paid and the benefits received.

Lastly, the media should assume some responsibility for the misunderstanding. It takes considerable time and effort to learn enough about Social Security to report on it in a meaningful way. Not enough people have been willing to invest that much time, and the result has been an undue amount of incomplete and confusing media coverage of the program.

If this general misunderstanding of Social Security continues, the inevitable result will be growing dissatisfaction and frustration among the taxpayers, and increasing reluctance to pay the taxes required to support the program. There is no excuse for permitting this lack of understanding to continue. Widespread understanding of the Social Security program may result in a certain amount of trauma and even disruption among the public, but even more disruption will result if the current misunderstanding is allowed to continue.

It is unlikely that rational changes can be made in the Social Security program as long as the present low level of understanding of the program exists. In the future, public understanding or misunderstanding will play a much more critical role in determining the shape of the program than it has in the past when the payroll tax was relatively low and when the taxpayer was in a less questioning frame of mind. If people understand Social Security, there is a much greater chance that the program will be modified to coincide with their desires and thus gain the public acceptance obviously necessary for a program that will pay over four trillion dollars in benefits, and require tax collections of almost five trillion dollars, during the next ten years.

Accordingly, a careful analysis should be made of the Social Security program, as well as of the various other governmental income maintenance programs, to determine exactly what policy is inherent in such programs. This rationale, once determined, should be explained clearly to the public. Everyone should understand the extent to which an individual is responsible for himself and his dependents in the event of his retirement, disability, death, or sickness and the extent to which the government (supported by the resources of the working segment of the population) is responsible.

In addition to the rationale, the cost of Social Security both now and in the future should be acknowledged and explained clearly to the public. No further attempts should be made to conceal the cost, to minimize the importance of the cost, or to apologize for the cost. Such efforts will not change the cost in any way.

After having been informed of the rationale, the cost, and other features of the Social Security program, the public will then be in a position to reaffirm the program or ask that it be revised. It is possible that some change will be called for as the real cost and significance of Social Security become known. It is entirely possible that the public will continue the trend begun in recent years of decreasing governmental intervention in private affairs and decide that the "government should provide" only those benefits that can be provided in no other way, and that the individual should be responsible for himself and his dependents to the fullest extent possible.

9

A Program of Future Promises— Fulfilled or Broken?

The actuary's job is to make forecasts about the future. Many other people do this in addition to the actuary: crystal ball gazers, seers, fortune-tellers, economists, weathermen, and so on.

All of these people have one thing in common. When they forecast good news, their audience is grateful and happy. When they forecast bad news, their audience is unhappy and sometimes even belligerent. People are sometimes so reluctant to believe bad news that either they refuse to listen or they label the forecaster as a panicmonger.

The actuary frequently has a thankless task. When he is making forecasts about possible future costs of pension benefits, his conclusion is almost always that future costs will be much higher than they are at present, that they will be much higher than most people expect, and that it may be difficult to pay for such pensions.

Why is it important to forecast the future costs of a program like Social Security? *Social Security is a program of future promises.*

Consider a retired husband and wife who are both aged 65 and receiving monthly Social Security benefits that total

$1,600. Social Security promises to continue paying this monthly check as long as both the husband and wife are alive; the program also promises to pay $800 a month as long as the man lives after the death of his wife; or to pay $800 a month to the woman as long as she lives after the death of her husband.

But that is not all: Social Security promises to increase these monthly benefits so that they will keep up with the cost of living as measured by changes in the Consumer Price Index. If the cost of living increases 5 percent a year, in just fifteen years this $1,600 check will more than double to $3,326. If the cost of living increases 8 percent a year, this $1,600 check will more than triple to $5,075 within fifteen years.

This is a substantial promise that involves a lot of money (its "present value" is roughly $260,000) and a long period of years (benefits could still be payable thirty to forty years from now).

Let's take another example. Consider a worker aged 20 who is just now entering the work force in employment covered by Social Security. The Social Security program makes the following promises:

  If the worker dies at an early age, leaving behind a dependent spouse and children, monthly benefits will be paid, not necessarily continuously, during the next fifty to seventy-five years.

  If the worker becomes disabled at an early age, monthly benefits will be paid to the worker (and possibly to the spouse and children) during the next fifty to seventy-five years.

  If the worker lives to retirement at age 67 (forty-seven years from now), monthly benefits will be paid for the remainder of the worker's life (and possibly for the reminder of the spouse's life after the worker's death), promises spanning the next seventy-five or more years.

In each of these cases, benefits will be related to the worker's average monthly earnings in the future, and benefits, once commenced, will be adjusted for changes in the cost of living.

Hundreds of other promises are made about benefits that will be paid during the next seventy-five to one hundred years. When we make these promises about the benefits Social Security will pay during the next seventy-five years or so, with respect to the millions of people now living and paying Social Security taxes, it is essential that we make every reasonable effort to determine whether we can make good on the promises. There are two basic approaches we can take.

The first one is what I call the "head-in-the-sand" approach. We can determine the type and level of benefits that we think people *need*. We can determine the costs of paying such benefits during the next *two or three years*, and if these costs don't seem too high, we can adopt the benefits and *let the future take care of itself.* Sad to say, many policymakers prefer this approach, although they might not describe it in quite these terms.

The other approach is to make a reasonable effort to look ahead throughout the period over which the promises have been made and determine their likely future costs. It can then be decided whether or not we can afford the cost of such promises, not only for the next two or three years, but for the period of approximately seventy-five years during which we will have to make good on our promises.

This is the task of the actuary: to do the best job possible of forecasting future expenditures under the program over a long period of years to determine whether it seems reasonable to make such promises in view of the income that is similarly forecast over the same period. It cannot be concluded, of course, that today's projections of future Social Security expenditures will be highly accurate. The cost of the program will depend on a variety of changeable factors such as the rate of future economic growth and future fertility levels. Social Security actuaries realize this fact, however, and make projections on the basis of alternative sets of economic and demographic assumptions that span a range considered reasonable by most professional analysts.

Our knowledge of the future is limited, to be sure; but it is not as limited as many people assume. Consider the following:

Eighty-five percent of the people who are going to receive old-age retirement benefits at any time during the next seventy-five years are alive today.

These people will receive 96 percent of the total old-age retirement benefits that are paid during the next seventy-five years.

Of the total Social Security taxes that will be paid during the next fifty years, 81 percent will be paid by people who are now alive. For the first twenty-five years the figure is 99 percent.

Thus, while many of the projection factors are subject to substantial variation, the basic numbers of people who will be tomorrow's workers and beneficiaries can be determined today with reasonable certainty. The purpose of long-range projections is not to predict the future with certainty (no one, obviously, can do that) but rather to indicate how the Social Security program would operate in the future under a variety of economic and demographic conditions, any of which could reasonably be expected to occur. Such projections provide a valuable test of the reasonableness and long-range viability of the Social Security provisions that we enact today.

The extent to which we are interested in projections of future income and outgo of the Social Security program and the prospects for its continued financial health depends in part upon our own age. A person just now retiring at age 65 may be content to worry about Social Security's financial health for about the next twenty years or thirty years. On the other hand, a person now aged 40 should be concerned about Social Security's financial health during the next fifty years at least. The Veterans' Benefits Administration is keenly aware of the long-range nature of pension promises. At the end of 1989 the government was still making monthly benefit payments to seven widows and forty-four needy children of Civil War veterans.

The "head-in-the-sand" approach is taken by far too many people. I have watched in amazement as prominent politicians, policymakers, and labor leaders have taken this approach. It is understandable, perhaps even forgivable, for a layman to make such a mistake, particularly if he has never had the situation properly explained to him. It is completely irresponsible, however, for a politician or a labor leader or a policymaker to take such an approach, especially when he has been informed about the long-range consequences of promises inherent in a social insurance program. There is no excuse for persons in responsible positions not to familiarize themselves with the possible long-range consequences of their actions.

It is important to note that the Board of Trustees of the Social Security program has not been consistent in assessing our nation's ability to fulfill the promises we have made under the various parts of Social Security. Specifically, consider the following:

Old-Age, Survivors, and Disability Insurance Programs: Projections are made for seventy-five years; however, there is occasional pressure from the "head-in-the-sand" devotees to reduce this to as short a period as twenty-five years and thus to ignore the consequences of the inevitable transition from the present youthful population to a future older population.

Hospital Insurance Program: Projections are made for seventy-five years; however, prior to 1985 projections were made for only twenty-five years. As yet, therefore, relatively little attention is being paid to the longer-range cost projections for the Hospital Insurance program. Hospital Insurance benefits are paid principally for persons aged 65 or over; thus Hospital Insurance benefits may be viewed as a form of retirement benefit. Accordingly, it is just as important that seventy-five-year projections be made for these benefits, and that they be heeded, as it is for the old-age benefits.

Supplementary Medical Insurance Program: Projections are made for *only three years.*[1] These benefits are paid for substantially the same persons who receive

Hospital Insurance benefits and thus are just another form of retirement benefit; hence, it is as important that seventy-five-year projections be made for these benefits as it is for the cash old-age benefits and the Hospital Insurance benefits. Any report that the SMI program is "actuarially sound" is practically meaningless since projections are made for only three years. If Social Security's Trustees continue to publish Supplementary Medical Insurance projections for only three years, they should include in their annual Trustees Report a disclaimer such as the following:

> The Trustees, who are responsible for reporting annually on the financial condition of Social Security, have not reviewed the long-range costs of the Supplementary Medical Insurance program and are therefore unable to say with any degree of certainty that the benefit promises now being made to millions of today's taxpayers will in fact be honored.

It seems clear that we should do a better job of recognizing the cost implications of the longer-term promises we have made under our Social Security program. As indicated in Chapter 4, the present Social Security program makes promises that we cannot keep unless tax rates are at least doubled within the working lifetime of today's young people. Although the history of Social Security is the story of a virtually uninterrupted expansion of coverage and benefits, it is indeed possible to make promises we cannot keep; witness, for example, these Social Security amendments made in 1977 and later that curtailed benefits:

Elimination of benefits for orphaned children and children of retired or disabled workers, who are aged 18–21 and full-time students.

Postponement of cost-of-living adjustment for six months in 1983 and later, and provision for the future retardation of such adjustments under certain conditions.

Increase in the "normal retirement age" for persons born after 1937.

Partial income taxation of benefits (thus an effective reduction in benefits) under certain conditions after 1983.

Elimination of the minimum benefit under most circumstances.

Restriction of the circumstances under which lump-sum death benefits are payable.

Because of the nature of Social Security's promises, the consequences of breaking those promises should not be underestimated. For example, the Social Security program promises a certain level of retirement benefits in exchange for the payment of taxes during one's working years. Moreover, the Social Security Administration emphasizes that Social Security retirement benefits are not sufficient to fully replace the earnings lost through retirement and encourages workers to participate in private pension plans and to save and invest on their own in order to provide a total retirement income that will be sufficient for their needs. If, after several decades of playing by these rules, a worker is abruptly notified that Congress has chosen to reduce Social Security retirement benefits, then the worker may well be unable to adjust his own savings and pension to compensate for the lower Social Security benefits. He may then face the difficult choice of delaying his retirement (if possible) or adjusting to a lower standard of living than planned. Apart from the immediate impact on the retirement plans of the worker and his family, such broken promises could have serious ramifications: namely, the erosion of public confidence in other government programs as well as the Social Security program, and eventually the complete loss of confidence in the government itself. Without the confidence and support of the public, the institution of orderly government cannot long survive.

It is important to note that Social Security involves two separate and distinct kinds of promises: one promise that specified benefits will be paid to the inactive segment of the population; and another promise that specified taxes will be collected from the active segment of the population. Both promises are equally important but, unfortunately, we have tended to place more emphasis on our promise to the inactive population than to the active population. This is partly because of the mistaken notion—discussed in Chapter 11— that a given generation of beneficiaries has "paid for its own benefits" with its past taxes. To promote public harmony and faith in government institutions, we should give appropriate emphasis to honoring our future *taxation promises* to the active segment of our population as well as our future *benefit promises* to the inactive segment. The integrity of both promises is essential.

The purpose of the long-range cost estimates made by an actuary is not to scare people or to cause unrest about the future viability of Social Security, although this sometimes happens. The purpose is to provide the information necessary to ensure that we do not make promises we cannot keep. The purpose is to make certain that Social Security is a program of *fulfilled promises*, not a program of *broken promises*.

10
Actuarial Assumptions

It is essential that projections of future income and outgo be made for the Social Security program. Otherwise, there can be no assurance that promises of future benefits can be kept. This is discussed at length in Chapter 9. Chapter 4 explains why, under a pay-as-you-go, or current-cost, financing method, the present cost is not representative of future costs. Chapter 4 also discusses the concept of making several projections based upon alternative sets of assumptions about the future to indicate the broad range within which it might reasonably be expected that income and outgo will fall during the coming years.

In the 1990 Trustees Reports, projections are made under four sets of assumptions designated as alternatives I, II-A, II-B, and III. These are usually referred to as "actuarial assumptions," at least among actuaries, but are sometimes separated into economic and demographic assumptions. Alternative I is the most optimistic and alternative III is the most pessimistic of the four sets of assumptions; thus projections based on these assumptions are usually referred to as "optimistic" and "pessimistic" projections. The two intermediate sets—alternatives II-A and II-B—share the same demographic assumptions but differ in their economic assumptions. More robust economic growth is assumed for alternative II-A than for alternative II-B. An assumption is

labeled "pessimistic" if it results in a relatively high projected cost; for example, lower mortality and longer life
spans would be pessimistic from a cost standpoint but would
obviously be favorable from other standpoints.

This range of assumptions and projections is usually derived as follows. First, the alternative II-B assumptions are
selected by the Board of Trustees as the basis for the "most
probable" projections of income and outgo—projections that
are termed "intermediate" and that come to be used by
Congress, policymakers, the news media, and the public in
assessing the financial viability of Social Security. Then,
alternative I and alternative III assumptions are selected to
bracket the alternative II-B assumptions. Finally, alternative II-A assumptions are added to represent the "targeted,"
or desired, economic performance of the nation as distinguished from the "probable" economic performance that the
alternative II-B assumptions are intended to represent.

Since this array of projections tends to be a little overwhelming, it is almost inevitable that most observers concentrate on only one projection: the intermediate, alternative II-B projection. Unfortunately, this tends to be an
optimistic rather than a true intermediate projection, and
the result is that the whole range of projections is skewed
toward the optimistic side of the spectrum. (This is my
strongly held, personal opinion for which some evidence will
be offered later in this chapter. The reader can, of course,
form his own opinion based on a detailed review of the latest
Trustees Reports and related material.)

Selecting actuarial assumptions is a matter of judgment
and is not simply a matter of studying past experience and
projecting it into the future. Past experience must be stud-
ied, to be sure. But the underlying factors that influenced
past experience must be analyzed to determine whether and
how such factors will influence future experience. Furthermore, new factors must be identified that may have had no
effect on the past but that may well affect the future.

Consider fertility rates, for example. The "total fertility
rate" is defined to be the average number of children that
would be born to a group of women during their lifetimes if
they were to experience the birthrates, by age, observed in,

or assumed for, the selected year, and if all were to survive the entire child-bearing period. The total fertility rate decreased from 3.3 children per woman after World War I to 2.1 during the Great Depression, rose to 3.7 in 1957, and then fell to 1.7 in 1976. Since then, it has risen to a level currently estimated at 1.9. During the twenty-year period from 1945 to 1965, the so-called baby-boom years, the total fertility rate rose from 2.4 to 3.7 (in 1957) and then declined to 2.9.

What caused these fluctuations in the fertility rate? There are many factors, including changes in social attitudes, economic conditions, and the use of birth-control methods. (Birth-control pills were not successfully developed until the 1950s and were not approved for use by the Food and Drug Administration until 1960.) What does the future hold with respect to these factors? Will economic conditions, particularly improvements in the standard of living, be better or worse than in the past? Will there be a smaller or larger proportion of women in the work force? Will birth control be forsaken or employed more widely? Will marriages become less or more stable? What new factors will influence future fertility rates? Perhaps government policy will encourage or discourage changes in fertility rates. This may depend upon immigration policy (or de facto immigration, regardless of official policy) which will depend, in turn, on world social and economic conditions. This same kind of analysis is appropriate for each of the hundreds of assumptions that must be made to project future Social Security costs.

There is an added difficulty in selecting actuarial assumptions that deserves mention: The assumptions must appear to be reasonable to the majority of the people who take action based on the results of using the assumptions; otherwise it will be fruitless to employ such assumptions. For example, if one could somehow divine that the fertility rate would drop from its present rate of 1.9 to 1.4 (the rate for 1988 in West Germany), very few people would accept that premise and the entire projection would be summarily rejected. In general, people tend to be wary—if not downright afraid—of change of any kind, and it is difficult to convince anyone that "the future is not what it used to be," particularly if the results are less favorable than previously projected or hoped for.

Public perception of Social Security and the nature of its promises should also be an important determinant of the assumptions that are used. As noted in the prior chapter, grave damage can be done to government credibility, as well as to an individual's financial circumstances, when a program's long-term commitments are scaled back without appropriate advance warning. If the public believes that the benefits that Social Security promises should be inviolable, then relatively "pessimistic" assumptions should be employed to help ensure that we do not promise more benefits than future generations of taxpayers will be willing to finance. While the young segment of today's population is skeptical about Social Security's ability to keep its benefit promises, the older population believes that Social Security's promises are sacred and must be kept. If there is any doubt about this, just propose a benefit cut for the retired or almost-retired population and observe the reaction. When the time comes for the baby boomers to begin receiving benefits, it is likely that they will consider Social Security's benefits to be just as inviolable as do today's recipients.

It is important to note that Social Security involves two separate and distinct kinds of promises: one promise that specified benefits will be paid to the inactive segment of the population; and another promise that specified taxes will be collected from the active segment of the population. Both promises are equally important but, unfortunately, we have tended to place more emphasis on our promise to the inactive population than to the active population. This is partly because of the mistaken notion—discussed in Chapter 11—that a given generation of beneficiaries has "paid for its own benefits" with its past taxes. The use of more judiciously selected assumptions about the future economic and demographic environment would enable us to give appropriate emphasis to honoring our future taxation promises to the active segment of our population as well as our future benefit promises to the inactive segment. The integrity of both promises is essential.

With this background, consider the following comments about the overoptimism, in my view, of the three assumptions used in the 1990 Trustees Reports that have the greatest impact on long-range projections of future income and outgo: total fertility rates, productivity rates, and mortality rates.

Total Fertility Rate

The higher the fertility rate, the lower the long-range Social Security cost expressed as a percentage of payroll during the 75-year projection period.[1] Although fertility rates have fluctuated widely in past years, the long-range trend has been downward in the United States. This is illustrated graphically in Chart 10.A, which shows actual rates since 1920 and the rates assumed until 2030 under the three alternative assumptions used in the 1990 Trustees Reports. During this period, as noted previously, the rate has ranged from a high of 3.7 in 1957 to a low of 1.7 in 1976. The average rate during the 15-year period from 1975 to 1989 is 1.8.

Chart 10.A

Comparison of Past United States Total Fertility Rates with Assumed Rates for the Future

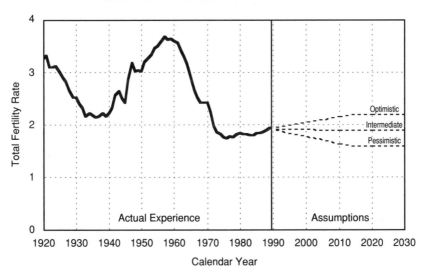

Note: The total fertility rate is defined as the average number of children that would be born to a group of women during their lifetimes if they were to experience the birthrates, by age, observed in, or assumed for, the given year.

In 1989–90 there were widespread reports in the media about a "new baby boom" because of an apparent rise in birth rates. The *birth rate* is the total number of births relative to the total population; it does not necessarily indicate a rise in the total *fertility rate* (the number of births during a woman's lifetime). Currently, for example, the total number of births is relatively high because there is a large number of women in their peak child-bearing years. The total fertility rate is estimated to have risen somewhat during 1987–89, although some analysts believe this is only a temporary effect, attributable to the recent tendency for women to bear their children later in life.[2]

According to the 1990 Trustees Report, the past "variations in fertility rates have resulted from changes in many factors, including social attitudes, economic conditions, and the use of birth control methods.... The recent historical and projected trends in certain population characteristics are consistent with a continued relatively low fertility rate. These trends include the rising percentages of women who have never married, of women who are divorced, and of young women who are in the labor force."

Fertility rates have declined during the past twenty-five years or so throughout much of the developed world. In 1988, for example, the total fertility rates in selected areas of the world[3] were as follows:

United States	1.9
Canada	1.7
Northern Europe	1.8
Western Europe	1.6

The fertility rates were particularly low in these countries: Denmark, 1.6; Belgium, 1.6; Switzerland, 1.6; Austria, 1.4; and West Germany, 1.4.

The Bureau of the Census prepares population projections for the United States using a series of alternative fertility rate assumptions. In their latest projections,[4] the alternative fertility rates ranged from 1.5 to 2.2, with an intermediate assumption of 1.8.

A review of the above points would seem to suggest that the long-term fertility rates will probably be lower, not higher, than the past 15-year average of 1.8. Accordingly, the alternative II rate of 1.9 seems optimistic and the alternative

III rate of 1.6 does not seem to be pessimistic—in fact, 1.6 is probably quite appropriate to use as an intermediate assumption, and it could even be optimistic.

Productivity Rate

The rate of increase in productivity is an important determinant of the future cost of Social Security. The cost of living, by itself, has little effect on future costs, expressed as a percentage of payroll, because cost-of-living changes affect Social Security taxes and currently paid benefits by approximately the same relative amount. On the other hand, productivity increases eventually result in wage increases that exceed cost-of-living increases; therefore, the Social Security tax base grows faster than current benefit payments—resulting in a lower pay-as-you-go cost expressed as a percentage of taxable payroll. (Benefit payments eventually increase, as a result of workers' higher earnings, but this effect is considerably delayed compared to the increase in earnings.)

Implicit in the ultimate economic assumptions employed in the 1990 Trustees Reports (i.e., those applicable from about 2010 onward) are the following average annual productivity rate increases:

alternative I	2.2 %
alternative II-A	1.9 %
alternative II-B	1.7 %
alternative III	1.4 %

According to the 1990 Trustees Report, "For the 30 years 1959–88, annual increases in productivity for the total U.S. economy averaged 1.6 percent, the result of average annual increases of 2.5, 1.4, and 0.9 percent for the 10-year periods 1959–68, 1969–78, and 1979–88, respectively." The average annual increase for the past twenty years 1969–88 has thus been about 1.1 percent; and for the past twenty-five years 1964–88, about 1.4 percent. The past levels of annual productivity gains are shown in Chart 10.B and compared to the assumed future levels.

As with all the other actuarial assumptions that must be made, past history is only a rough guide to the future. Furthermore, the linkage between productivity increases and wage increases is complex and to look at only the past

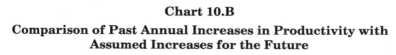

Chart 10.B

Comparison of Past Annual Increases in Productivity with Assumed Increases for the Future

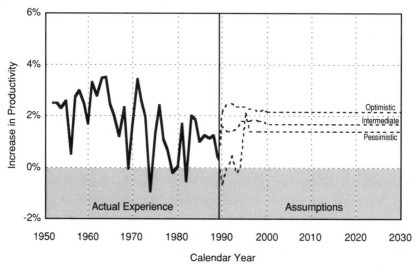

productivity increases is to oversimplify the situation. Nevertheless, the assumptions being made in the 1990 Trustees Reports about future productivity rate increases appear to be overly optimistic.[5] According to the experience of the past twenty to twenty-five years, the alternative III assumption of a 1.4 percent annual increase in the ultimate productivity rate does not seem to be pessimistic; to the contrary, it appears to be quite appropriate to use as an intermediate assumption and it may even be optimistic.

Mortality Rate

Mortality rates, or death rates, above age 50 or so have an important effect on the cost of Social Security: the lower the death rate, the longer the life span and the higher the cost.

Lower death rates at younger ages have the opposite effect, by increasing the number of workers. This effect, however, is small compared to the effect at the higher ages.

Historically, death rates in the United States have declined fairly steadily over the years, as shown in Chart 10.C. The age-sex-adjusted death rate—which is the crude rate that would occur in the enumerated total population as of

April 1, 1980, if that population were to experience the death rates by age and sex for the selected year—declined at an average rate of 1.2 percent per year between 1900 and 1989. This death rate declined at an average rate of 1.4 percent per year between 1969 and 1989.

These reductions in death rates have resulted from many factors, including increased medical knowledge and availability of health-care services, improved economic conditions and living standards, and improvements in personal health-care practices such as diet and exercise. Based on consideration of the likelihood of continued progress in these and other areas, the 1990 Trustees Reports assumed that the age-sex-adjusted death rate would decline each year between 1989 and 2064 by the following average amounts:

alternative I	0.3%
alternative II-A and II-B	0.6%
alternative III	0.9%

Chart 10.C

Comparison of Past Reductions in Mortality Rates with Assumed Reductions for the Future

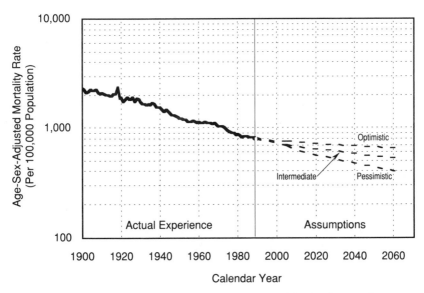

Note: The age-sex-adjusted mortality rate is the number of deaths that would occur per 100,000 persons in the U.S. population during 1980, if that population were to experience the mortality rates by age and sex observed in (or assumed for) the given year. A "semi-log" scale is used on the chart to clarify the trend of actual experience versus the assumed future trend.

These rates of decline in the death rates represent a considerable slowdown in the improvement in mortality experienced thus far during the 20th century. There is a limit, of course, to how much mortality can improve; but there is also the possibility of major breakthroughs in health care or improved understanding of the aging process that could result in significant increases in life spans.

This is not to suggest that such breakthroughs should be assumed in projecting future income and outgo for the Social Security program; but rather to indicate that if such changes in longevity should occur, the normal retirement ages in the present Social Security program would be totally inappropriate and would almost certainly need to be increased. This is something that should be understood by the public to minimize the problems associated with increasing the retirement age. Even though the remaining life expectancy at age 65 has increased from 13 years when Social Security was adopted in 1935 to 17 years in 1990 (and is expected to increase to about 20 years in the next century), suggestions for an increased retirement age are not usually well received.

Conclusion

In deciding upon a set of economic and demographic assumptions on which to rely, it is not a question of selecting the "correct assumptions" since that is clearly impossible. The question is this: For the Social Security program, which makes promises about benefits and taxes that will be payable for as many as fifty to seventy-five years in the future, what set of assumptions should be used to assess whether future income will likely be approximately equal to future outgo— and whether both benefit and taxation promises can be fulfilled? In making this test, it seems to me that the alternative III assumptions are the most appropriate of the four sets of assumptions shown in the 1990 Trustees Reports—and even they may be somewhat optimistic.

11
Do We Get
Our Money's Worth
from Social Security?

A question that is being asked more and more often is "Do we get our money's worth from Social Security?" This question can be answered from several different points of view, and each produces a different answer.

Taxes, Benefits, and Administrative Expenses

First, consider the Social Security program from the viewpoint of the nation as a whole, taking into account only the dollars involved. The total income and outgo, including interest earnings and administrative expenses, of the trust funds since the program's inception are summarized in Table 11.1 for the three parts of Social Security that are supported primarily by payroll taxes. Table 11.1 shows that over the years $3,380.4 billion has been collected in payroll taxes. Normally, as these taxes were collected, they were used almost immediately to pay benefits. This procedure is known as "current-cost" or "pay-as-you-go" financing and, in the past, has been one of the fundamental characteristics of our Social Security program, as discussed in Chapter 6. For a variety of reasons, the taxes collected plus other trust

Table 11.1

Summary of Cumulative Income and Outgo under the Old-Age, Survivors, Disability, and Hospital Insurance Programs, 1937–89
(amounts in billions)

	Old-Age and Survivors Insurance[a]	Disability Insurance[b]	Hospital Insurance[c]	Total
	(1)	(2)	(3)	(4)
Payroll Taxes	$2,498.6	$287.8	$594.0[d]	$3,380.4
Income from Taxation of OASDI Benefits	18.5	0.8	—	19.3
Interest Earnings	75.3	12.3	40.6	128.2
General Revenue	16.2	3.5	18.8	38.5
Total Income	$2,608.6	$304.4	$653.4	$3,566.4
Benefit Payments	$2,425.2[e]	$286.7[f]	$558.2	$3,270.1
Administrative Expenses	28.3	9.8	9.7	47.8
Total Expenditures	$2,453.5	$296.5	$567.9	$3,317.9
Excess of Income over Expenditures (Value of Trust Funds on 12-31-89)	$ 155.1	$ 7.9	$ 85.5	$ 248.5

[a] Taxes were first collected in 1937; monthly benefits were first paid in 1940.

[b] Taxes were first collected and benefits first paid in 1957.

[c] Taxes were first collected in January 1966; benefits were first paid in July 1966.

[d] Includes $4.7 billion in transfers from the Railroad Retirement program and $0.4 billion in HI premiums paid by uninsured voluntary enrollees.

[e] Includes $37.1 billion in net transfers to the Railroad Retirement program.

[f] Includes $0.8 billion in net transfers to the Railroad Retirement program.

fund income are not exactly equal to benefits and administrative expenses paid in a given period. Any excess of income over expenditures is maintained in the appropriate trust fund for the payment of future benefits during periods when income is less than outgo. As indicated by Table 11.1, total income to the OASI, DI, and HI trust funds from 1937 through 1989 exceeded total expenditures by $248.5 billion— and this amount was present in the three funds at the beginning of 1990.

Trust fund assets are invested in U.S. Treasury securities, primarily "special issues" yielding interest at the same rate as the average of all outstanding long-term Treasury securities. During the twelve months ending June 30, 1989, the effective annual rate of interest earned by the combined assets of these three trust funds was approximately 9.8 percent. Total OASDHI interest earnings in 1937–1989 were $128.2 billion. The reason the interest earnings appear relatively small compared to the $3,380.4 billion in tax income is that the amount in the trust funds at any given time has been small relative to the total amount of benefit payments. The relatively low level of trust fund assets at any given time is consistent with the fund's traditional purpose as a contingency reserve to cover any temporary shortfalls that occur as a result of current-cost financing. Table 11.1 also indicates that administrative expenses have been low, amounting to only 1.5 percent of the benefit payments for all three trust funds combined.

Table 11.2 summarizes similar information on income and outgo for the Supplementary Medical Insurance trust fund. This program is not supported by payroll taxes, but rather by premiums paid by those electing to participate and by general revenue derived from all taxpayers (not just Social Security taxpayers).

There is no mismanagement of the trust funds, there is no

Table 11.2

Summary of Cumulative Income and Outgo under the Supplementary Medical Insurance Program, 1966–89 (amounts in billions)[a]

Premiums from Enrollees	$ 80.9
General Revenue	214.7
Interest Earnings	9.8
Total Income	$305.4
Benefit Payments	$277.6
Administrative Expenses	14.3[b]
Total Expenditures	$291.9
Excess of Income over Expenditures	$ 13.5
(Value of SMI Trust Fund on 12-31-89)	

[a] Premiums were first collected in January 1966; benefits were first paid in July 1966.

[b] SMI administrative expenses are higher (relative to benefits) than under OASDI or HI due to the many benefit claims, often involving small amounts.

significant waste in administering the programs, and there is no significant misapplication of the funds. That is, benefits are generally determined correctly and are paid to those who are entitled to receive them according to Social Security law. Mistakes are made, of course, but most of the spectacular stories of fraud and abuse that have appeared in recent years are about Supplemental Security Income and Medicaid, welfare programs which are more difficult to administer than the Social Security benefits being discussed here. Accordingly, an examination of the past financial operation of the four major parts of the Social Security program could easily lead one to conclude that "Yes, we do get our money's worth from Social Security."

Individual Equity

A second viewpoint from which to consider whether we get our money's worth is the viewpoint of the individual. Chapter 3 explained the types of benefits that are payable under Social Security, and Chapter 5 explained how taxes are assessed in order to pay for those benefits. A careful reading of those sections will indicate that there is relatively little connection between what an individual pays in taxes and receives in benefits. The system was not designed to pay an individual benefits that are equivalent to his tax payments. Accordingly, it is a futile exercise for individuals to attempt to determine whether they can expect to receive benefits from Social Security that are commensurate with their tax payments. The answer is "No." As illustrated below, many participants can expect to receive much *more* in benefits than can be provided by their taxes, and many can expect to receive much *less*. This does not mean the system has failed because it is "unfair"; it means simply that the system was never designed on the principle of individual equity or "fairness" for each participant—even if many people thought it was.

Therefore, if one ignores the value to the nation as a whole of the existence of our Social Security program and is concerned only with the direct value a particular individual receives in terms of benefits or benefit protection, the answer to the question of whether we get our money's worth from

Social Security is "No, some people get more and some get less."

Ample support for this conclusion is provided in a recent study by actuaries at the Social Security Administration.[1] This study considered the value of benefits payable under Social Security throughout the lifetime of more than 100 hypothetical workers. The study took into account only the principal benefits: those payable in the event of retirement, death, and disability, including benefits payable with respect to a spouse and children, as well as to the worker. "Secondary benefits" were not taken into account by this study: for example, benefits to dependent parents or divorced spouses. These secondary benefits, although valuable to those who receive them, are not a significant part of the overall cost of Social Security. Medicare benefits were excluded to simplify the calculations.

After the value of the benefits was computed, it was determined how much the worker and the employer would have to pay in taxes to finance such benefits. The cost was expressed as a level percentage of the worker's earnings that are subject to Social Security tax. Administrative expenses, which amount to less than 2 percent of benefit payments, were ignored. Also ignored was the extent to which general revenue finances benefits because it is estimated to account for no more than 2 to 3 percent of the benefit cost during the projection period.[2]

The results of this study are not surprising to anyone who understands how Social Security works; however, they will be astonishing to those who think "you get what you pay for" when you pay Social Security taxes. Table 11.3 briefly describes four hypothetical workers[3] and shows the tax rates that would be payable by each worker and his employer if total taxes were equivalent to the total benefits during the lifetime of the worker and his dependents. *The theoretical tax rate is as low as 4 percent of earnings for some workers and as high as 29 percent of earnings for others.* In each case the employee tax would have to be matched by an equal employer tax. By way of contrast, the actual OASDI tax rate for all employees is currently 6.2 percent (in 1990), with a matching employer tax rate. Of course this tax rate excludes Medicare taxes since Medicare benefits were excluded from the benefit values used in preparing Table 11.3. While these examples may not be typical of persons covered by Social Security, they do show that it is only by sheer coincidence that a worker receives benefits that are equivalent to the taxes that he or she pays. This statement is true whether we consider employee taxes only, employee and employer taxes combined, or taxes of the self-employed.

It should be noted that the calculations shown in Table 11.3 are strictly theoretical, and it cannot be assumed that an individual or a group of individuals with the characteristics indicated in Table 11.3 can duplicate Social Security benefits by means of private savings and insurance for the costs that

Table 11.3

Theoretical Tax Rate Payable by Workers and Employers, Each, If Taxes Are to Be Equivalent to Benefits for Selected Workers Entering the Work Force[a] in 1990

Brief Description of Worker[b]	Tax Rate Payable by Worker (with Matching Rate Payable by Employer)
Unmarried male who enters work force at age 21, works in steady employment at the maximum taxable earnings under Social Security, remains single, retires at age 70	4%
Unmarried female who enters work force at age 21, works in steady employment at the average earnings level for all workers covered by Social Security, remains single, retires at age 67	7%
Married male with dependent wife and two children, who enters work force at age 21, works in steady employment at about the federal minimum wage, retires at age 67	16%
Married male with dependent wife who enters work force at age 55, works in steady part-time employment at high salary (that produces about the same annual income as full-time employment at the federal minimum wage), retires at age 65	29%

[a] In employment covered by Social Security.

[b] Retirement age shown in each example represents age at which worker is assumed to retire if he or she has not died or become disabled prior to that age.

are shown. Many benefits provided under Social Security are virtually impossible to duplicate outside a system that covers practically the entire working population and mandates the payment of taxes necessary to support the system, and thereby makes it feasible to provide benefits that are not based principally on individual equity.

Equity among Generations

A third viewpoint from which to consider whether we get our money's worth is that of the various generations of persons covered by Social Security. Under the current-cost method of financing, used throughout most of the Social Security program's history, the amount of taxes collected each year is intended to be approximately equal to the benefits and administrative expenses paid during the year plus a small additional amount to maintain the trust funds at an appropriate contingency reserve level. This means that the taxes paid by one generation of workers are used to provide the benefits to an earlier generation of workers. Therefore, the taxes paid by a particular generation of workers are not necessarily equivalent to the cost of the benefits that generation will eventually receive.[4]

For example, if benefit levels are increased over time (in addition to adjustments made for inflation), then any particular generation may receive benefits of greater value than the taxes it paid to become eligible for such benefits. On the other hand, if benefits are decreased or "deliberalized" over time, any particular generation may receive benefits of lesser value than the taxes it paid to become eligible for such benefits.

Also, the size of the working population relative to the retired population, now and in the future, is an important determinant of whether a given generation will receive benefits equivalent to the taxes it pays. Even if benefits are not increased from their present levels in relation to preretirement earnings, current projections indicate that future generations of workers must pay considerably higher tax rates than today's workers (at least 50 percent higher), because in the future the ratio of beneficiaries to taxpayers will be higher.

Past generations have benefitted extremely well from the Social Security program, as the well-known case of Miss Ida Fuller illustrates. Miss Fuller, the program's very first beneficiary, paid only about $22 in Social Security taxes prior to her retirement but lived to collect more than $20,000 in retirement benefits. Most early participants, of course, did not receive "actuarial bargains" of this magnitude. Still, on average, they have done remarkably well. Specifically, during the first fifty years of Social Security's existence, the total taxes paid by employees and employers combined have amounted to only one half of the value of the benefits that have been paid or promised with respect to this period of participation. In other words, during the past fifty years, if the Social Security tax rates had been twice what they were, they would have been adequate to pay for the benefits that were "earned" during that period. (This concept is discussed in more detail in Chapter 7.)

Present and future generations will not fare as well. Social Security actuaries have estimated that the generation of workers currently entering the work force will receive benefits that in total are roughly 10 percent greater than those that can be provided by their Social Security taxes and those of their employers (based upon taxes scheduled by present law and ignoring Medicare benefits and taxes).[5] Future generations should probably expect to receive less in benefits than can be provided by the total of employee and employer Social Security taxes; however, this will depend to some extent upon the timing of future changes in the benefits and upon fluctuations in future birth rates.

This question of equity among various generations is not as simple as it seems and it should be considered from a broad point of view. In recent American history, for example, each generation has enjoyed a better standard of living than the prior generation. At least some of the credit for this steady improvement in the standard of living should be given to the work, savings, and sacrifice of prior generations. Thus, it could be considered that the receipt by today's beneficiaries of benefits of greater value than could have been provided by their past taxes is a partial repayment for the sacrifices they made which resulted in a higher standard of living for later generations of workers. The point in mentioning this question of intergenerational equity is not to resolve it but rather to note that any consideration of money's worth from Social Security should be viewed from a broad perspective, taking into account much more than Social Security taxes paid and benefits received by a particular individual or group of individuals.

Are Benefits Appropriate?

There is yet a fourth point of view from which to consider the question of money's worth: whether we are buying the proper benefits with our Social Security tax dollars. Just because there is no significant waste in administering the Social Security program, it does not follow automatically that we get our money's worth from our tax dollars. Similarly, just because we may not be discontent with questions of equity among generations or among individuals within each generation, it does not follow automatically that we get our money's worth.

Perhaps we are providing the wrong benefits to the wrong people. To the extent that this is true, it can be said we do not get our money's worth from Social Security. It is difficult, if not impossible, to find a simple answer to questions about whether we are collecting the right taxes from the right people and paying the right benefits to the right people. The answer depends upon one's philosophy of right and wrong and, for better or for worse, there is no agreement among all Americans as to exactly what this philosophy should be.

I would suggest that the answer to the question "Do we get our money's worth from Social Security?" depends upon the ultimate effect of Social Security on the American social and economic structure. Will the effect be favorable or unfavorable? Will the effect be what we intended, or will there be unforeseen consequences? My opinion is that we will get our money's worth from Social Security if it is designed to be consistent with the following principles:

> An individual should have freedom of choice to the fullest extent possible consistent with the interest of the nation as a whole.

An individual should be afforded maximum opportunity and incentive to develop and utilize his abilities throughout his lifetime.

A government (federal, state, or local) should provide those benefits, and only those benefits, that an individual (acting alone or as part of a group of individuals utilizing some form of voluntary pooling or risk-sharing arrangement) cannot provide for himself. In meeting this responsibility, the government should become involved to the least extent possible consistent with the interest of the nation as a whole.

The development of a system like the Social Security program is a continuing and evolutionary process. A program that was appropriate for yesterday may not be appropriate for today. A program that is appropriate for today will probably not be appropriate for tomorrow. The present Social Security program is a product of decisions made by past generations of policymakers who lived in a different social and economic environment and who were trying to resolve problems different from those that will exist in the future. When Social Security was enacted some fifty-five years ago, the nation had been in a serious depression for almost six years. The social and economic conditions existing at that time included the following:

More workers than jobs and a consequent high unemployment rate

A small elderly population relative to the younger potential working population

Relatively undeveloped reliable institutions through which an individual could invest and save for the future

An almost completely undeveloped system of private pensions and other employee benefits provided by employers

When the bulk of today's population approaches retirement—some twenty to forty years in the future—social and economic conditions can be expected to be quite different from what they are now or were fifty-five years in the past.

Accordingly, the nation need not and should not be forever influenced by past decisions made to solve past problems. On the contrary, it is the responsibility of today's generation to begin now to make any changes that might be necessary so that the Social Security program will be appropriate for the probable future social and economic environment. In designing a Social Security program for the future, full recognition should be given to the extent to which the design of the program itself will influence the future environment, to ensure that more problems will not be created than resolved. It must be borne in mind that a social insurance system, if not properly designed and communicated, can:

> effectively dictate the retirement-age patterns followed by the nation and thereby encourage earlier retirement at a time when later retirement may be in the best interest of the nation;

> discourage individual initiative and private saving for retirement, yet fail to provide adequate retirement benefits; and

> create unrealistic expectations for retirement that, when unfulfilled, will result in frustration and dissatisfaction.

In my opinion, our present Social Security program exhibits these unsatisfactory characteristics in varying degrees.

So, what is the answer? According to the needs of society, do we get our money's worth from Social Security? With regard to the past fifty years: "Perhaps." But it does no good to worry about what is past. With regard to the next fifty years: "No, unless we change the program."

Even if the present Social Security program were appropriate for the conditions that existed in the past, it will not be appropriate for conditions that are likely to exist in the future when the young working population of today is ready to retire. Although the present Social Security program may have given us our money's worth in the past, it will not give us our money's worth in the future because, unless the program is changed, *we will be using our tax dollars to buy benefits that are inappropriate for the future.*

12
The Earnings Test

You work and pay taxes all your life and finally retire on Social Security and, perhaps, a company pension. Things are going all right until you encounter some unexpected medical expenses—and inflation. You locate a temporary job that will put your finances in order, but then learn that because of your new job you must forfeit some of your Social Security benefits and you will not be as much better off as you thought.

You are a widow with small children and are glad to be receiving Social Security benefits but would like to resume your career. This will give you extra money to send the children to college and will also make your future life happier. But then you find out that, since you are so successful in your job, you will lose most of your Social Security benefits and you will not have as much extra money for the children's college as you had planned.

The culprit is the "earnings test," sometimes called the retirement test, an often misunderstood feature of Social Security designed to reduce or even eliminate benefits when a beneficiary has more than nominal earnings.

The earnings of a retired worker can reduce both his own benefit *and* the benefits of dependent beneficiaries, but the earnings of a dependent beneficiary or a survivor beneficiary can reduce only his own benefit and not the benefit of any other beneficiary. The earnings test does not apply to disabled beneficiaries; other standards are used to determine the continuance of disability. Also, eligibility for Medicare benefits is not affected by the earnings test.

The earnings test is complicated but its essential features can be summarized as follows:

> The test applies only to beneficiaries under age 70 whose benefits are not based on disability.
>
> Certain types of income are not counted in applying the earnings test (investment earnings, rental income, pension benefits, etc.).
>
> A beneficiary may have annual earnings up to a specified amount—the annual exempt amount—without having any benefits withheld:
>
> For persons aged 65 to 69, the annual exempt amount is $9,360 in 1990, automatically adjusted after 1990 to reflect increases in average wage levels.
>
> For persons under age 65, the annual exempt amount is $6,840 in 1990, automatically adjusted after 1990 to reflect increases in average wage levels.
>
> If earnings of a beneficiary aged 65 to 69 exceed the applicable annual exempt amount, $1 in benefits is withheld for each $3 of excess earnings. For example, a beneficiary over 65 (but under age 70) who earned $12,000 in 1990 would have $880 withheld from his benefits because his earnings exceeded his annual exempt amount ($9,360) by $2,640. For beneficiaries under age 65, benefits are reduced by $1 for every $2 of earnings in excess of the exempt amount. Accordingly, such a beneficiary with earnings of $12,000 in 1990 would have $2,580 withheld from his benefits (one-half of the excess of $12,000 over $6,840).
>
> Beneficiaries can have relatively high earnings and still get some benefits.
>
> A beneficiary aged 65 to 69 could earn an amount equal to the total of the applicable exempt amount and three times his annual benefit before all his benefits would be withheld.

For example, a 66-year-old worker who is eligible for benefits of $8,000 per year could earn $33,360 in 1990 before all his benefits would be withheld. This is considerably more than the level of pre-retirement earnings that produced the $8,000 annual benefit.

There is a provision that permits a person who retires to receive benefits in the remainder of the year regardless of his earnings before retirement (assuming that is the first time he has retired). In the first year a beneficiary has a nonwork month (a month in which he earns less than one-twelfth the annual exempt amount), and does not provide substantial services in self-employment, benefits are not withheld in any nonwork month even if annual earnings exceed the annual exempt amount. A similar monthly earnings test is applicable in the final year of benefit receipt for children and for adults who receive benefits because of having an eligible child in their care.

Since the exempt amount of earnings is a flat amount for all beneficiaries within each age group, it favors the lower paid workers. For example, a worker who has always earned the federal minimum wage is not affected by the earnings test after age 65 and can continue working at the same earnings level and receive full Social Security benefits. On the other hand, a worker who has always earned the maximum taxable amount under Social Security and who continues to work past age 65 at the same earnings level will not receive any benefits while still working prior to age 70.

The reason for the earnings test lies in the traditional view of the purpose of the Social Security program; namely, to replace, in part, earnings that are lost when a worker becomes disabled, dies, or retires in old age. The earnings test is used as a measure of whether a loss of income has occurred. The test also applies to dependents and survivors who have earnings, although the rationale for this is not as clear. It is sometimes stated that earnings of dependents and survivors offset partially the loss of a worker's income to the family.

This reasoning is faulty, however, in the case of dependents and survivors who worked prior to becoming eligible for benefits. More generally, the reasoning follows the concept that Social Security benefits are based partly on "presumed social need." Thus dependents or survivors with significant earnings of their own are presumed not to need Social Security benefits as much as dependents or survivors without earnings.

The fact that the earnings test is based only on work earnings, and not on other income such as private pension benefits, interest and dividends, etc., is often criticized. Many consider that the test "favors the rich" while discriminating against poor, aged workers. As noted above, however, the general purpose of the Social Security program is to replace a portion of the earnings lost when a worker becomes disabled, dies, or retires. If a worker continues to work and earn significant income, the program will pay lower benefits (or none at all) based on the grounds that no earnings have been lost. Furthermore, Social Security cash benefits are intended to represent a "floor of protection"; that is, they are not intended to replace fully a worker's lost earnings. Accordingly, workers are urged to provide on their own for additional income in the event of disability, death, or retirement. It would thus be inconsistent to reduce Social Security benefits because of a private pension or income from savings. (Nevertheless, such a reduction has been practiced indirectly since 1984, when a portion of Social Security cash benefits became subject to federal income tax if total income from all sources exceeds certain limits.)

The original earnings test in 1940 was simple but stringent: If monthly earnings in covered employment were $15 or more, the entire monthly benefit was forfeited. Over the years the retirement test has been liberalized continually as a result of public pressure for change.

There is no provision in the present Social Security law that is subject to such consistent public and Congressional criticism as the earnings test. In each session of Congress in recent years scores of bills have been introduced to change the earnings test.

The reason for this public criticism and misunderstanding of the earnings test is not hard to find. For some fifty years the government described Social Security with rhetoric that has led people to believe that their "contributions" were placed in a "trust fund" under an "insurance program" to create an "earned right" to benefits payable upon old age, disability, death, or illness. Little emphasis was given to explaining that the "earned right" was to a benefit payable only if the beneficiary did not have substantial earnings when otherwise eligible for benefits. After a while the public began to believe that they had in fact "bought and paid for" their benefits (as they believed them to be defined) and that it was inconsistent with fifty years of rhetoric, if not downright unfair, to withhold benefits just because the beneficiary continued to work (particularly if the work was to supplement an inadequate benefit in a time of frustrating inflation).

The result of this misunderstanding of the nature of Social Security should not be surprising: pressure by the public to liberalize the earnings test, a yielding to this pressure by Congress, and a substantial change in the very nature of Social Security (to conform more with what the public thought Social Security was all along). This process will probably continue until the earnings test is eliminated altogether and the original design of this part of the Social Security program is transformed completely. There comes a time when misunderstanding is too deeply imbedded to be reversed.

In theory, at least, the original concept of the earnings test was a sound one. In effect, it provided for a flexible retirement age for each individual. Retirement benefits were not to be paid to everyone at an arbitrarily determined age; rather they were to be paid whenever a person was no longer both willing and able to work (but not earlier than age 65 originally, reduced later to age 62). Accordingly, the earnings test has helped to facilitate changes in the size of the work force as the nation's work opportunities have varied. Such changes can be necessary because of shifts in the relative size of the aged and young populations caused by fluctuations in the birth rate and because of changes in the nation's production needs. We shall see a striking need for higher effective retirement ages during the first half of the next century as today's youth reach their 60s and the size of the work force (as we now define it) declines relative to the total population.

It is often alleged that the earnings test provides a strong disincentive to work once a person becomes eligible for Social Security benefits. Every dollar of earnings in excess of the annual exempt amount will, within certain limits, result in a reduction of 33-1/3 or 50 cents in Social Security benefits (depending on the age of the beneficiary). In addition, such earnings will be subject to federal, state and local income tax (as much as 40 percent or so in 1990), as well as the Social Security tax on the first $51,300 of earnings in 1990 of 7.65 percent for an employee, or 15.3 percent for a self-employed person. Therefore, after all these reductions it is possible for one dollar of earnings to yield no increase in net income whatsoever—and, in some cases, even a decrease in net income. If total income is at the point that Social Security benefits first become taxable, it can result in an even poorer return on additional work earnings.

But an important point seems to have been overlooked by critics of the earnings test. It is not the earnings test that, by reducing Social Security benefits, creates a disincentive to work. Rather, it is the payment of Social Security benefits in the first place that creates the disincentive to work. Eliminating the earnings test will not resolve any legitimate concern that we may have about the Social Security system:

> If we are concerned about treating retired workers fairly and giving them the benefits they have "bought and paid for" with their Social Security taxes, we need worry no longer because to date benefits have significantly exceeded those that can be provided by such taxes.

> If we are concerned about the high cost of Social Security, we should not eliminate the earnings test and thus increase the cost by spending more money on those who are able to work; instead, we should spend our retirement dollars only on those who *cannot* work.

If we are concerned about the dwindling work force and want to encourage people to work longer, we should not pay benefits at all to relatively young persons, say those under age 65, unless they are unable to work. (This limiting age would be subject to change, of course, as economic and demographic factors change.)

It is tempting to suggest that the trend toward elimination of the earnings test be reversed and that the original concept of a strict earnings test be restored. This could be achieved simply by freezing the exempt amounts of earnings at present levels instead of raising them as average wages increase, and retaining age 70 as the maximum age for applying the earnings test instead of continually reducing it. (This maximum age did not exist prior to 1951, and it was age 75 from 1951 through 1954 and age 72 from 1955 through 1982.) In a relatively short time, inflation would effectively restore a strict earnings test to Social Security, which would then provide flexible retirement ages to accommodate the nation's changing needs. This would, of course, reduce the ratio of beneficiaries to active taxpayers after the turn of the century.

For those higher retirement ages to result in reduced benefit costs, however, another revision would be required: the delayed retirement credit (the actuarial increase in benefits when the receipt of retirement benefits is postponed) would have to be reduced or eliminated. Under current law, this delayed retirement credit is scheduled to increase gradually, for persons reaching their normal retirement age during the twenty-year period 1990 to 2009, from 3 percent a year to 8 percent a year—thus negating any cost saving from delayed retirement.

It may be too late to restore a strict earnings test and to scale back the delayed retirement credit, however, since that would require the population to view Social Security in a considerably different way than it has become accustomed: namely, that taxpayers have paid for their own benefits with their Social Security taxes and that it is unfair to withhold benefits just because they elect to work past normal retirement age.

13
Integration of Private Benefit Plans with Social Security

Social Security was not designed to meet all the financial needs that arise from a person's old age, disability, death, or illness. It is still necessary to supplement Social Security with personal savings and employee benefit plans. Supplemental employee benefit plans are sometimes designed without regard to the benefits provided under Social Security. It is preferable, however, to coordinate any supplemental plans with Social Security so that the combined benefits from all sources will form a rational package. This process of coordination is usually called "integration."

In theory, integration is not very difficult. In practice, however, it is quite complicated, largely because of:

the design of the Social Security program itself; and

the requirements of the Internal Revenue Service that supplemental plan benefits be designed in certain ways in order to be a "qualified plan" and thus be accorded favorable tax treatment.

A discussion of the integration of supplemental retirement benefits and Social Security benefits upon retirement at age 65 will illustrate some of the problems.

167

Social Security retirement benefits are based largely on the principle of "social adequacy" and thus provide benefits for persons with low earnings that are higher, relative to preretirement earnings, than for persons with higher earnings. For example, consider four workers retiring in January 1990 at age 65 after a steady work history, each at a different level of earnings. A worker whose past earnings have always been a little less than half the average annual wage for all workers would receive benefits during the first year of retirement of approximately 60 percent of his or her average earnings in the three years prior to retirement.[1] This percentage is frequently called a "replacement ratio" because it represents the proportion of average preretirement earnings that is replaced by the retirement benefit.[2] This replacement ratio would be 45 percent for a worker whose past earnings have equaled the average earnings of all employees covered by Social Security, 26 percent for a worker whose past earnings have equaled the maximum taxable wage base in effect during prior years, and 13 percent for a worker whose earnings have been twice the maximum taxable wage base in effect during prior years. These replacement ratios represent the basic benefit payable to a worker alone. For a worker with an eligible spouse (also aged 65), the replacement ratios become 90 percent for the low-wage earner, 67 percent for the average-wage earner, 39 percent for the maximum-wage earner, and 19 percent for the high-wage earner (one earning twice the maximum taxable wage base). These replacement ratios for the various categories of workers retiring at age 65 in 1990 may be summarized as follows:

	Annual Earnings in 1989	Social Security Benefits as a Percentage of the Last Three Years' Average Earnings	
		Worker Alone	Worker and Spouse
Low Wage	$ 9,224	60%	90%
Average Wage	20,497	45	67
Maximum Taxable Wage	48,000	26	39
High Wage	96,000	13	19

An examination of these figures makes it obvious that income replacement needs at retirement are not met uniformly for all of the workers in the example and that for most workers some kind of supplemental plan is called for. This need for supplementation is not a deficiency of the Social Security program; it was always intended that Social Security provide a basic floor of protection upon which additional protection could be built. Also, it has always been a characteristic of Social Security to provide more adequate benefits for workers earning lower than average wages than for workers earning higher than average wages. Furthermore, since 1939, Social Security has provided additional benefits in the case of a retired worker with an eligible spouse.

It is not unusual to find a supplemental retirement plan that provides benefits that are a uniform percentage of average preretirement earnings and that are the same whether the worker does or does not have a spouse. Such a plan *supplements* Social Security, yet it is not *integrated* with Social Security. As an example, consider a supplemental plan that provides a career worker with retirement benefits of 60 percent of average earnings in the three years prior to retirement. The benefits under such a plan are summarized below for the same workers used as an example in the preceding table:

	Annual Earnings in 1989	Supplemental Plan Benefits as a Percentage of the Last Three Years' Average Earnings	
		Worker Alone	Worker and Spouse
Low Wage	$ 9,224	60%	60%
Average Wage	20,497	60	60
Maximum Taxable Wage	48,000	60	60
High Wage	96,000	60	60

If this supplemental plan is superimposed on the Social Security program, the total benefits may be summarized as follows:

	Annual Earnings in 1989	Total Benefits as a Percentage of the Last Three Years' Average Earnings	
		Worker Alone	Worker and Spouse
Low Wage	$ 9,224	120%	150%
Average Wage	20,497	105	127
Maximum Taxable Wage	48,000	86	99
High Wage	96,000	73	79

This table illustrates the wide discrepancy in benefits relative to preretirement earnings that can occur when a supplemental retirement plan is simply *added to* Social Security but not *integrated with* Social Security. Such a situation is not uncommon, particularly among supplemental plans covering public employee groups.

If a supplemental retirement plan is to be integrated with Social Security, the plan must comply with the Internal Revenue Code as well as with rules and regulations of the Internal Revenue Service if the plan and its participants are to be accorded favorable tax treatment. The Internal Revenue Service requirements for integration permit a supplemental plan to provide benefits, relative to preretirement earnings, that favor more highly paid workers in order to offset, in part, the effect of the Social Security program which favors lower paid workers.

Assume, for example, that a benefit level of 70 percent of the final three-year average earnings is considered to be the desired goal for all workers regardless of their earnings level. Assume further that the supplemental plan benefits are modified toward that goal within the limits of the integration rules of the Internal Revenue Service. The benefits under such a plan may be summarized as follows:

	Annual Earnings in 1989	Supplemental Plan Benefits as a Percentage of the Last Three Years' Average Earnings	
		Worker Alone	Worker and Spouse
Low Wage	$ 9,224	36%	36%
Average Wage	20,497	39	39
Maximum Taxable Wage	48,000	52	52
High Wage	96,000	57	57

If these integrated supplemental plan benefits are added to Social Security benefits, the total benefits may be summarized as follows:

	Annual Earnings in 1989	Total Benefits as a Percentage of the Last Three Years' Average Earnings	
		Worker Alone	Worker and Spouse
Low Wage	$ 9,224	96%	126%
Average Wage	20,497	84	106
Maximum Taxable Wage	48,000	78	91
High Wage	96,000	70	76

A review of this table indicates that it is not possible to achieve simultaneously for all employee categories the stated goal of replacing 70 percent of the final three-year average earnings. Even if a supplemental plan is integrated to the full extent permitted by Internal Revenue Service requirements for a tax-qualified plan, there is still a wide variation in benefits. Lower-wage earners receive relatively larger benefits than high-wage earners. Workers with spouses receive relatively larger benefits than single workers. If adequate benefits are provided the high-wage single workers, excessive benefits must be provided all other workers.

Of course, not everyone would agree that the combined benefits from Social Security and a supplemental retirement plan should be a uniform percentage of gross preretirement earnings. Some would argue that it is "equitable" for such a percentage to decline as average earnings increase—to reflect, if for no other reason, the progressive nature of the federal income tax and the nontaxability of Social Security benefits (except for beneficiaries with high incomes who pay some tax on their Social Security benefits). These features tend to make a declining replacement ratio for gross preretirement earnings equivalent to a level replacement ratio for net (after tax) preretirement earnings. In any event, it would seem that more uniformity of retirement benefits relative to preretirement earnings is desirable than is permitted by current integration requirements of the Internal Revenue Service.

This entire subject may seem complicated, and it is. Nevertheless, the following observations seem reasonable:

Social Security alone does not meet all the financial needs that arise from a person's old age, disability, death, or illness. It meets those needs more completely for lower wage earners than for higher wage earners and more completely for married workers than for single workers.

Supplemental plan benefits must be provided if income replacement needs are to be met adequately. Supplemental benefits should be *integrated with* and not just *added to* Social Security benefits. Otherwise, the extreme unevenness with which financial needs are met will be continued but at a higher level.

Under present laws and regulations, it is not possible to integrate supplemental benefit plans with Social Security to the extent necessary to satisfy uniformly the financial needs of all workers at the various earnings levels. If appropriate benefits are provided for workers with average earnings, less than adequate benefits are provided for the more highly paid workers; if adequate benefits are provided for the more highly paid workers, excessive benefits will be provided for lower paid workers. This situation can be corrected only if the Internal Revenue Service integration rules are revised, or if the Social Security program is revised, or both.

Many employee groups that do not participate in Social Security (e.g., employees of state and local governments) have established employee benefit plans that satisfy uniformly the financial needs of all participants regardless of their earnings level. If these employee groups elect to participate in Social Security or are required to do so, significant revisions will be necessary in their existing employee benefit plans if rational balance is to be maintained in the benefits provided employees at the various earnings levels. The extent to which these revisions can be implemented is seriously hampered by the Internal Revenue Service laws and regulations, assuming they are in fact applicable to public as well as to private benefit plans.[3]

Providing rationally coordinated benefits under two systems, Social Security and supplemental employee benefit plans, is quite difficult in view of the nature of Social Security itself and the Internal Revenue Service rules for integration. Nevertheless, proper coordination of benefits is essential if income replacement needs are to be met at an affordable cost. To achieve this coordination within the framework of the present laws and regulations requires that tax-qualified supplemental employee benefit plans be integrated as completely with Social Security as is allowed by Internal Revenue Service rulings, and that a portion of the retirement benefits for the more highly paid employees be provided separately from tax-qualified retirement plans so as to minimize the limiting effect of integration rulings.

It is unfortunate that federal tax laws are not more consistent and are not more conducive to the formation of rationally conceived supplemental employee benefit plans. Many tax laws are designed to encourage the adoption of supplemental plans while others tend to discourage their adoption. The Internal Revenue Service integration rules in particular make it virtually impossible to design a supplemental retirement plan that fits together with Social Security to form a sensible combination of retirement benefits. On the other hand, many supplemental plans are not as completely integrated with Social Security as is permitted under existing tax laws, imperfect though such laws are.

14
Inflation and Automatic Benefit Increases

Social Security payments for 40 million beneficiaries were increased by 5.4 percent in December 1990. This benefit increase corresponded with the increase in the Consumer Price Index of 5.4 percent from the third quarter of 1989 to the third quarter of 1990 and was granted automatically in accordance with Social Security's automatic adjustment provisions. These provisions were enacted in 1972 and were scheduled to take effect in January 1975, but it was June 1975 before they were permitted to operate without modification. Increases in Social Security benefits in the course of payment for each year since 1974 are summarized in Table 14.1.

These benefit increases have provided valuable protection against inflation for Social Security beneficiaries. The cumulative increase in benefits during the seventeen-year period from 1973 to 1990 was 189 percent; that is, benefits almost tripled. At first glance, the automatic adjustment provisions may appear to have solved the problems of inflation. There are many factors to consider, however, and in attempting to alleviate the various problems caused by inflation, the government faces a dilemma because not all of these problems

175

Table 14.1

Automatic Increases in Social Security Benefits

Calendar Year of Benefit Increase[a]	Percentage Benefit Increase
(1)	(2)
1974[b]	11.0%
1975	8.0
1976	6.4
1977	5.9
1978	6.5
1979	9.9
1980	14.3
1981	11.2
1982	7.4
1983[c]	3.5
1984	3.5
1985	3.1
1986	1.3
1987	4.2
1988	4.0
1989	4.7
1990	5.4

[a] For the years 1974 through 1982 the benefit increases were effective with benefits for June (generally payable on the following July 3). For the years after 1982 the benefit increases were effective for December (generally payable on January 3).

[b] Automatic benefit increases did not become effective until 1975. The 1974 benefit increase shown is approximately the same amount that would have resulted if the automatic increase provision had been in effect.

[c] The 1983 increase was with respect to the 18-month period from June 1982 to December 1983 but was based on the CPI increase for the 12-month period from the first quarter of 1982 to the first quarter of 1983.

can be resolved simultaneously. In fact, resolving one problem often aggravates another—as indicated below.

Responsibility and Opportunity

It can be argued that the government has a responsibility to maintain the purchasing power of any Social Security benefit it provides if the program is to carry out the purpose for which it was established. The individual pensioner did not cause the inflation which is robbing him of purchasing power. In most cases, at least some of the blame must be placed on governmental economic policies. To the extent that external forces or actions by the nation's active workers have caused inflation, it is true that the government may not have played a role—but then neither did the individual pensioner. Consequently, the government may still be considered responsible for finding a solution.

Moreover, the retired pensioner is out of the active work force and usually is powerless to protect himself against inflation. The government is the only logical protector of pensions provided by Social Security. The government enacted the Social Security law in the first place; it is the government that can and must amend the law as necessary to preserve the pensioner's standard of living. Finally, if the government does not protect pensioners against inflation, who will do so?

These are powerful arguments in favor of governmental action, and they do in fact usually lead to governmental intervention such as Social Security's 1972 automatic adjustment provisions. But what does governmental intervention entail? Can the government really solve the problems caused by inflation?

Who Bears the Burden of Inflation?

It is easy to make casual references to "governmental responsibility" or to having the "government pay" for all or part of a social insurance program, without pausing to realize what this truly means. The government has no magic wand. If social insurance benefits are made inadequate by inflation and the government responds by increasing benefits, this simply means that the active workers and their employers must pay higher taxes to provide such benefits. Many analysts believe that higher payroll taxes result in more inflation and that increased benefits to pensioners will reinforce, if not aggravate, inflation. If this is true, the net result is still further increases in inflation, and then in pensions and taxes, resulting in an ever-increasing upward spiral. This is particularly so if the wages of active workers are adjusted for inflation. And if the government adjusts *pension benefits* for inflation, to be consistent it must endorse adjustment of *wages* for inflation.

Table 14.2

**Comparison of Yearly Increases in Consumer Price Index and
Average Earnings of Social Security Taxpayers**

Calendar Year	Percentage Increase in Consumer Price Index[a]	Percentage Increase in Average Earnings of Social Security Taxpayers[b]
(1)	(2)	(3)
1973	6.2%	7.1%
1974	11.0	7.1
1975	9.2	6.7
1976	5.7	8.5
1977	6.5	7.0
1978	7.6	9.8
1979	11.4	9.4
1980	13.5	8.0
1981	10.2	9.1
1982	6.0	5.8
1983	3.0	5.1
1984	3.4	7.0
1985	3.5	4.5
1986	1.6	4.2
1987	3.6	5.3
1988	4.0	5.6
1989	4.8	3.9[c]
1990	5.3	4.4[c]

[a] The figure for 1973 represents the relative increase in the average CPI for 1973 over the average CPI for 1972, and so on.

[b] The figure for 1973 represents the relative increase in the average earnings for 1973 over the average earnings for 1972, and so on.

[c] Preliminary estimate.

Note: CPI data are based on the Consumer Price Index for Urban Wage Earners and Clerical Workers (CPI-W).

The problem of maintaining the purchasing power of the active worker is a difficult one. It usually requires wage increases that exceed the rate of inflation to avoid reductions in the real level of workers' net incomes after taxes. Table 14.2 compares the average increase in the earnings of persons who pay Social Security taxes and the increase in the Consumer Price Index during recent years. Historically, average earnings have increased faster than prices. This is a reflection of an increased productivity of the nation's workers and thus an improved standard of living. For example, from 1952 through 1972, average wages increased faster than prices by an average annual amount of more than 2 percent. This was not true during the period from 1973 to 1990 when, as indicated in Table 14.2, the average earnings of Social Security taxpayers increased at virtually the same rate, on average, as the Consumer Price Index. For the ten-year period from 1973 to 1982, the average earnings of Social Security taxpayers increased less than the Consumer Price Index by an average annual rate of 1.0 percent. During this same period, a comparison of the increase in net earnings after taxes (instead of gross earnings) with the Consumer Price Index would show a substantially larger gap, or a loss of purchasing power among the active workers.

On the other hand, Social Security benefits have generally been adjusted fully to reflect increases in the Consumer Price Index—putting the Social Security recipient at an advantage over the active worker during times when inflation outstrips earnings growth. If this phenomenon were to continue for a significant period, the result would be an eventual conflict between the working and nonworking populations, since it would not be possible to protect the nonworking population against the ravages of inflation, except at the expense of the working population. Similarly, there could easily be a conflict among the various segments of the working population, since it is virtually impossible to distribute the burden of inflation "equitably." If high inflation were to persist, these realities would be more widely recognized and strong efforts would be made to require all segments of the population to share more equally in bearing the cost of inflation. This could result in less than a full adjustment in Social Security benefits for inflation.[1]

There are other problems in adjusting pensions and wages for changes in the cost of living. For example, some methods of compensating for inflation may, in fact, overcompensate and thus accelerate the very inflation for which adjustment is being made. In some cases this is because of faulty methods in designing the cost-of-living index; in other cases it may result from failing to apply different adjustments to the active and the retired populations, although there is little reliable information available on whether different adjustments should be applied. Accordingly, extreme care must be taken in constructing an index (or indices) to be used in adjusting pensions and wages.

The Real Solution

Although the problems posed by inflation are complex, it is clear they must be addressed in some way. It is generally accepted that the purchasing power of social insurance pensions (and other benefits) should be restored if eroded by inflation. Increasing the benefits, however, should be viewed as a temporary stopgap measure. A government cannot simply increase social insurance benefits and thereby presume to have resolved the widespread problems caused by inflation, or even to have alleviated them, except temporarily for a limited segment of the population.

In the final analysis, there is only one action a government can take that will be in the best interests of the most people and keep social and economic turmoil to a minimum. The government must identify the underlying *causes* of inflation, attack those causes, and keep inflation under control to the maximum possible extent. This is a large order, but to do otherwise will be to permit inflation to fester into such a complex problem that there will be no acceptable solutions.

15
Should
Social Security
Cover Everyone?

Approximately 84 percent of the nation's workers are in jobs automatically and mandatorily covered by Social Security and are therefore required to pay Social Security taxes.[1] Of course this entitles them to receive Social Security benefits if they meet the eligibility requirements. About 3 percent of the nation's workers are in jobs that are not covered by Social Security, hence they neither pay Social Security taxes nor receive its benefits. The remaining 13 percent of the working population have the option of paying or not paying Social Security taxes and thus receiving or not receiving its benefits. Approximately 72 percent of the workers with this option have chosen to participate in Social Security. (Generally speaking, the option must be exercised by groups of employees and not by individuals; and, once a group has elected to participate, the election is irrevocable for the group and new members of the group must participate.) The reasons for this varying treatment of different segments of the population are outlined in Chapter 2.

Is this situation of nonuniversal and partly optional coverage by Social Security a fair arrangement? Is it in the best interest of the nation?

The purpose of Social Security is to ensure that everyone with a significant work history is assured a basic standard of living in the event of retirement because of age or disability and that the dependents of every such worker are also assured a basic standard of living in the event of the worker's retirement, disability, or premature death. In theory it may be acceptable to exclude a portion of the population from the protection offered by Social Security, provided there is reasonable assurance that this excluded segment will have alternative protection and thus not become a "charge on society." Most of the persons who do not participate in Social Security do in fact have a variety of employee benefit programs that provide much of the benefit protection offered by Social Security. Of course, no alternative system can be as financially stable as Social Security, publicity to the contrary notwithstanding. Furthermore, even though a person may be protected adequately under an alternative system, there is no assurance that such protection will continue as long as it is needed: either the system could change or employment could terminate. Accordingly, it should be anticipated that some of the persons who do not participate in Social Security and who rely upon other systems of benefit protection will die or become disabled or reach old age without receiving benefits equivalent to those that would have been afforded under Social Security. This will in turn create some situations in which society (more specifically, the taxpayers) will have to step in and provide financial support through one of the welfare programs—the very situations that Social Security was adopted to prevent.

Another point to consider is the fairness, actual as well as perceived, of a nonuniversal system. If Social Security were a system whereby an individual received benefits with a value approximately equal to his tax payments, then it might be considered fair, or "actuarially sound," to permit optional participation or to exclude certain groups from participation. As we saw in Chapter 11, however, this is not the case. Benefits are not equivalent to taxes. It is natural, therefore, for persons for whom participation is optional to select their options in such a way as to take maximum advantage of

Social Security, leaving the bulk of the taxpayers—who have no choice in the matter—to make up any extra cost this may entail. This is in fact what is happening. When a career federal civil servant (hired before 1984 and not participating in Social Security) takes a part-time job in employment covered by Social Security, he generally receives benefits of considerably greater value than his tax payments. When a policeman or fireman (whose job is not covered by Social Security) retires at age 50 and then works in a job covered by Social Security, upon his "second" retirement he receives benefits that can exceed the value of his tax payments. This same situation exists for many other employees of state and local governments, including public school teachers, when their jobs are not covered by Social Security.[2] This is not the fault of the career federal civil servant or the policeman or fireman or the public school teacher; it is the fault of the Social Security system which was designed to cover all of the nation's workers but which, because of a series of "loopholes," excludes a significant portion of the population.

If groups of employees in different parts of the nation were given the option of paying or not paying the taxes necessary to support the national defense effort, it would be reasonable to expect that certain groups would elect not to pay such taxes. Similarly, if persons were given the opportunity not to provide any support for the nation's educational system, it would be reasonable to expect that some persons would elect to discontinue paying taxes that are used to educate our youth. In both of these cases, persons who elected to discontinue tax payments would nonetheless receive benefits, admittedly indirect and difficult to appreciate, from the national defense effort and the national educational effort, since both of these efforts would be continued by other taxpayers—perhaps at a slightly reduced level because of slightly reduced tax receipts. The difference between these examples and the option for certain groups of persons not to participate in Social Security is not very great. There is an indirect, although substantial, benefit to the nonsupporter of the Social Security system by virtue of its continuing to pay benefits to some 40 million persons—retired and disabled persons and their dependents, as well as widows and orphans. Were it not for the Social Security program, the burden of supporting a large proportion of these beneficiaries would fall directly upon all taxpayers regardless of whether they paid taxes to the Social Security program.

Social Security was not designed to be a neatly defined package of benefits that a particular group of persons can elect to buy or not buy in exchange for the payment of Social Security taxes. It was designed to provide a wide range of benefits to the bulk of the nation's workers and their dependents based upon their presumed need. The benefits are based upon prior earnings levels, the worker's type and number of dependents, the ability of the beneficiary to work, and so on. Benefits are not related, except incidentally, to the taxes paid by the participant. Since the program is operated on close to a pay-as-you-go basis (with relatively little advance funding), the taxes paid by one generation of workers are used to provide benefits for an earlier generation of workers. Therefore, the taxes paid by a particular generation of workers are not equivalent to the cost of the benefits that will be provided eventually to that generation of workers.

These characteristics of Social Security result in a significant redistribution of income: intragenerational transfers as individuals within each generation receive benefits with a different value than the taxes paid by such individuals, and intergenerational transfers as benefits received by one generation taken as a whole are more or less than the value of the taxes paid by that generation.

On the other hand the provisions regarding optional participation for certain groups of workers were designed as if the employee group concerned would pay taxes equivalent to the benefits it receives. This is obviously not the case under our present Social Security program; therefore, such provisions are poorly conceived and inappropriate. Apparently, when the provisions were designed, it was presumed that most of the people who had the option to join Social Security would elect to participate.

One of the reasons frequently given for requiring everyone to participate in Social Security is that it will help solve Social Security's financial problems. This is not an appropriate

SHOULD SOCIAL SECURITY COVER EVERYONE? 185

reason. For one thing, if more people are added to Social Security, they will not only pay more taxes but will also receive more benefits. The net effect of bringing everyone into Social Security would be to decrease the required tax rate paid by employees and employers by only about 0.125 percent each on the average over the next seventy-five years. This is not very much compared with the present tax rate of 7.65 percent and the much higher tax rates of 12 to 20 percent that will be required by the middle of the next century if no changes are made in the program. But this phenomenon of reduced payroll tax rates deserves closer study. Even though universal coverage may result in slightly lower payroll tax rates, and therefore may appear to alleviate Social Security's financial problems, *it would not reduce the total tax burden— direct and indirect—imposed on the nation as a whole to support Social Security.* On the contrary, it would most likely *increase* the tax burden.

This paradox may be explained as follows by considering the effect of bringing all state employees into Social Security. State employees would pay the same Social Security tax rate as all other participants; however, because of the characteristics of state employees, their Social Security taxes relative to their benefits would be higher than the average for all other participants, yielding a "gain" to Social Security. This gain would result in lower average benefit costs relative to taxable payroll and lower average tax rates for all participants. It should be obvious, however, that the cost of benefits for present participants would not be lowered by adding state employees; it is simply that "excess" Social Security taxes paid by state employees would permit slightly reduced taxes by present participants. But who pays the Social Security taxes for state employees, including any "excess" taxes? It is the taxpayers of the states involved. Accordingly, any reduction in Social Security payroll taxes made possible by including state employees would be offset by an exactly corresponding increase in other taxes paid by taxpayers of the states that are affected.

One might argue that the state employee—not the general taxpayer—would pay half the Social Security tax, hence there would be a saving to the general taxpayer. Any such tax saving would be unlikely for the following reasons. Most state employees already contribute a percentage of their salary to their own retirement system. Inclusion of state employees in Social Security would almost certainly be made on the basis of no increase in employee cost; therefore, existing employee contributions to state retirement plans would be reduced by the amount of any Social Security taxes imposed on state employees. Therefore, state employees would not pay any more under Social Security and their state retirement plan combined than they now pay under the state retirement plan alone. (A minor exception, perhaps, is with respect to short-term employees, since Social Security taxes are not refundable as are contributions to retirement plans; therefore, some short-term employees would in effect pay higher contributions if participating in Social Security.) Any diversion of present employee contributions from a state retirement plan to Social Security would have to be restored by added general revenue paid by the state's taxpayers.

One might argue alternatively that state retirement plan benefits could be reduced by the amount of any Social Security benefits newly provided, resulting in a saving to the general taxpayer. It is true that the substitution of largely pay-as-you-go financed Social Security benefits for advance-funded state retirement plan benefits may give an apparent reduction in costs in the short run, but it cannot reduce costs in the long run; it can only shift part of the costs to later generations. Providing identical benefits through different vehicles cannot change the cost, taking into account the time-value of money.

Finally, universal coverage would actually increase the total tax burden because state retirement plan benefits can be reduced by some but not all the benefits provided by Social Security. This is because Social Security provides some benefits that are not provided by state retirement systems. Therefore, if state employees are included in Social Security on the basis of not receiving lower total benefits than the present benefits provided under the state retirement system, it follows that there would be an increase in total benefits (to the extent Social Security provides benefits not provided by a state retirement system). This increase in benefits for state employees would result in increased costs for the general taxpayer in the state affected.

The same general reasoning concerning the financial implications of requiring state employees to participate in Social Security also applies to the inclusion of employees of local governments, although the particular taxpayers affected may be different. For example, lowered Social Security taxes for the nation as a whole would probably be offset by increased local income taxes or increased real estate or other taxes paid by taxpayers in the localities affected.

In summary, with regard to the financial aspect of universal coverage, although there are certain financial inequities in nonuniversal coverage, which should probably be corrected, universal coverage cannot possibly reduce the total tax burden—direct and indirect—of supporting Social Security (unless, in the process, someone suffers a benefit reduction). Universal coverage can result only in the shifting of Social Security costs among taxpayers brought about, generally speaking, by substituting general revenue for part of the payroll tax. In addition, universal coverage could result in a shift among generations of some of the costs of the affected public employee retirement systems. This would result from substituting part of the Social Security benefits for part of the public employee retirement system benefits, which could in turn cause a change in the financing patterns since Social Security is generally financed on a pay-as-you-go basis and a given public employment retirement system is generally financed on some form of advance-funded basis. Universal coverage could also result in higher long-range total costs of benefits for public employees since they would, in some cases, receive a broader array of benefits by participating in Social Security.

Universal coverage would, of course, pose many problems. Most employee groups not now covered by Social Security have their own employee benefit programs. These programs would need to be revised in the event of universal coverage so that the employees affected would receive neither smaller nor appreciably larger benefits after inclusion in Social Security than before inclusion. There would also be certain technical as well as legal problems in revising existing employee benefit plans. All of these problems can be resolved, however, should coverage under Social Security become universal.

Based upon the present design of Social Security, there should be no optional participation; everyone should participate in both the payment of its taxes and the receipt of its benefits, direct and indirect. If it is desired that participation be optional, the Social Security program should be redesigned so that the benefits paid to each group of workers are approximately equivalent to the taxes paid by such group. Unless such a basic change is made, there can be no satisfactory basis for optional participation.

Compulsory participation by all state and local government employees has been successfully opposed in the past largely because of legal questions regarding the constitutionality of mandatory participation. This barrier seems to have eroded or become irrelevant in recent years: perhaps because such a large proportion of state and local employees have elected Social Security coverage; perhaps because it has been perceived to be in the public interest that coverage be universal. Participation in the Hospital Insurance portion of Social Security is now required for all federal civilian employees, and for all state and local employees hired after March 1986. The movement toward mandatory, universal coverage by Social Security appears to be inexorable.

16
Should You Opt into Social Security If You Can?

There are just over four million employees of state and local governments whose present jobs are not covered by Social Security—jobs that could be covered if the workers and their employers so desired. They include all state employees in Alaska, Colorado, Louisiana, Maine, Massachusetts, Nevada, and Ohio, and all state teachers in Alaska, California (except San Francisco), Colorado, Connecticut, Illinois, Kentucky, Louisiana, Maine, Massachusetts, Missouri (with certain exceptions), Nevada, Ohio, and Puerto Rico.

On the other hand, there are approximately eleven million state and local government employees, including state teachers, who *are* covered by Social Security.

Which group made the correct decision—the eleven million workers who decided to participate in Social Security or the four million workers who decided not to participate?

This chapter presents some of the many considerations to be taken into account by employee groups that are considering whether or not to exercise their option to participate in Social Security. In order for the chapter to stand on its own as much as possible, there is some duplication of material contained in other parts of the book.

189

General Background Information

The Social Security Act originally excluded from Social Security coverage all employment for state and local governments because of the question of whether the federal government could legally tax such employers.

Legislation enacted in the early 1950s provided that employees of such organizations could be covered by Social Security on a voluntary basis under certain conditions. For example, Social Security coverage is available to employees of state and local government systems on a group voluntary basis through agreements between the Secretary of Health and Human Services and the individual states.

Approximately 72 percent of the 15 million state and local employees are covered by Social Security under these voluntary participation arrangements.

Until the 1983 amendments to Social Security, an employee group that elected to participate in Social Security could, after meeting certain requirements, elect to terminate its participation, or "opt out." Once having opted out, the group could never rejoin Social Security. The 1983 amendments prevented further opting out and permitted groups that had opted out to rejoin the system.

During the ten-year period from 1973 to 1983 approximately 600 coverage groups representing some 125,000 employees opted out of Social Security (about 1.5 percent of those eligible to opt out). Coverage groups in Alaska, California, Louisiana, and Texas accounted for 86 percent of the terminations.

The State of Alaska was the first and only state to withdraw all of its employees from Social Security. The termination of the coverage agreement for Alaska state employees became effective December 31, 1979, and ended participation for about 14,500 employees.

These withdrawals came at a time of increasing public doubt about the financial viability and fairness of Social Security—a time of financial crisis and rising taxes. The government's response to this situation was to strengthen Social Security's financial condition by increasing taxes and reducing benefits; and to make it impossible for an employee group to discontinue participation.

Difficulties in Making Cost Comparisons of the Social Security Program with Alternative Private Systems

For state and local government employee groups considering coverage under Social Security, a natural question is how much do Social Security benefits cost versus alternative retirement systems. A major problem with answering this question is that Social Security provides many benefits and has many characteristics that are difficult, if not impossible, to duplicate for subgroups of the population. It is only through a mandatory program with practically universal coverage that it is feasible to provide many of the benefits that are available under Social Security. Therefore, it is almost impossible to make a valid comparison of the cost of Social Security benefits as provided under:

the Social Security program financed primarily through its payroll taxes; and

a private program providing the "same benefits" but financed in a different way.

Some of the characteristics of the Social Security program that make it virtually impossible to duplicate are listed below.

Benefits being accrued for payment in the future increase automatically as increases occur in the Consumer Price Index, in the average wages of the nation's employees, and in the average covered wages of a particular employee.

Benefits in the course of payment increase with the CPI.

The type and level of benefits change automatically as an employee's family status changes (without any change in the Social Security taxes payable). For example:

A single worker marries.

The family has children.

A couple divorces after ten years of marriage (the former spouse continues to be eligible for certain benefits).

All of these changes—and others—result in automatic extensions in benefit protection. Certain other changes in family status result in contractions in benefit protection.

When an employee changes employers, he takes his "accrued benefits" with him regardless of his length of service. If he has satisfied part but not all of the participation requirements for a particular benefit (say the disability benefit) and his new employment is covered by Social Security, his previous participation will be added to his new participation in determining eligibility for future benefits. Changes back and forth between employed and self-employed status have no effect on benefits (but do affect Social Security taxes paid).

Survivorship protection and disability protection are provided without regard to an individual's health, occupational and avocational hazards, or other factors affecting his "insurability." The same amount of Social Security tax is paid by an individual regardless of any of these factors.

Medicare benefits are payable to persons aged 65 and over who are eligible for monthly cash benefits under Social Security and to disabled persons under age 65 after they receive disability benefits for twenty-four months. Special medical expense benefits are payable to an insured person or to his dependents in the event of kidney disease.

Social Security benefits are largely exempt from federal income tax as well as state and local income tax. Only when a person's (or couple's) total income rises above a certain threshold does as much as one-half of his or her Social Security benefits become subject to income taxes.

Social Security benefits for retired workers, their dependents, and their survivors are, in general, either reduced or not paid when the beneficiary is engaged in substantial employment or self-employment. Whether benefits are eliminated completely or simply reduced depends upon the individual's level of earnings. Different earnings levels apply for persons under age 65 than apply for persons at ages 65 to 69. This "earnings test" is no longer applied after an individual reaches age 70. There are special rules, which include medical considerations, for disabled beneficiaries who work.

The Social Security program has experienced dramatic changes over the years with the addition of survivors benefits, disability benefits, Medicare, automatic adjustment provisions, and so on. Although future changes are certain to occur, they cannot be predicted with certainty.

As a result of these special characteristics of the Social Security program, there are no private income-security plans available that exactly duplicate Social Security.

Any comparison of the costs of a private system with those of Social Security must recognize that the cost of Social Security is not limited to the direct Social Security tax. In addition, there is general revenue including the federal income tax on the growing portion of Social Security benefits that is taxable.

The financing procedures followed by social insurance systems and private pension systems are usually quite different; therefore, the same set of benefits may appear to have different costs depending upon whether the benefits are provided through social insurance or a private system. This is discussed at length in Chapter 6.

Under the method of financing currently used for the Social Security program, the amount of taxes collected each year is somewhat greater than the benefits and administrative expenses paid during the year, but it is considerably lower than the total value of benefits currently accruing for future payment. Most or all of the taxes paid by one generation of workers are used to provide the benefits to an earlier generation of workers. Therefore, the taxes paid by a particular generation of workers are not necessarily equivalent to the cost of the benefits that will eventually be paid to it.

For example, if benefits are liberalized over time (in addition to adjustments made for inflation), then any particular generation may receive benefits of greater value than the taxes it paid to become eligible for such benefits. On the other hand, if benefits are deliberalized over time, any particular generation may receive benefits of lesser value than the taxes it paid to become eligible for such benefits.

Also, the size of the working population relative to the retired population, now and in the future, is an important determinant of whether a given generation receives benefits equivalent to the taxes it pays; that is, whether the apparent cost of benefits represents the true cost of benefits. Even if benefits are not increased from their present levels in relation to preretirement earnings, current projections indicate that future generations of workers must pay considerably higher tax rates than today's workers (at least 50 percent higher) because in the future the ratio of beneficiaries to taxpayers will be higher.

Nature of Social Insurance: Social Adequacy

Because of the characteristics of Social Security listed above, it is probably possible to find a group of employees who could rightfully maintain that they receive less in benefits relative to their Social Security taxes than some other group of employees. For example, compare the following two hypothetical Groups A and B. (This example is for illustrative purposes only; it is not suggested that groups having precisely these characteristics exist.)

Group A

Woman employees married to men who are in employment covered by Social Security

Relatively high salaries for the husbands and low salaries for the wives

Relatively small number of children

Short working career for the wife

Group B

Male employees

Hazardous working conditions

Wives who do not work outside the home, with a relatively large number of children

Relatively low wages

Obviously Group B will be paid more in benefits relative to their Social Security taxes than will Group A. Is this fair? It depends upon your standard, the yardstick by which you measure.

According to social insurance standards, it is fair and just that Group B will receive relatively more from the program than will Group A. Social Security is a program of social insurance. It emphasizes social adequacy. It pays benefits according to presumed need: A married worker who dies leaving behind a spouse and three young children is presumed to need survivorship benefits; a single person who dies is presumed not to need survivorship benefits (unless there are dependent parents). Yet, the Social Security tax rates paid by single and married persons are the same. That is social insurance.

It costs more to provide survivorship protection and disability protection for persons in Group B than it does for persons in Group A, yet the Social Security tax rates are the same for Group A and Group B. That is social insurance.

In a social insurance program that emphasizes the principles of social adequacy, no attempt is made to relate the benefits that a particular group of persons receives to the taxes paid by that group of persons to become eligible for such benefits.

There is, of course, an indirect relationship between the taxes an individual pays and the benefits he receives since benefits are related to the earnings on which taxes are paid— among numerous other factors. But this relationship is more tenuous than most people have realized, and this misunderstanding is an important factor in any public dissatisfaction with the Social Security program.

Can a Particular Group of Persons Duplicate Their Private Benefits at a Lower Cost by Joining Social Security?

In some instances a group of employees could elect to participate in Social Security and duplicate the benefits previously provided through a private system; however, this would not always be a tidy procedure and would not always result in a saving in costs.

Social Security provides a package of benefits, as noted above, and in order to obtain the benefits that are desired one must also take benefits that may not be desired but that must be paid for nonetheless. Moreover, some participants would be eligible for the new Social Security benefits and would retain rights to certain benefits under the superceded private system, resulting in some redundancy in benefits and in the costs thereof. This problem could be minimized by operating a dual system for a while: present employees would continue in the private system and forego Social Security coverage and new employees would forego the private system and participate only in Social Security. This would create a new problem: employees working side-by-side could have different employee benefits.

One group that might be able to duplicate its benefits by joining Social Security and still save on pension costs (at least in the near term), in spite of the added benefits provided under Social Security, is a group with a relatively large number of employees nearing retirement age, particularly if there is no existing retirement plan or if it is not well-funded.

Relative Financial Stability of the Social Security Program and Private and Public Systems

Despite the financial problems—specifically the need for additional income—the Social Security program will face during the coming years, there is little reason to expect that private and public employee benefit systems will not also face difficult financial problems, particularly if they attempt to provide benefits roughly comparable to those provided under the Social Security program. The financial problems of many of these private and public systems have become evident recently as a result of the maturing of some of the systems and as a result of the preparation of appropriate actuarial studies for others.

It stands to reason that a national social insurance program supported by the taxes of and operated for the benefit of over 90 percent of the working population has greater financial stability and has a greater chance of meeting any financial challenge it may face than any smaller system covering only a few hundred or a few thousand employees in a limited geographical area or in a single industry.

Better from Whose Point of View?

Consideration of whether or not a particular group of employees should participate in Social Security should take into account the viewpoints of a number of interested parties, some of whose preferences can be expected to be conflicting:

Employer

Present employees and their families who may or may not have Social Security coverage from other employment

Future employees and their families who may or may not have Social Security coverage from other employment

Taxpayers who support Social Security and those who support the retirement system in a particular state

The nation as a whole

At the time a group of employees elects to participate in Social Security, the employees who are affected usually have a voice in the decision (and individuals can usually elect not to join Social Security even though most of the group joins); however, once the decision is made, future employees have no choice as to participation. This fact gives a multiple level of responsibility to those making such a decision today.

Similarly, an employer has a heavy responsibility in deciding whether a particular employee group should participate in Social Security. Abiding by the wishes of a majority, or a vocal minority, of the present employees will not necessarily be in the best long-range interest of both present and future employees.

Miscellaneous Considerations

Social Security has changed considerably in the forty years since optional participation first became possible. These changes may make participation more desirable than it was when the last serious consideration was given by a particular group to joining Social Security. Disability and Medicare benefits have been added. A new method of determining benefits (based on indexed earnings) has been adopted and benefits in general have been increased. Automatic cost-of-living benefit adjustments have been in effect since 1974—a significant change in this era of inflation. Some of Social Security's benefits may be more important now than they were in the past: for example, benefits for divorced spouses and benefits that are largely tax exempt (at least at the present time). All things considered, Social Security offers a very different package of benefits now than it did several years ago.

For some groups of employees it may be desirable to replace an existing system of employee benefits—partially, if not completely—with the Social Security program. Characteristics of the employee group may have changed since the decision not to participate was made. The financial situation of the employer may have changed. And, as already noted, Social Security has changed.

Despite adverse publicity in recent years, Social Security is a good buy for many groups. For some employees, it may provide almost all the employee benefits that are needed, except preretirement health insurance. Also, there are some employee groups that still have no pension plan and would be well advised to consider Social Security along with the other systems that are available when choosing an employee benefit system. A small group of employees, most of whom have average earnings or less, should look seriously at the option of joining Social Security. If the group has a limited number of employees with higher earnings and special needs, supplemental benefits outside of Social Security can be arranged easily.

As noted earlier, groups with a relatively large number of employees nearing retirement age would probably find Social Security a good buy, particularly if there is no existing retirement plan or if it is not well funded.

Not participating in Social Security is sometimes a handicap in hiring the more experienced and mature employees who are employee-benefit-plan conscious and whose former jobs were covered by Social Security.

Most employees whose jobs are not covered by Social Security have had some covered employment in the past and are thus entitled to some Social Security benefits. An employer who does not participate in Social Security but who wants to integrate its supplemental plan benefits with Social Security benefits may have difficulty in justifying such a procedure and may thus have to provide larger benefits than otherwise necessary.

Every year Congress considers financing some part of Social Security with general revenue. In 1984 it began taxing a portion of Social Security benefits and using such taxes to help finance Social Security—a form of general revenue financing. As this practice expands, and it almost certainly will, more of the cost of Social Security will be borne by the general body of taxpayers and less of the cost will be borne directly by the participants themselves. In such an event, Social Security will become a much better buy for the participants (considering only the direct payroll taxes). In fact, if a large enough portion of Social Security is financed by general revenue, the only sensible course of action for an employee group—from an economic viewpoint—would be to participate in Social Security since it would already be paying for a significant part of the program's cost.

Conclusion

In view of the above commentary, it would seem desirable for each employee group not now participating in Social Security to reevaluate its position. It would be unfortunate if sheer inertia prevented an employer and a group of employees from modifying past decisions—made under past conditions to solve past problems—and thus handicapped the group in appropriately satisfying its employee benefit needs of tomorrow.

Careful consideration of all the factors mentioned above will give important guidance for making decisions about whether to participate in Social Security; however, it will not eliminate the role of judgment—as well as a certain amount of luck—in predicting the future course of Social Security and the actions and needs of the particular employees affected. The problem is complex and its resolution depends upon diverse factors and future events, many of which cannot be predicted with certainty. Furthermore, because of the different interests of the various parties involved, a decision that appears to be advantageous for one party may not be advantageous for another party. Accordingly, there can be no assurance that a particular decision will turn out to be "correct" in the long run for the majority of persons much less for each person affected.

It is vexatious to ponder a question that has no clear-cut, unqualified answer. As indicated in Chapter 15, this dilemma arises because Social Security was designed to be compatible only with universal, mandatory participation. The imposition of optional participation on such a system could not have been expected to work for very long, and it is probably only a matter of time before virtually all persons will be covered by the Social Security program.

17
Is Social
Security Enough?

Social Security is a complex program providing a vast array of benefits which very few people comprehend. It is costly and will become even more costly. Accordingly, much of the public has come to believe that the government (through Social Security) is providing, or should provide, for most of our needs in the event of retirement, disability, sickness, or death.

Despite its complexity and cost, however, Social Security does not meet all of these needs uniformly for all sectors of the population. Some needs are met more adequately than others; for example, retirement needs are better satisfied for low-income workers than for high-income workers. Some needs are not met at all; for example, income maintenance during short-term illness and long-term partial disability. Some needs that appear to be satisfied may not be met in reality; for example, survivors benefits that are forfeited if the survivor has earnings in excess of the "earnings limitations."

It should be noted that there are currently some seven million employees who are not covered by Social Security

201

except through occasional employment (mainly, employees of the federal government hired before January 1, 1984, and some employees of state and local governments; low-income, self-employed persons; and farm and domestic workers with irregular employment). This discussion of whether Social Security by itself provides adequate benefits obviously does not apply to these seven million employees.

For an individual to determine the status of his protection, a careful analysis of benefits from all sources—not just Social Security—is necessary. This is a difficult task, however. The Social Security Administration will provide, upon request, estimates of benefits payable upon retirement, disability, or death. The personnel department of your employer can usually give information about employer-provided benefits (group life insurance, disability and sickness benefits, retirement benefits, etc.) but may or may not be equipped to provide detailed information about Social Security benefits. Your employer may also be able to give you information about benefits under programs it does not directly administer, such as workers' compensation and state cash sickness plans. Your life insurance agent can provide information about any individual life insurance, disability insurance, health insurance, or retirement policies you may have. Putting all this information together is not an easy matter, but it is something you must do if you are to meet your various needs and those of your family on the most economical basis possible.

Where do you start? If your income is high, you may want to hire a financial advisor—a new breed of consultant specializing in analysis of your total financial picture. Some life insurance agents are qualified to help you organize your financial affairs. You stand a better chance with an experienced, well-trained agent—perhaps one who has completed the study program offered by the American Society of Chartered Life Underwriters and has thus received the C.L.U. designation. It is reasonable to expect your employer—probably through the personnel department—to provide some help in comparing your financial needs with the coverage offered under employer-provided plans. In the final analysis, however, you will have to get heavily involved in comparing what you have with what you need, and thus be able to fill any voids that may exist. The following sections of this chapter are intended to help you identify these voids in income security for you and your family. Although the emphasis is on gaps in protection, in some cases there may be duplications that can be eliminated. The threats to income security are presented under four general headings: sickness, disability, death, and retirement.

Sickness

It is possible, of course, for you and members of your family to become ill or to suffer an accidental injury at any time throughout life. This can result in loss of income because of inability to work, as well as hospital and medical expenses. This section deals only with the expenses of illness or injury; loss of income is covered in the following section on disability.

It should not be surprising that Social Security provides less protection against the expenses of illness or injury than it provides against the loss of income upon retirement, disability, or death. Social Security, as originally designed, was intended to replace a portion of lost income upon retirement and not to provide any reimbursement for the expenses of illness. It was only when Medicare was added in 1965 that Social Security began to pay any of the costs of illness. Medicare benefits are provided only in the following relatively limited circumstances:

> For a person after he or she reaches age 65 if eligible to receive cash payments under the Social Security (or Railroad Retirement) program.

> For the spouse (aged 65 or older) of a person eligible for such cash payments, or the widow or widower (aged 65 or older) of someone who had been eligible for such payments.

> For a disabled person less than age 65 after having been entitled to Social Security disability benefits for

twenty-four months. (This could be a disabled worker, a disabled widow or widower, or a person receiving childhood disability benefits. A person who has received a disability annuity under the Railroad Retirement Act for twenty-four months is also eligible.)

For a person of any age with chronic kidney disease who is fully or currently insured under Social Security (or the afflicted spouse or dependent child of a person so insured).

Generally speaking, therefore, you and your spouse will be eligible for Medicare benefits after each of you reaches age 65 but not before. Your healthy children are not eligible for Medicare benefits. This leaves many circumstances in which hospital and medical expenses are not covered by Social Security and in which supplementary health care arrangements may be advisable for you or your family members. Here are a few examples of when this is true:

If either you or your spouse is less than age 65 and you do not have adequate employer-provided health insurance (covering family members as well as yourself).

If you are older than age 65, but your spouse is less than age 65 or you have dependent children.

If you are younger than age 62, but your spouse is aged 65 or older and is excluded from employer-provided health insurance yet ineligible for Medicare.

If you are older than age 65 and you live outside the United States or travel abroad.

If you are older than age 65 and are an alien with less than five years' permanent residence in the United States (and thus are ineligible for Part B of Medicare).

If you retire earlier than age 65 and your employer-provided health insurance terminates.

If you become disabled earlier than age 65 and your employer-provided health insurance terminates.

In most of these situations you would be well advised to make arrangements for supplementary health care coverage. This could be in the form of individual or group health insurance, Blue Cross-Blue Shield coverage, or group pre-paid health care such as is offered by a health maintenance organization. If you are a regular full-time employee of an established company, you probably have such health insurance as one of your fringe benefits. Supplemental coverage is sometimes advisable even if health care benefits are provided by your employer, particularly to protect you in the event of a catastrophic or extended and high-cost illness.

After you reach age 65 and are covered by Medicare (Supplementary Medical Insurance as well as Hospital Insurance) you will probably still need to make special provision for the expense of illness. This is because Medicare does not pay the total health care expenses of those who participate.[1] By way of example, here are just a few of the expenses *not* paid for by Medicare (the dollar amounts apply in 1990 and are subject to increases as average costs increase):

> The first $592 of hospital expenses in a "spell of illness" (as defined in Chapter 3).

> $148 per day for hospital charges for the 61st day through the 90th day and $296 per day for the 91st through the 150th day, and all costs thereafter plus all hospital room charges that exceed the cost of a semiprivate accommodation. (If you have previously exhausted your "lifetime reserve" of 60 days, you must pay all hospital costs after the 90th day.)

> $74 per day for skilled nursing facility charges for the 21st day through the 100th day, and all costs thereafter.

> The first $75 of covered medical expenses in a year plus 20 percent of subsequent covered medical expenses and all costs in excess of "reasonable charges" as determined by the Health Care Financing Administration.

> 50 percent of the cost of covered medical expenses of out-patient treatment for a mental illness and all costs

in excess of "reasonable charges" as determined by the Health Care Financing Administration.

The hospital and medical expenses that are not covered by Medicare can easily amount to thousands of dollars, particularly in an extended illness. Accordingly, even if you are covered by Medicare it is advisable to obtain supplemental protection against catastrophic illnesses and the need for long-term nursing-home care.

Furthermore, you will still need a cash reserve to pay for part of the expenses of illness, even if you are covered by Medicare and even if you have appropriate supplemental health insurance coverage. Most insurance programs have features of "non-covered services," "deductibles," and "coinsurance" which require that you pay at least a portion of the costs.

Social Security is not intended to provide for all hospital and medical expenses in your old age. Furthermore, it provides for virtually none of these expenses for you and your family during your working years. In order to protect yourself and your family against the high costs of illness, as well as to ensure that proper medical care is available, it is essential that you make appropriate arrangements for supplemental health care or insurance of one kind or another and that you accumulate a suitable cash reserve.

Disability

The financial problems caused by disability, particularly long-term permanent disability, are sometimes more severe than those accompanying death, or even old age. Yet, acquiring protection against disability usually receives the lowest priority. In this section, disability means the inability to perform part or all of one's normal work as a result of sickness or injury; hence, disability may be partial or total. Also, it may be temporary, lasting only a few days or weeks, or it may be permanent, lasting a lifetime.

Social Security began providing disability benefits in 1957. Since then eligibility for benefits has changed from time to time. Currently, the provisions may be summarized as follows (stated in a negative way to highlight the conditions under which benefits will *not* be available):

Disability benefits will not be paid unless you are so severely disabled that you cannot perform any substantial gainful work, and the disability is expected to last at least twelve months or result in death.

Disability benefits will not be paid until you have been disabled for five full consecutive months. Since the benefit for a particular month is not paid until the end of that month, the first benefit payment will not be made until sometime between six and seven months after the disability begins.

Disability benefits will not be paid unless you have paid Social Security taxes for a specified number of quarters, the number varying based upon your date of birth and disability. This is usually referred to as acquiring "quarters of coverage." For example, if you become disabled in 1990 the appropriate requirements are:

Age at Disability	Quarters of Coverage Required
50	28 with 20 earned in last 10 years
40	20 earned in last 10 years
30	18 or 19 earned after age 21
20	6 earned in last 3 years

Therefore, persons in these examples will not be eligible for disability benefits until they have paid Social Security taxes for at least one and one-half years and, possibly, as long as seven years. For disabilities occurring at higher ages, even more quarters of coverage are required.

You can see that there are many circumstances in which you could become disabled without being eligible for Social Security benefits. These voids in disability income protection may or may not be filled by other disability benefit programs in which you participate.

Many employers have formal or informal sick-pay plans which continue part or all of one's pay in the event of short-term sickness or disability. Some employers have sick-pay plans that provide benefits for six months, after which Social Security is presumed to be effective—at least for severe and probably long-lasting disabilities. Still other employers have comprehensive arrangements that meet a large proportion of the financial needs of a disabled person throughout his life-time. The period of time during which employer-provided disability benefits are payable usually increases as the employee's service with the employer increases.

Five states (California, Hawaii, New Jersey, New York, and Rhode Island) and Puerto Rico require that employers participate in mandatory state-operated cash sickness benefit programs or that they establish comparable programs on a private basis. Employees are usually required to pay a large part of the cost of such plans. These programs provide cash payments for short-term periods (up to twenty-six weeks) in

Table 17.1

Ratio of Initial Social Security Disability Benefits to Average Earnings Prior to Disability for Illustrative Workers

| Earnings Level of Worker[b] | Replacement Ratio[a] When Disability Began at... | |
	Age 25	Age 50
(1)	(2)	(3)
	Single Worker	
Low	64%	64%
Average	48	47
Maximum	32	28
Twice Maximum	16	14
	Married Worker with Eligible Family[c]	
Low	91%	90%
Average	72	71
Maximum	48	42
Twice Maximum	24	21

[a] Replacement ratio equals the disability benefits payable in the first year divided by the average of the last three full years of earnings prior to disablement. In each example it is assumed that the worker become disabled in July 1989 and that he begin to receive benefits in January 1990.

[b] "Low" and "average" denote earnings in each year equal to 45 percent and 100 percent, respectively, of the average wage for all employees. "Maximum" and "Twice Maximum" refer to the level of the maximum contribution and benefit base under Social Security.

[c] A family is assumed to consist of worker, spouse, and one or more children.

the event of sickness or injury that is not work-connected. All fifty states require that employers participate in state-operated workers' compensation programs, or that they otherwise provide comparable benefits to compensate employees for job-related injuries, sickness, or death.

Few plans that provide disability benefits take into account the number and type of dependents of a worker. Social Security is a notable exception. Furthermore, hardly any program except Social Security provides disability benefits for members of a worker's family who become disabled. (In the case of Social Security, such benefits are limited to the surviving spouse over age 50 of a deceased worker, and the children of retired, disabled, or deceased workers when such children are disabled before age 22.)

Even after you meet all the eligibility requirements for Social Security disability benefits, you may still need to make special provision for supplemental disability benefits. This is because Social Security benefits are sometimes adequate, but more often they are not. It depends upon your earnings level, family responsibility, and—to a certain extent—your age at disability.

Table 17.1 illustrates the wide range of benefits payable under various circumstances. In each case it is assumed that the worker became disabled in July 1989 and began receiving benefits for January 1990. Benefits are not shown in dollar amounts, but rather as a percentage of average earnings during the three full years of work prior to disablement (1986–1988). This percentage is referred to as the replacement ratio. Since Social Security disability benefits are not fully taxable and since many work-related expenses are eliminated, a replacement ratio of less than 100 percent will usually maintain the pre-disability standard of living (depending, of course, upon the level of medical care required).

Assume, for example, that you are a single worker who became eligible to receive disability benefits in January 1990 at age 50. Assume further that you have participated in Social Security throughout your adult lifetime and have always had maximum earnings covered by Social Security. Your monthly disability benefit during the first year would average $1,008, or about 28 percent of your average earnings during the three full years prior to disability. This benefit, taken by itself, is probably not adequate to support you, and it will certainly not preserve your pre-disability standard of living; therefore, supplemental disability benefits should be provided through a pension plan, group or individual disability insurance plan, accumulation of personal savings, or by some other means. If your average earnings during the three-year period prior to disability had been about $87,000 (twice the maximum amount taxable for Social Security earnings), your disability benefit would be the same dollar amount but would be only 14 percent of your pre-disability average earnings. In this example, supplemental disability benefits are essential unless a substantial decrease is made in the standard of living.

In other situations, the Social Security disability benefit—once it commences—may be adequate, or even more than adequate, to continue the pre-disability standard of living. Consider a worker who earned low wages and who becomes disabled at age 25 with a spouse and one or more small children. Social Security disability benefits during the first year would average $625 per month, or about 91 percent of average earnings during the three years prior to disability, assuming the spouse and children did not have earnings at a high enough level to forfeit any of their benefits because of the "earnings limitation."

For a single person who began to receive Social Security disability benefits in January 1990, the monthly benefit could have been anywhere between a few dollars and $1,156, depending on the circumstances. The monthly benefit payable to a married person with a family could have been as high as $1,734.

It is a rare case when an employee is adequately protected, from the first day of employment, against the various kinds of disability he may suffer. It is even more rare for family members to be protected against the possibility of their becoming disabled. The risk of loss of income because of disability may well be the most neglected area of personal financial planning. It is time-consuming and difficult, but not impossible, to summarize the benefits provided from all sources in the event of disability: Social Security, employer plans, workers' compensation, personal insurance, etc. Such a survey must be made, however, to identify gaps in coverage and to enable you to obtain the supplemental disability insurance and plan the personal savings program necessary to protect you and your family from the catastrophe of disability.

Death

When someone who has been contributing to the support of a family dies, a variety of expenses may have to be met: burial costs, liquidation of personal debt (including home mortgage repayment), estate taxes, transitional costs while the surviving family adjusts to a different standard of living, and so on. If the decedent provided the principal support to a family, it may be necessary to replace part or all of the lost income for an extended period.

Social Security, as originally enacted in 1935, provided no death benefit when a covered worker died except a guaranteed return of employee-paid Social Security taxes. In 1939, this type of death benefit was eliminated; instead, a lump-sum benefit and monthly benefits to survivors were adopted. Subsequent legislation broadened and extended these benefits so that, today, Social Security provides much more in death benefits than is commonly realized. In fact, the value of the death benefit can amount to as much as $500,000 depending on the circumstances.

The lump-sum death benefit paid by Social Security is $255. This was the maximum benefit payable in 1954, and it was intended to cover only the expenses of a modest funeral; however, the benefit has not been increased since then. The benefit is payable only if the deceased worker leaves a spouse with whom he had been living, or a spouse or child who is eligible for immediate monthly survivors benefits.

Survivors benefits, on the other hand, are relatively substantial and can be paid to:

a spouse caring for an eligible child;

a divorced spouse caring for an eligible child;

an eligible child;

a spouse aged 60 or older (50 or older, if completely disabled);

a divorced spouse aged 60 or older (50 or older, if completely disabled), if the marriage lasted at least ten years; or

dependent parents aged 62 or older.

The amount of the benefits and the conditions for payment are based upon a seemingly endless set of conditions. These conditions are discussed briefly here and in more detail in Chapter 3. Eligibility for some death benefits requires that

Table 17.2

Ratio of Initial Social Security Survivors Benefits to Deceased Worker's Average Earnings Prior to Death for Illustrative Surviving Families

Earnings Level of Worker[b]	Replacement Ratio[a] Where Worker's Death Occurred at...	
	Age 25	Age 50
(1)	(2)	(3)
	Surviving Spouse and Two or More Children	
Low	92%	91%
Average	83	82
Maximum	54	47
Twice Maximum	27	24
	Surviving Spouse and One Child (or Two Surviving Children)	
Low	92%	91%
Average	69	67
Maximum	46	40
Twice Maximum	23	20
	One Surviving Child	
Low	46%	45%
Average	34	34
Maximum	23	20
Twice Maximum	12	10

[a] Replacement ratio equals the survivors benefits payable in the first year divided by the deceased worker's average earnings in the last three full years prior to death. In each example the worker is assumed to have died in January 1990.

[b] "Low" and "average" denote earnings in each year equal to 45 percent and 100 percent, respectively, of the average wage for all employees. "Maximum" and "Twice Maximum" refer to the level of the maximum contribution and benefit base under Social Security.

the worker be "currently insured," while eligibility for others requires the worker to be "fully insured."

To be currently insured, you need six quarters of coverage during the last thirteen quarters ending with the quarter in which you die. This would qualify your survivors for the lump-sum death benefit and monthly benefits for an eligible child and a spouse (or divorced spouse) caring for an eligible child.

To be fully insured, you must have between six and forty quarters of coverage depending on when you were born and when you die. This requirement is not difficult to meet if you have been working in fairly steady employment. Fully insured status would qualify your survivors for monthly benefits for a spouse (including divorced spouses) and dependent parents, as well as the benefits mentioned above for currently insured participants.

Table 17.2 presents examples of benefits for several workers and their families. Benefits are expressed as replacement ratios; that is, the ratio of the first year's benefits to the average earnings in the last three full years prior to death. Consider, for example, a 25-year-old worker who has always had earnings equal to the average amount earned by those covered under Social Security and whose family consists of a spouse (who is not currently working in paid employment) and two children. Such a worker who has at least six quarters of coverage would be both currently insured and fully insured, and his death in January 1990 would result in a lump-sum benefit of $255 and monthly benefits payable to the family of 83 percent of the worker's average earnings in the last three years. Since Social Security benefits are not fully taxable, this benefit would virtually equal the worker's average take-home pay.

The amount of this benefit, payable in future years, would vary depending on many factors. It would increase as the Consumer Price Index increased. It would decrease when the first child reached age 18, decrease further when the younger child reached 16, and would terminate altogether when the younger child reached age 18. Benefits would resume to the spouse at age 67 (or as early as age 60 if a reduced benefit is elected). The monthly benefits payable to any of these beneficiaries under age 65 would be reduced by $1.00

for every $2.00 of earnings *by that beneficiary* in excess of the "earnings limitation," which is $6,840 in 1990. For beneficiaries aged 65 to 69, the benefit reduction is $1.00 for every $3.00 of earnings in excess of the "earnings limitation," which is $9,360 in 1990. Finally, the remarriage of the surviving spouse or the marriage of a child beneficiary would normally terminate benefits for that beneficiary.

The survivors' benefits in this example are substantial and are worth over $300,000 at the death of the worker. In other words, on the average, it would take roughly $300,000 invested at interest to provide these survivors benefits. Most of the surviving family's needs in this example are well satisfied by Social Security in the early years following the worker's death. Once the children have reached maturity, there will be a period when the spouse will have no income (from age 40 or 45 until age 67). At age 67 benefits to the spouse would resume at about 46 percent of the worker's average earnings in the last three years (adjusted for changes in the level of average wages for all workers occurring since then). Supplemental income for the spouse during this period before age 67, as well as after age 67, may be necessary since Social Security benefits alone will not be adequate to maintain the earlier standard of living.

This particular example was chosen to illustrate a situation in which Social Security almost "does it all." Other situations require substantial provision for supplemental benefits through private saving and private insurance, either group or individual. Most workers with above-average incomes need supplemental benefits unless their families' living standards are to suffer in the event of their death. The examples in Table 17.2 illustrate that the initial replacement ratio ranges from 10 percent to 92 percent, depending on the circumstances of the worker and his or her family; for persons with higher earnings than illustrated, the replacement ratio can be even lower than 10 percent. Obviously, the amount of survivors benefits payable under Social Security can vary widely and is not easy to determine; however, a basic understanding of such benefits and their payment provisions is essential in determining an appropriate level of supplemental coverage.

Many employees are covered under group life insurance plans sponsored by their employers (partially paid for by the employee in some cases). Some people obtain group life insurance benefits through membership in unions or professional organizations, purchase of "credit insurance," and so forth. Many persons buy individual life insurance to supplement their other benefits or to cover specific obligations such as home mortgage loans. Life insurance benefits are normally described by their face amount, such as $25,000 or $100,000, but in most cases a variety of payment methods is available in the event of death. In determining your supplemental insurance needs, it will be helpful to determine the monthly income that can be provided by these insurance policies. This can be added to the monthly income paid by Social Security to indicate any gaps that should be filled to protect your family adequately. Remember that a large part of Social Security benefits and most life insurance benefits are tax free and that family expenses are usually lower after the death of a breadwinner.

When deciding how much supplemental life insurance protection and personal savings should be provided, several key decisions must be made regarding the surviving family's life-style. Would a spouse who was not working in paid employment begin working? Would the family's house or other major possessions be kept? How long are the children likely to need support, and what financial arrangements will be necessary for their education? Once these and other personal decisions are worked out within the family, attention can be turned to evaluating the overall financial needs that would result from a breadwinner's death, the level of benefits payable by Social Security, employee benefit plans, etc., and the need for any supplemental benefit protection. The effect of future inflation must also be considered. What might seem like an adequate benefit in the first two or three years could prove to be inadequate in later years.

Just as in making contingency plans for sickness and disability, in planning for the possibility of death you must absorb an array of facts and figures to decide what financial alternatives should be devised. Your responsibility in making such plans is more awesome, of course, since you will not be around to modify any arrangements that need adjusting.

Retirement

Retirement is somewhat different from the events just discussed—sickness, disability, and death—which result in extraordinary expenses or loss of income. Barring premature death, everyone will experience old age, and, for most of us, there will come a time when retirement must be considered—and probably will be necessary for one reason or another. Knowing that we must one day retire, however, does not make it any easier to plan for and make the necessary financial arrangements. A person who reaches age 65, a common retirement age at the present time, can expect to live another fifteen to twenty years, on the average, and

Table 17.3

Ratio of Initial Social Security Retirement Benefits to Average Earnings Prior to Retirement for Illustrative Workers

Earnings Level of Worker[b]	Replacement Ratio[a] for Worker Retiring at...		
	Age 62	Age 65	Age 70
(1)	(2)	(3)	(4)
	Single Worker		
Low	48%	60%	65%
Average	36	45	49
Maximum	20	26	29
Twice Maximum	10	13	14
	Worker and Spouse		
Low	71%	90%	95%
Average	53	67	71
Maximum	30	39	41
Twice Maximum	15	19	21

[a] Replacement ratio equals the retirement benefits payable in the first year divided by the average of the last three years of earnings prior to retirement. In each example, the worker is assumed to have reached the indicated age in January 1990.

[b] "Low" and "average" denote earnings in each year equal to 45 percent and 100 percent, respectively, of the average wage for all employees. "Maximum" and "Twice Maximum" refer to the level of the maximum contribution and benefit base under Social Security.

perhaps as long as thirty-five years or more. This uncertainty itself makes planning for retirement difficult.

Social Security, as originally enacted, was designed solely to replace a portion of the income that was lost because of old age. Social Security has expanded over the years and now provides a wide variety of benefits in the event of a worker's retirement; for example, benefits may be paid to:

    a retired worker aged 62 or over;

    the spouse aged 62 or over of a retired worker, if the retired worker is also receiving benefits;

    the spouse of a retired worker who is receiving benefits, if the spouse is under age 65 and caring for an eligible child;

    a divorced spouse aged 62 or over, who was married to the insured worker for at least ten years, if the insured worker is at least 62; or

    an eligible child.

Table 17.3 illustrates the benefits payable upon the retirement of a worker at different retirement ages and in different family situations. The examples reflect the actuarial reduction of benefits for retirement before age 65 and the effect of the "delayed retirement credit" for retirement after age 65. Benefits are shown as a percentage of the average earnings in the last three years before retirement, and are therefore referred to as replacement ratios. It was assumed that the benefits began in January 1990; examples for later years would reflect additional variations for different ages at retirement because the "normal retirement age" increases from 65 to 67 and the delayed retirement credit increases from 3 percent per year to 8 percent.

As indicated in Table 17.3, there is an extremely wide variation in the replacement ratios, depending on the age at retirement, earnings level, and family status. The replacement ratios shown range from 95 percent for a low wage earner and spouse who retire late to 10 percent for a high wage earner who is single and retires early. The replacement ratio would be even lower for persons with higher earnings.

The replacement ratio that is necessary to permit suitable retirement depends on a variety of factors including preretirement earnings level, family status, and post-retirement standard of living. Also, Social Security benefits are largely tax free, income taxes are lower for persons over age 65, Social Security taxes stop when earned income stops, expenses associated with employment cease, personal savings after retirement may be lower, medical costs for the elderly are usually higher, and so forth.

If one's preretirement standard of living is to be maintained, retirement benefits of some 60 to 85 percent of average preretirement earnings are probably necessary—depending on the factors mentioned above. Furthermore, these benefits must be adjusted periodically to reflect changes in the cost of living. Social Security benefits satisfy these criteria reasonably well for many workers toward the lower end of the earnings scale, provided they retire at age 65 or later. Even for these workers, there may be some need for supplementation through private saving or a job-related retirement plan. This need, however, is relatively small compared with that of the above-average wage earner for whom substantial supplementation is needed if preretirement living standards are to be maintained.

Supplemental retirement income is available from several sources. The majority of full-time permanent employees in private employment are covered by a pension or profit-sharing plan sponsored by their employer. Most public employees are covered by employer-sponsored retirement systems. Many self-employed persons have so-called "Keogh" or "HR 10" retirement programs. Some employees have established Individual Retirement Accounts for themselves and, in some cases, for their spouses. Many people have cash value life insurance, as well as endowment and retirement income insurance policies that are earmarked for retirement purposes. Finally, personal saving (investments, equity in a home, etc.) is accumulated for general purposes but may be used eventually for support in retirement years.

Just as in analyzing the needs discussed earlier, it is quite difficult to compare your retirement needs with the various sources of income that will be available and, therefore, to determine what level of supplementation is required. In studying your needs it is well to keep in mind that Social

Security and other benefits may be less than they appear; the following examples indicate this.

A wife may appear to be protected by Social Security by reason of her marriage to a person in Social Security covered employment. An untimely divorce (particularly before ten years of marriage) would normally terminate this financial protection. In some cases, a portion of Social Security benefits is subject to federal income tax. Furthermore, if you or your dependents or survivors work in order to supplement Social Security benefits, it may result in a reduction or complete loss of such benefits (as discussed earlier). A retirement income that is adequate for a couple may be reduced upon the death of one of the members (as is the case with Social Security), leaving the survivor with an inadequate income. Retirement benefits that are not adjusted for inflation (unlike Social Security, which is so adjusted) may be adequate at their inception but inadequate just a few years later because of continuing inflation.

If you receive a pension under a government pension plan as a result of being an employee of a federal, state, or local government (this includes policemen, firemen, and public school teachers) and you were not under Social Security in such employment, you may not receive the Social Security benefits that you thought you would receive. This is because Social Security benefits payable to you as a dependent or survivor will generally be reduced by two-thirds of any benefits under such a government pension plan, thus reducing or completely eliminating your Social Security benefits. This provision does not apply to anyone entitled to Social Security benefits before December 1977 and to certain other cases. Social Security benefits payable to you as an insured worker will be calculated using a less-generous formula if you also qualify for a pension based on employment not covered under Social Security.

The net result of an analysis of Social Security retirement benefit protection is that most persons need some supplemental protection, and workers with above-average earnings need substantial additional protection unless a significant reduction is made from their preretirement standard of living. Even workers with average earnings or less may need to make provision for supplemental retirement benefits if they desire to retire earlier than the standard set by Social Security.

Conclusion

In the event of the sickness, disability, death, or retirement of any member of your family, the family's financial situation will change—sometimes drastically. None of these events can be predicted with certainty. The only certainty is that at least one such event will occur, probably at a time when it is least expected.

It is tempting to assume that one's financial needs in a time of crisis will be met by Social Security or some other government program or by a job-related fringe benefit program. This is a dangerous assumption and is not one that can be relied on.

To protect your family from financial stress, you must compare what you need with what you have—much easier to say than to do. If you provide the principal financial support for your family, define your needs and those of your family in the event of your sickness, disability, death, or retirement. Do the same for other family members who provide financial support. Also define the needs that will arise if a member of your family becomes sick or disabled.

Then analyze all the programs that will provide benefits in any of these events: Social Security and other government programs, job-related fringe benefit plans, personal insurance and saving, and so forth. A surprising number of unmet needs will be revealed. In some cases there may be duplications in benefit protection. You can then set about to fill the gaps in protection and to eliminate the duplications.

You can get help in making this analysis and taking corrective action; but in the end, you must get heavily involved and do much of the work yourself. Perhaps this is as it should be. Your family financial situation is a unique and personal matter, and you cannot expect a stranger to have the same level of interest as you.

18
Social Security as a Determinant of Behavior

Most people think of Social Security as a program that collects taxes from the active working population and provides benefits in the event of old age, disability, illness, or death. This is certainly true, but it may be useful to look at Social Security from another point of view that may be of even greater importance in the long run.

Social Security is, in effect, a complex system of rewards and penalties for various kinds of social and economic behavior among its participants. As such, it is an important determinant of the behavior of the individual participants; thus it will ultimately shape the habits of the nation as a whole. Here are some examples of how Social Security affects our behavior.

Normal Retirement Age

We usually think of age 65 as the "normal retirement age." If we retire before age 65, it is called "early retirement." If we retire after age 65, it is called "late retirement."

Why is age 65 the normal retirement age instead of 66, or 67, or 70, or 60? It is because the planners of Social Security back in the 1930s thought this was a good compromise between the high cost of paying full benefits at age 60 and the limited usefulness of a retirement age of 70 for combatting unemployment. Since then, Social Security has been changed to permit retirement benefits to commence as early as age 62, but on a reduced basis. Age 65 remains the normal retirement age, the earliest age at which unreduced benefits are payable.

Most private and many public employee pension plans have followed the Social Security practice of normal retirement at age 65. This is partly for convenience and consistency but also because the Internal Revenue Service regulation of private pension plans is related to the standards set by Social Security.

Social Security, then, started it all and has effectively defined the retirement age pattern for the nation. After fifty-five years of being told that normal retirement is at age 65, most people have begun to believe it. In fact, many people believe that it is their inalienable right to retire at age 65 and that it is absurd to suggest they should work longer, even if they are in good health.

Social Security was amended in 1983 to provide for a gradual increase in the normal retirement age from age 65 to age 67 during the twenty-five-year period 2003 to 2027. This change has not yet become part of our thinking and not very much of the population is even aware of the change.

Whether or Not to Work

Decisions about whether or not to work depend largely on a person's financial situation, state of emotional and physical health, and the availability of work that the person considers suitable. Social Security plays an important role in this decision by virtue of the benefits it provides or does not provide. Furthermore, the existence of Social Security has significantly influenced the birth and growth of the private pension movement. Social Security, directly and indirectly, has thus spawned an entirely new way of thinking about work and retirement.

The influence of Social Security on our acceptance of age 65 as the normal retirement age has already been noted. Through its various provisions concerning the payment of benefits, Social Security also influences early and late retirement practices. Social Security pays full benefits at the "normal retirement age," currently 65. Benefits may begin as early as age 62, in which event they are "actuarially reduced" to offset their expected payment over a longer period of time; however, the method of calculating benefits favors retirement at age 62, and the worker receives greater total value in relation to Social Security taxes paid by retiring at age 62. Benefits may be deferred until after age 65, in which event they will be increased to reflect partially, not fully, the shorter remaining lifetime during which they will be paid. The worker thus receives relatively less value if benefits begin after age 65.

Social Security was amended in 1983 to provide for an increase in this "delayed retirement credit" to be phased in during the twenty-year period 1990 to 2009. When fully implemented, this provision will make the value of Social Security benefits approximately the same for all retirement ages between ages 62 and 70 (ignoring the added Social Security taxes paid in the case of later retirement and any benefit adjustments that might result from the additional years of earnings).

Chapter 12 discusses in some detail the retirement test, or earnings test. If the worker begins to receive benefits but also continues in paid employment, his Social Security benefits are reduced if his earnings exceed certain "exempt amounts." These exempt amounts are lowest below the normal retirement age, next lowest between the normal retirement age and age 70, and are highest after age 70 when there is no limit on earnings. The provisions of the current law would seem to encourage a person to retire at age 62, to engage in limited paid employment until age 65, to increase the level of his activity in paid employment from age 65 to 70, and then to work in full-time paid employment after age 70—an apparent irrational set of provisions.

Spouses and children who receive benefits based on the work record of a retired worker, or because of the death or disability of a worker, are also subject to the earnings test. Accordingly, they may lose part or all of their benefits if their earnings exceed the exempt amount. In cases where the maximum family benefit is in effect, however, a family member could earn more than the exempt amount and lose part of his or her own benefit without causing a reduction in the total amount received by the family. This is because the reduction in family benefits as a result of excess earnings is made before the maximum family benefit is determined.

Social Security's influences on the decision of whether or not to work are subtle and are different for each type of beneficiary. Unfortunately, many of the beneficiaries, particularly the worker's family members, are not aware of the effect of their working on the receipt of benefits early enough to make informed decisions about related financial matters.

Whether to Marry or Remarry

Many benefits are paid under Social Security to wives, husbands, widows, and widowers. Of course the payment of such benefits presupposes that marriage has taken place. Even though common-law marriages are recognized, this is frequently an ambiguous situation. Just living together will not necessarily create an entitlement to these benefits— benefits that may be quite important in the event of death, disability, or illness, particularly if dependent children are involved. The failure to formalize a de facto marriage could result in substantial financial hardship.

If you are the widow (nondisabled) of a worker covered by Social Security, your eligibility for widow's benefits will cease if you remarry prior to age 60 (except if you are receiving a mother's benefit and you marry an adult who is a Social Security beneficiary). Remarriage at age 60 or later does not affect a widow's benefit. The same rules apply to widowers.

If you are receiving benefits as a result of being a dependent parent of a worker covered by Social Security, your benefits will cease if you remarry after the worker's death (except if you marry a person who is entitled to a widow's, widower's, mother's, father's, divorced spouse's, parent's, or disabled child's benefit).

If you are receiving benefits as a result of being a divorced widow of a worker covered by Social Security, your benefits will cease if you remarry at any age (unless you marry a person who is entitled to a widower's, father's, parent's, or disabled child's benefit).

If you are receiving benefits as a result of being a divorced spouse of a worker covered by Social Security, your benefits will generally cease if you remarry someone other than the worker; however, your benefits will not be terminated if you marry an adult individual entitled to Social Security cash benefits.

Some children receive benefits because one of their parents is receiving retirement or disability benefits, or because one or both of their parents have died. To continue receiving these benefits, such a child must be *unmarried* (generally) and:

> under age 18; or
>
> any age, if disabled before age 22.

In any of these circumstances, marriage could result in a substantial loss of benefits.

Whom to Marry

Some people marry to attain financial security. If this is your objective, all other factors being equal, it may be preferable to marry someone who will work in employment covered by Social Security. This excludes about 6 percent of the nation's workers at any given time: some federal government employees; some state and local government employees, including public school teachers; and so forth.

If you are a divorced wife who was married at least ten years to a man who will become entitled to Social Security benefits, you may eventually be entitled to benefits yourself based upon his work record. You will lose this benefit right if you remarry prior to beginning to receive benefits. Once receiving benefits, however, you can remarry and continue to receive payments—but only if your new husband is a certain type of Social Security beneficiary. These rules apply to a divorced husband as well as to a divorced wife.

If you are a disabled person aged 18 or over and are receiving benefits as a result of being a child of a worker covered by Social Security, your benefits will cease if you

Chart 18.A

Effect of One Beneficiary's Marriage to Another Beneficiary

1853.   THE EFFECT OF ONE BENEFICIARY'S MARRIAGE TO ANOTHER is summarized in the following chart:

Type of beneficiary	Effect of marriage to a Social Security beneficiary
Retired or disabled worker, widow(er), disabled widow(er), surviving divorced spouse or disabled surviving divorced spouse	No effect on entitlement.
Child under age 18 or student	Always terminates entitlement.
Parent or divorced spouse	No effect on entitlement unless marriage is to a retired or disabled worker, a child under age 18, or a student, in which case benefits of the parent or divorced spouse terminate.
Mother, father, surviving divorced mother/father or childhood disability beneficiary	No effect on entitlement unless marriage is to a child under age 18 or a student, in which case both benefits terminate.

1854.   IF A MARRIAGE WAS VOID, benefits may be reinstated as of the month they were terminated because of the marriage, subject to the rules on administrative finality. (See § 2016.)

If the marriage was voidable and has been annulled *from the beginning* in accordance with State law by a court having jurisdiction over the matter, benefits can be reinstated as of the month the decree of annulment was issued provided a timely application is filed.

A divorced spouse, a mother, a father, a widow(er), a surviving divorced spouse, or surviving divorced mother or father whose right to benefits was ended by remarriage, may also have benefits on the prior spouse's Social Security earnings record.

marry (except if you marry another disabled child aged 18 or over who is receiving child's benefits, or if you marry a person entitled to old-age, widow's, widower's, mother's, father's, parent's, disability, or divorced spouse's benefits).

These comments about whether and whom to marry, taking into account the Social Security benefits that may be gained or lost, may appear to be somewhat overdrawn. There is, perhaps, an element of satire in the exposition in the sense it is "used for the purpose of exposing folly." Consider, however, Chart 18.A, which is a copy of page 303 of the following government publication: *Social Security Handbook 1988*, U.S. Department of Health and Human Services, Social Security Administration, SSA Publication No. OS-10135, October 1988.

Whether (or When) to Divorce

A divorce at any time will result in a potential loss of future benefits. A divorce *prior* to ten years of marriage can result in the *total loss* of benefits a person may have become eligible to receive based on the other person's coverage by Social Security. A divorce *after* ten years of marriage will result in a *partial loss* of such benefits. From the standpoint of receiving Social Security benefits, it is obviously preferable to divorce after ten years and one month of marriage rather than after nine years and eleven months. The difference in a few days could amount to a loss of more than one hundred thousand dollars.

Consider, for example, a recently divorced wife, aged 30, with one child aged one month, whose former husband died in January 1990 leaving her with maximum Social Security benefits. The actuarial value of these benefits at the time of the former husband's death would be:

Divorced Mother's benefits	$ 142,000
Divorced Widow's benefits	137,000
Child's benefits	156,000
Total	$ 435,000

The actual dollar amount payable over the years would be more than six times these amounts.

The example above assumes that the divorce occurred after at least ten years of marriage. If the divorce had occurred just prior to ten years of marriage, no divorced widow's benefits would have been payable, and $137,000 worth of benefits would have been lost, probably unwittingly. The divorced mother's benefits would still be payable, but they would usually terminate upon remarriage. The child's benefits, worth about $156,000 and payable in any event, would be controlled by whichever party is given custody of the child.

Generally speaking, a divorced wife of a marriage that endured at least ten years will receive the same benefits as if the divorce had not occurred. There are, however, at least three exceptions:

> The spouse of a person entitled to disability or retirement benefits will receive monthly benefits if he or she is caring for a child entitled to benefits who is under age 16 or disabled, even if the spouse is less than age 62. A divorced spouse in these circumstances will receive no such benefit.

> The spouse of a worker eligible to receive retirement benefits cannot actually begin to draw spouse's benefits until the worker is receiving benefits himself. A divorced spouse, however, can begin to receive benefits as early as age 62 whether or not the worker is drawing retirement benefits (so long as the worker is fully insured and at least age 62).

> The spouse's benefits may be reduced if the total family benefits would otherwise exceed the family maximum. A divorced spouse's benefits are not subject to such a reduction.

Therefore, the benefits payable to a divorced wife may be equal to, less than, or greater than the benefits payable if the divorce had not occurred, depending on the circumstances. Even though a divorced wife may be entitled to the same benefits she would have if the divorce had not occurred, these benefits can be forfeited completely in the event of her remarriage; and the amount of Social Security benefits resulting from the remarriage may be equal to, less than, or greater than, the benefits forfeited.

A divorce frequently has significant financial consequences as a result of lost Social Security benefits. Oftentimes, these consequences are not fully recognized until it is too late to prevent the loss (sometimes they are never recognized), in large part because the myriad of benefits provided by Social Security is not widely appreciated.

Whether to Recover from Disability

Social Security pays disability benefits to persons who are so severely disabled, mentally or physically, that they cannot perform any substantial gainful work. Needless to say, it is not always possible to determine conclusively whether a person is disabled. Subjectivity is sometimes involved, not only on the part of the administrator who is assessing the disability but also on the part of the potential beneficiary.

I shall ignore the question of whether a potential beneficiary feigns disability just to collect benefits. Undoubtedly some do, but most people are not inclined to go to such lengths and are not aware of the relatively generous benefit levels that are sometimes payable, so let us assume most disabilities are determined fairly at their inception. Once benefits commence, however, there may not always be sufficient incentive to recover.

Consider the following example: A married couple, both aged 35, with two children under age 18. Each adult earns the same as the average worker in the United States: that is, $20,500 in 1989 for combined gross earnings of $41,000 per year. The annual net take-home pay after federal, state, and Social Security taxes is $31,640 (based on the standard deduction and an average of representative state tax rates). Assume that one of the spouses qualified early in 1990 for disability benefits of $13,032 per year payable monthly (for the disabled spouse and the children). The disability benefit is not taxable because the family's income falls below the threshold for the taxation of Social Security benefits. The family's net take-home pay after federal, state, and Social Security taxes would now be $29,840. This is only $1,800 per year less than when both parents worked. After disability benefits have been paid for two years, the disabled spouse would receive Medicare, free of charge except for a nominal premium for Supplementary Medical Insurance ($28.60 per month in 1990). Furthermore, the disabled spouse would not be subject to the earnings test applied to retired persons; under rules followed by Social Security, a disabled person can generally earn about $500 per month without jeopardizing the disability status. Finally, the disability benefits are automatically and fully adjusted for changes in the Consumer Price Index—which may be more than can be said of the working spouse's earnings.

Some attempt is made by Social Security to rehabilitate disabled workers. For such an attempt to be successful in the example given, however, the rehabilitation effort would have to be Herculean, the disabled person would need an overwhelming desire to reenter paid employment, and both the man and wife would need to perceive Social Security as a fair program and not one that they should try to take advantage of.

Which Employer to Select

Social Security has the potential to influence our selection of employers in many ways. If it does not, frequently it is because of our failure to appreciate how much variation exists in the employee benefit plans provided in various jobs and how this may affect our future security.

Suppose you are a public school teacher in a state that provides Social Security coverage for its teachers. Suppose further that you would like to move to another state and continue teaching, and you believe that Social Security provides appropriate benefits for you because of your circumstances at this time (and there are many valid reasons this can be true). There are twelve states you may not want to consider any further because their teachers are not covered by Social Security. Alternatively, perhaps you would like to leave the teaching field and get a job in state or local government. There are six states that do not provide their public employees with Social Security. True, state employees have their own benefit plans, but these may not provide adequate benefits for short periods of service and you may not plan to make a career with the state government.

On the other hand, you may not now be in a job that is covered by Social Security, but you may want such a job at some point in your career so that you can obtain at least some of the benefits Social Security provides. For example, you may be a career employee with the Commonwealth of Massachusetts (not now participating in Social Security) who plans to retire from government service at age 55 but to work in other employment until age 65. In this event, you would probably choose as your next job one that is covered by Social Security.

In some cases a person may want to spend the last few years of his career in a job *not* covered by Social Security, particularly if covered by Social Security during the first part of his career. The reason is that such employment frequently provides larger retirement benefits than employment covered by Social Security, and the effect on Social Security benefits may be relatively minor. Accordingly, the total benefit at retirement may be larger than if one continued to work in a job covered by Social Security.

Each year thousands of employment decisions are made that reflect, or should reflect, factors similar to those mentioned.

To Save or Not to Save

The existence of Social Security discourages individuals and their employers from saving for their eventual retirement needs. Whether this affects the total saving habits of the nation is debatable; however, it seems reasonable to assume that it does.

Imagine that your employer does not provide a pension plan and that there is no Social Security program. Under these conditions would you save any of your current earnings for a time when you may not be able to work because of poor health or old age? Any prudent person past middle age would almost certainly answer yes. On the other hand, if you participate in Social Security, do you make less provision for your retirement than if you were not covered by Social Security? Again, the only reasonable answer is yes.

If you are covered by Social Security and your employer also provides a pension plan, are the benefits lower under this employer plan than they would be if you were not covered by Social Security? Once again, the most common answer is yes.

Accordingly, it seems clear that the existence of Social Security results in individuals' and employers' making less provision for retirement than if there were no Social Security. And this means less saving by individuals and employers for retirement. This reduced saving by individuals and employers is not offset by increased saving under Social Security since Social Security is operated on close to a pay-as-you-go basis and does not generate substantial saving.[1]

Since the existence of Social Security results in less saving for retirement purposes, it is logical to assume that total national saving for all purposes is reduced. This has not been, and probably cannot be, proved conclusively. Furthermore, if there is no capital shortage in the nation, it may not matter whether total national saving is reduced. However, if there is a capital shortage in the nation, now or in the future, the negative influence exerted by Social Security on saving may be very important.

Whether to Feel Responsible for One's Self and One's Family

Social Security is changing our attitudes about our responsibility for saving and providing for our own future needs and those of our extended family. Part of this change in attitude is justified by the facts about how Social Security is now satisfying some of our financial needs. Another part of this change in attitude is not justified by the facts; rather it is based upon confusion concerning what Social Security is all about.

The average individual does not know what to expect from Social Security. Should he expect it to meet all of his needs (and those of his dependents) in the event of old age, disability, death, or sickness? Or should he expect it to be merely a floor of protection in meeting these needs, a floor upon which he and his employer should build through supplemental private saving and insurance and some form of retirement program? Apart from his expectations, what type and level of benefits does Social Security actually provide in meeting these various needs? Most people don't know. Under a system as complex as the present Social Security program, it is doubtful that a clear delineation of such responsibility will ever be possible—*a situation almost certain to result in people's expecting more and thus eventually receiving more from the government (that is, from the active working taxpayers).*

A number of factors, not the least of which is the general misunderstanding about the role of Social Security, have caused more and more people to believe that their economic needs in time of adversity should and will be met by someone else, namely the government. This change in attitude about responsibility for one's self is alarming. Its consequence has been and will probably continue to be a decline in individual initiative and self-reliance and thus a decline in the productivity of the nation as a whole.

Conclusion

Our Social Security program plays an important role in satisfying the population's economic security needs. While satisfying these needs, Social Security exerts strong influences, both good and bad, on the social and economic behavior of the nation's citizens. We must recognize that the design of Social Security is not only a reflection of our nation's existing social and economic structure, it is an important determinant of that structure in the future.

The nation must decide the extent to which it wants its citizens to have freedom of choice and the extent to which it wants to regulate their activities. It can then design an appropriate public policy as to the optimum roles to be played by the three natural sources of retirement income: government, employers and trade unions, and individuals. By properly designing and implementing such a policy, the nation can ensure that its citizens' basic economic security needs are met by methods that are consistent with a social and economic environment in which the nation will flourish, not wane. The challenge of finding and implementing the optimum mix that is the most favorable to this given end is considerably greater than merely satisfying the population's economic security needs during the next few years.

19
The Great American Retirement Dream

Many Americans believe that if they work until about age 60 or 65 they will then be able to live the balance of their lives in carefree and leisurely retirement, occupying themselves with hobbies, sports, and travel—activities for which they had neither the time nor the money in their earlier years. They believe this will be possible because of some combination of Social Security benefits, employer-paid pension benefits, and private savings in one form or another (a paid-for house, personal life insurance and annuities, etc.).

Not everyone really believes that this period of carefree and leisurely retirement will actually occur; however, most people want it to happen, hope that it will happen, and, after a few years of nourishing such wants and hopes, begin to believe it *should* happen—that they are *entitled* to a leisurely retirement after having worked a lifetime in a job they consider difficult, or frustrating, or boring, or unsatisfying in some way. Indeed, this Great American Retirement Dream serves as a kind of opiate in making life more tolerable in the face of a sometimes onerous job, not to mention the everyday difficulties of living.

The Great American Retirement Dream has failed to materialize for most people in the past. Within a few years after retirement, many people experience significant financial difficulties. In an inflation-plagued economy, fixed pension benefits lose their purchasing power, and the cost of maintaining a "paid-for house" escalates unduly as real-estate taxes and other costs increase; increased sickness in old age and skyrocketing medical costs combine to produce extremely high health-care costs; personal savings do not prove to be as significant as planned, dissipated perhaps by unexpected health-care expenses or high education costs for children; Social Security benefits and employer-provided pension benefits prove to be less than hoped for. Moreover, retirees are frequently disappointed because of the ill health of themselves or their immediate family, the loss of friends and relatives, or their inability to disengage from work-related activities and substitute new activities.

Just as the Great American Retirement Dream has failed to materialize in the past, it will probably fail in the future. It is not a goal that can be achieved for the majority of the population. It is not affordable, at least at a price the nation will be willing to pay. It is not a healthful concept, particularly if there is so little chance it can be achieved. It is a sad commentary on our way of life that anyone would spend most of his or her adult life looking forward to retirement.

The nation's concept of work, education, leisure, and retirement must be revised. It must be presumed that an individual will engage in gainful employment suitable to his physical and mental condition until well beyond age 60 or 65 and possibly until the end of his life. A trend toward later retirement may be a natural development as health and life expectancy improve and as the growth in the work force slows because of the low fertility rates now being experienced and expected to continue in the future. For this trend to be consummated, however, significant changes will be required in existing social and economic arrangements. Jobs must be structured to be more meaningful and satisfying to the individual. Persons must undergo training and retraining to enable them to have not just second careers, but third and fourth careers. In some instances jobs must be designed to fit the capabilities of the human resources available. For older persons as well as disabled persons, less strenuous jobs and part-time employment must be made available. Significant advances will be required in our ability to match persons with jobs. Sometimes this complete utilization of an individual's capabilities can be achieved with one employer, but in some cases it will involve many different employers and may require geographical relocation as well. Attitudes must change to make these new concepts possible.

These changes must begin to take place during the next five years, and they must be well under way by the turn of the century when the children of the post-World War II baby boom begin to reach their 40s and 50s. Bringing about these changes will be a slow process that will require the cooperation of many institutions, not just Social Security.

Congress took the first step in the process—in a series of actions from 1967 through 1986—by prohibiting an employer from imposing mandatory retirement because of age (with exceptions for military, law enforcement, and firefighter personnel; tenured faculty at colleges and universities; and certain executive and "high policy making" employees).

The next step should be to revise the Social Security program itself so that it is consistent with a policy of more complete utilization of the nation's human resources. It is sometimes said that the Social Security program has no particular influence on the nation's retirement policy since it does not specify the age at which a person can retire and it does not impose a mandatory retirement age. Nevertheless, the Social Security program effectively dictates the retirement policy of the nation.

It does this in part through the manifold and complicated conditions under which benefits are payable. Currently, full benefits are payable at age 65, the "normal retirement age" selected somewhat arbitrarily in the 1930s by the program's designers. Benefits may begin as early as age 62, in which event they are "actuarially reduced" to offset their expected payment over a longer period of time; however, the method of calculating benefits under the present law favors retirement at age 62, since the worker receives greater total value, relative to his Social Security taxes, by retiring at age 62. The commencement of benefits may be deferred until after age 65 in which event benefits will be increased to reflect partially, but not fully, the shorter remaining lifetime during which they will be paid. The worker thus receives less value if benefits begin after age 65.

If the worker continues in paid employment after Social Security benefits begin, these benefits will be reduced if his earnings exceed certain levels. These levels of "permitted earnings" are lowest between ages 62 and 65, next lowest between ages 65 and 70 and are highest after age 70 when there is no limit on earnings.

The Social Security program's influence on other retirement systems and thus on the nation's employment practices is pervasive. Private and public employee pension plans must as a practical matter follow the retirement patterns fostered by Social Security. Internal Revenue Service regulation of private pension plans is related to the standards set by Social Security. Practices followed by Social Security in determining eligibility for disability benefits influence the practices of private pension plans and private insurers.

Although the Social Security program is influencing the retirement policy of the nation through these many complicated provisions, it is rather difficult first to determine and then to state in a concise way exactly what that retirement policy is. The provisions of the current law would seem to encourage a person to retire at age 62, to engage in limited paid employment until age 65, to increase the level of his activity in paid employment from age 65 to 70, and then to work in full-time paid employment after age 70.

These retirement incentives will change in the years ahead, of course, as the normal retirement age is increased from age 65 to 67 and as the delayed retirement credit is increased from 3 percent to 8 percent for each year the receipt of benefits is postponed. (This is discussed in more detail in Chapter 3.)

From a broader perspective, the mere existence of the Social Security program sets a standard—and thus creates an expectation that fosters a presumption of entitlement— for retirement in a person's early to mid-60s, regardless of the condition of his health and his ability to continue as a productive and useful member of society.

This retirement policy, which is inherent in the Social Security program and which effectively sets the nation's retirement policy, should be reviewed carefully to determine whether it is in fact the retirement policy that is appropriate for the nation at this time as well as in the future. Moreover, and more importantly, careful attention should be given to the question of the extent to which the Social Security program should set the retirement policy for the nation and the extent to which such a policy should be determined otherwise. The nation's retirement policy should vary from time to time depending upon a variety of factors, not the least of which is the fluctuating birth rate which causes shifts in the proportions of the population that are aged and young—the principal reason for the substantial projected Social Security cost increase beginning about twenty years from now. The present Social Security program may not be flexible enough to accommodate a variable retirement policy. In this connection it should be noted that one important reason for adopting Social Security in the first place was to alleviate the hardships of the widespread unemployment that prevailed in the 1930s. Much of the present design of the program is thus attributable to conditions that existed fifty-five years ago.

Finally, work must begin on training and retraining individuals to meet existing job opportunities, as well as designing and redesigning jobs so they can be performed by available human resources. More sophisticated ways must be developed to match individuals and jobs appropriately.

The nation should provide an environment in which the capabilities of each individual can be utilized effectively, an environment that fosters meaningful activity, not empty idleness. Both the incentive and the opportunity should exist to enable every individual to work and produce throughout his lifetime in a series of endeavors compatible with his changing physical and mental abilities. Government policies should be directed toward these goals and not toward the removal of able-bodied persons from the active work force—persons who must then be supported by the remaining active workers.

It will not be easy for the nation to move in this direction of full utilization of its human resources. The alternative will be continued high unemployment and underemployment, an ever-increasing pool of idle "disabled persons" and "aged persons," and a total cost to society that will become increasingly unbearable and that will eventually become destructive.

20

The Retirement Age

What the normal retirement age should be for a particular individual or a group of individuals is a complex question. The answer depends on social custom, an individual's physical and mental health, and numerous economic factors relating to the individual and to the nation as a whole.

The concept of retiring on a pension at a given age has evolved over the past 100 years or so as the proportion of the population engaged in agriculture has declined and as industry has been taken out of the home and workshop. Germany adopted the first program of old-age pensions for all workers in 1889, with a normal retirement age of 70 (later reduced to age 65).

When the U.S. Social Security system was adopted in 1935, a normal retirement age of 65 was selected, more or less arbitrarily. Because of the earnings test (see Chapter 12), Social Security might be considered to now have a variable retirement age ranging from age 62 to age 70, depending upon an individual's earned income during that period.

Trends in Prevailing Retirement Age

In the United States, the average age at retirement has declined fairly steadily for the past fifty years. This average is a difficult statistic to define and calculate, because "retirement" itself has become somewhat nebulous. For example,

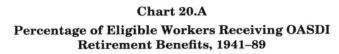

Chart 20.A

**Percentage of Eligible Workers Receiving OASDI
Retirement Benefits, 1941–89**

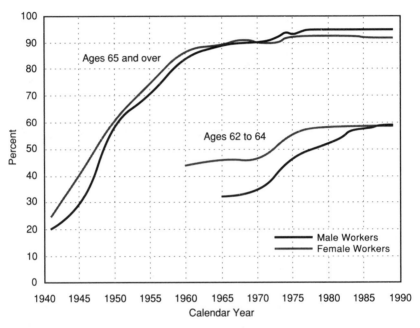

Note: Percentages are based on actual numbers of retired worker beneficiaries and
estimated numbers of workers insured for retirement benefits. Women became
eligible for retirement benefits before age 65 as a result of legislation in 1957;
men became so eligible through subsequent legislation in 1961.

does changing from full-time employment to part-time con-
stitute retirement? Or should the initial receipt of Social
Security retirement benefits be the test—although some
people are able to receive such benefits while continuing to
work? Despite these difficulties in defining and measuring
retirement age, by virtually any standard there has been a
major trend toward earlier retirement.

This trend is illustrated in Chart 20.A, which shows the
proportion of workers at age 62 to 64, and 65 or older, that is
receiving Social Security benefits. This ratio has increased
substantially over the years for both men and women, although its rate of growth has slowed somewhat in recent
years. Currently, almost 60 percent of workers at ages 62 to
64 who are eligible to receive benefits are, in fact, drawing

them. For such persons at ages 65 and above, the ratio is 95 percent for men and 92 percent for women.

As a general rule, people probably retire from full-time paid employment as soon as their financial condition permits it—or in many instances, as soon as they *think* it does. The exceptions to the rule are people who truly enjoy their work and for whom work is an essential, defining part of their life. Several developments since the end of World War II in 1945 have resulted in economic and other conditions favorable to the trend toward earlier retirement.

> Economic times were unusually good from 1945 until the early 1970s. Productivity and therefore wages increased significantly; unemployment was low; two-wage-earner families increased; inflation was relatively low.

> Social Security paid its first monthly benefits in 1940 and steadily became a significant factor in providing retirement benefits, indeed in fostering the very idea of retirement.

> The private pension system expanded significantly during World War II and continued to grow thereafter.

> The baby boom from 1946 through the mid-1960s provided an abnormal increase in the potential work force from the mid-1960s through the mid-1980s. This resulted in pressure for older workers to retire and make room for the baby boomers, frequently at a saving in payroll cost.

In view of the above factors, the recent trend toward early retirement should not be a surprise. Neither should it be a surprise if this trend moderates and reverses itself in the years ahead as a result of the following factors:

> Economic times will probably be less favorable in the years ahead than during the post-World War II boom period. Productivity and real wage increases will be lower; inflation will be higher; and the two-wage-earner family is already commonplace.

> Further significant expansion in Social Security and the private pension system seems unlikely. In fact, if

inflation is not slowed, these combined systems will probably play a smaller role in meeting retirement needs than they do now.

The baby boom was followed by a baby bust beginning in the 1960s. The decline in the size of the pool of workers entering the work force is already evident and employers are turning to older workers to meet their needs.

Effect of Increased Longevity and Improved Health

Additional factors that will influence the nation's average retirement age are the continued increases in life expectancy and improved health at the higher ages.

Life expectancy measured from birth has increased but this is not relevant to the question of retirement age since much of this increase has been attributable to decreased infant mortality. It is the increase in life expectancy measured from age 65 that is of interest in considering the question of retirement age. Table 20.1 compares the remaining life expectancy for a 65-year-old person in the past with that for such a person in the future based upon the

Table 20.1

Remaining Life Expectancy, Past and Projected

Calendar Year	Remaining Life Expectancy for Persons Reaching Age 65 in Designated Calendar Years[a]	
	Male	*Female*
(1)	(2)	(3)
1910	11.4	12.1
1930	11.8	12.9
1950	12.8	15.1
1970	13.1	17.1
1990	15.0	18.9
2010	16.0	19.9
2030	16.8	20.8
2050	17.6	21.7

[a] Projections are based on the intermediate set of assumptions.

"intermediate" actuarial assumptions (discussed in Chapters 4 and 10). In 1930 the life expectancy of the average 65-year-old male in the United States was just under 12 years; for a female, it was slightly less than 13 years. In the mid-21st century, the life expectancies for 65-year-olds are projected to be almost 18 years for males and 22 years for females under the "intermediate" assumptions. According to the "pessimistic" assumptions, the mid-21st century life expectancies for 65-year-olds are projected to be 20 years for males and 24 years for females. (Recall that the "pessimistic" assumptions are so named because of their effect on Social Security costs—not because of their underlying social desirability.) With major breakthroughs in health care, these life expectancies could be even longer.

Some analysts maintain that just because people live longer, they are not necessarily in better *health* at older ages than were persons at the same age in the past. While there may not yet be any hard evidence on this point, both common sense and anecdotal evidence suggests that the average 65-year-old today is in better health and is more able to work than was the case fifty years ago.

Chart 20.B shows the percentage of the population at the older ages that was in the active work force during the past 45 years. For older men, there has been a marked decline in labor force participation—particularly at ages 62 and above, when Social Security retirement benefits become payable. Participation in the labor force for women has generally increased, although at age 62 and over this pattern changed to one of decline beginning in the 1960s. It seems highly unlikely that this general decline in work force participation by older workers is attributable to declining health. It appears far more likely that the other factors described previously (relating to availability of retirement benefits and demographic pressures) are the correct explanation for the prevailing retirement patterns.

Other Determinants of Age at Retirement

It is probably fair to say that people work as hard and as long as they have to in order to provide whatever level of food,

Chart 20.B

Labor Force Participation Rates by Age and Sex, 1947–89

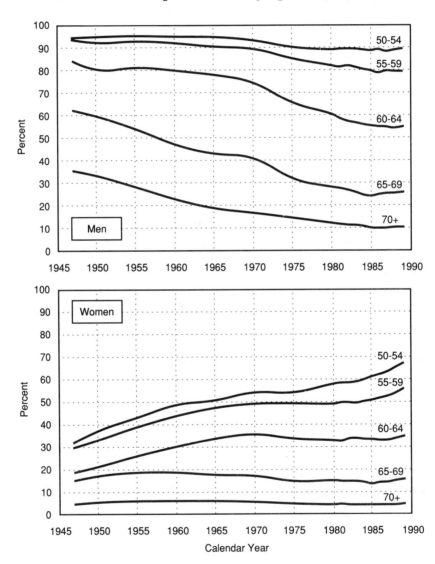

clothing, and shelter they consider desirable. Once having satisfied these basic needs, however, people work to satisfy other less tangible needs that range from "keeping up with the Joneses" to working toward the betterment of mankind. These latter needs are subjective and personal and hence vary greatly among individuals and groups of individuals.

In a 1981 survey,[1] this subjective side of the retirement decision was examined by comparing the percentage of men over 60 still in the labor force for several advanced nations. The results were as follows: 57 percent were still working in Japan, 33 percent in the United States, 13 percent in the United Kingdom, and 8 percent in France. The study concluded that cultural and personal values—basic attitudes toward life, work, and leisure—were the most important determinants of how long people work.

If each person were completely responsible for himself and received financial rewards directly related to his efforts, the question of retirement age would be self-regulatory; and the retirement age would be different for each person depending upon his personal circumstances. Societies usually modify these conditions, however, by redistributing earnings and establishing norms for behavior, with the result that individual responsibility tends to be diminished and social uniformity encouraged. For example, when Social Security, in 1935, adopted age 65 as the normal retirement age and later introduced 62 as an optional retirement age, it established a pattern and expectation for retirement that has grown remarkably strong: many people (perhaps most) now believe they are entitled to retire in their early 60s, even if it requires government support (that is, support from the active working taxpayer).

One possible problem with government intervention in setting norms for retirement ages and benefit levels is that unsuitable norms may be established, resulting in unrealistic expectations or an inappropriate size of the work force. For example, in the mid-21st century it may be impossible for a work force consisting only of persons younger than their early 60s to produce all the goods and services needed or desired by the entire population; hence it may be unrealistic for the baby-boom generation to count on retiring in their early 60s—the early 70s may be a more likely average retirement age.

Until recent years, retirement was generally an all-or-nothing situation; that is, it was customary to work full time until retirement and then not work at all. A recent trend has been to partially retire, with part-time paid employment continuing in one job or another after full-time employment ceases. This trend will probably continue as a natural consequence of the following factors: the need for older employees in the work force as the growth in the labor force slows because of the lower fertility rates since the mid-1960s; the need for retired workers to supplement their pensions as inflation and taxation continue to erode their purchasing power; and the sense of self-worth and the feeling of belonging that part-time employment can provide for older workers. Full-time retirement does not always provide the rewards and satisfactions needed for a contented life.

Related to this trend toward part-time employment will be more flexibility in the age at which full-time employment ceases. This will be compatible with a fuller implementation of age-discrimination-in-employment laws, two-wage-earner families, job-sharing arrangements, and a general work environment that is more accommodating to individual preference.

Conclusion

Whatever method is used to determine the customary retirement ages for a generation of workers—whether it be by government mandate or by individuals acting in their own self-interest—this is certain: there is no magic retirement age that is appropriate for all individuals within a given generation; each generation of workers must evolve its own unique range of retirement ages that is compatible with the social, demographic, and economic conditions of the time; and the appropriate retirement ages for the baby-boom generation will be different than the retirement ages for retirees of today and yesterday.

To the extent the government plays a role in setting retirement ages—through the Social Security program, for example—the challenge is to find the optimum range of retirement ages that will accommodate each individual's capacity to work with the type and size of work force required to produce all the goods and services needed and/or desired by the nation's population. The prevailing age at retirement is far more significant than it may at first appear, because of its pervasive effect on every aspect of national life ranging from economic size and strength to cultural and personal values.

21
Medicare

The Social Security program in the United States may be divided into two parts for analytic purposes: the Old-Age, Survivors, and Disability Insurance programs, which provide monthly cash benefits; and the Medicare program, which provides a partial reimbursement of medical expenses.

This commentary deals primarily with the Medicare program, a program that is significantly underfinanced and that will be in turmoil for at least the balance of the century and probably well into the next century. There are two basic parts to Medicare:

Hospital Insurance (HI), which pays for inpatient hospital care and other related care of those aged 65 and over and of the long-term disabled; and

Supplementary Medical Insurance (SMI), which pays for physicians' services, outpatient hospital services, and other medical expenses of those aged 65 and over and of the long-term disabled.

The HI program is financed primarily by payroll taxes (popularly called Social Security taxes) of equal amounts paid by employees and employers. Of the total employee and employer Social Security payroll tax of 15.30 percent in 1990, 2.90 percent is allocated to finance the HI program. The HI program's financing is "pay-as-you-go" with a small contingency fund to accommodate minor deviations of actual from expected experience.

251

The SMI program is also financed on a pay-as-you-go basis with a small contingency fund. Approximately 25% of the financing currently comes from "premiums" paid by persons eligible for the benefit protection and the remaining 75 percent comes from general revenue.

The assets of both the HI and SMI trust funds are invested in interest-bearing obligations of the U.S. government. The funds are thus available for use by the government until required for benefit payments.

During 1989, an average of some 30 million people over age 65 and 3 million disabled people under age 65 were covered by the HI and SMI programs. Program expenditures amounted to $60.8 billion under the HI program (1.3 percent of which was for administrative costs) and $39.8 billion under the SMI program (3.7 percent of which was for administrative costs). Approximately 95 percent of all persons aged 65 and over in the United States and its territories are covered by the HI and SMI programs.

The Importance of Medicare to Retirees

Insufficient attention is paid to the Medicare program. The beneficiaries fail to appreciate the value of the benefits (until they actually become ill). The Congress fails to give appropriate attention to the program's virtually unaffordable projected future cost and to the public outcry that will result in the years ahead when Social Security taxes, as well as general taxes, have to be increased to support this expensive Medicare program. Such tax increases are inconsistent, of course, with the current repeated assurances to the public that "Social Security" financing problems have been resolved for the next forty years or so.

To illustrate the importance of Medicare to the retired person, it may be useful to think of the retirement benefits provided by Social Security as follows. A person who retires at 65 receives monthly benefits under the Social Security program, made up of two parts:

> A cash annuity, payable monthly for life, adjusted explicitly to reflect changes in the Consumer Price Index (CPI).

A medical care annuity, payable monthly for life, which increases implicitly as the cost of medical care increases.

The medical care annuity is not paid in cash, of course; it is paid in kind: in the form of medical care insurance protection under the HI and SMI programs.

The approximate monthly value of this insurance protection for HI and SMI benefits can be determined from the annual Trustees Reports. Here are some examples of average monthly medical care annuities compared with average monthly cash annuities for 1989.

	Retired Worker over Age 65	Retired Worker and Spouse
Cash Annuity	$ 549	$ 922
Medical Care Annuity		
– HI	152	304
– SMI	100	200
	$ 252	$ 504
Total	$ 801	$ 1,426

For the retired worker alone, the medical care annuity of $252 is 46 percent of the cash annuity of $549. For the retired worker and spouse, the medical care annuity of $504 is 55 percent of the cash annuity of $922. (These examples are based on averages and ignore the differences in male and female per capita medical care costs.)

Medicare is thus a very important part of every retired person's benefits. A reduction in Medicare benefits may be even more burdensome to the beneficiary than a reduction in cash benefits, since it may be more difficult to replace benefits lost as a result of Medicare cuts than it is to replace reductions in cash benefits. Despite this, the beneficiary outcry has usually been less when Medicare benefit reductions have been proposed than when cash benefit reductions (particularly in cost-of-living adjustments) have been proposed. The value of Medicare benefits is more difficult to comprehend since such benefits are paid in kind and represent insurance protection that may or may not result in the provision of tangible benefits.

The Projected Cost of Medicare

Previous chapters present the projected cost of Medicare, sometimes alone but usually as an inherent part of the total Social Security program. This chapter shows Medicare costs alone, separately for the HI and SMI segments.

Hospital Insurance

Chart 21.A and Table 21.1 illustrate the range of projected expenditures for the HI program under the optimistic, pessimistic, and intermediate "II-B" sets of alternative assumptions used in the 1990 Trustees Reports. The expenditures

Chart 21.A

Projected Expenditures for Hospital Insurance Program under Alternative Demographic and Economic Assumptions,[a] and Tax Income, Expressed as a Percentage of Taxable Payroll[b]

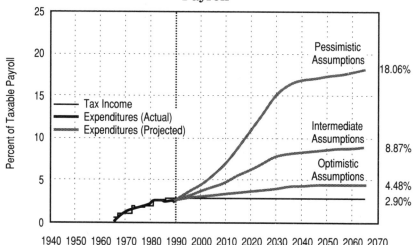

[a] See Chapter 10 and Appendix I for discussion of alternative sets of assumptions.

[b] "Taxable payroll" consists of the total earnings subject to Social Security taxes, after adjustments in applicable years to reflect (i) deemed wages based on military service, and (ii) the lower tax rates on self-employment income, tips, and multiple-employer "excess wages." This adjustment is made to facilitate both the calculation of tax income (which is thereby the product of the tax rate and the payroll) and the comparison of expenditure percentages with tax rates.

Table 21.1

Projected Expenditures for Hospital Insurance Program under Alternative Demographic and Economic Assumptions,[a] Expressed as a Percentage of Taxable Payroll[b]

Calendar Year	Optimistic Assumptions	Intermediate Assumptions	Pessimistic Assumptions
(1)	(2)	(3)	(4)
1990	2.54%	2.56%	2.61%
1995	2.83	3.13	3.50
2000	3.06	3.69	4.52
2010	3.26	4.67	6.85
2020	3.60	6.18	10.86
2030	3.99	7.69	15.12
2040	4.19	8.32	16.88
2050	4.30	8.52	17.29
2060	4.42	8.75	17.80

[a] See Chapter 10 and Appendix I for discussion of alternative sets of assumptions.

[b] "Taxable payroll" consists of the total earnings subject to Social Security taxes, after adjustments in applicable years to reflect (i) deemed wages based on military service, and (ii) the lower tax rates on self-employment income, tips, and multiple-employer "excess wages." This adjustment is made to facilitate both the calculation of tax income (which is thereby the product of the tax rate and the payroll) and the comparison of expenditure percentages with tax rates.

include both benefits and administrative costs and are shown as a percentage of taxable payroll. Chart 21.A also shows actual past expenditures as well as past and projected tax income. In sharp contrast to the steadily rising projected expenditures, the supporting tax income is scheduled to remain level at 2.90 percent of taxable payroll. The comparison of projected income and expenditures depicted in Chart 21.A makes clear the difficulty we face in financing future HI benefits.

Table 21.2 provides another way of assessing the financial viability of the HI program by showing the proportion of benefits that can be financed by scheduled tax income under each of the alternative sets of assumptions for three 25-year periods beginning in 1990 as well as for the entire 75-year projection period. The comparisons are only approximate since they are based on the average of the tax income and the benefit outlays during each year in the period under study.

Table 21.2

Proportion of Hospital Insurance Benefits That Can Be Financed by Scheduled Tax Income

| | Alternative Assumptions | | |
Time Period	Optimistic	Intermediate	Pessimistic
25-year averages			
1990-2014	95%	76%	59%
2015-2039	75	41	22
2040-2064	67	34	17
75-year average			
1990-2064	79	47	27

These figures indicate that under the optimistic assumptions, there would be enough tax income to finance about 95 percent of the promised benefits during the next twenty-five years or so, but that tax income would average only about 79 percent of benefits throughout the 75-year projection period. Thus, even under very favorable circumstances, HI income would soon be woefully inadequate to cover costs.

Under the intermediate assumptions, tax income would average about 76 percent of benefits during the next twenty-five years, and the situation would worsen during the ensuing time periods. Over the entire 75-year projection period, tax income would average only 47 percent of benefits. This set of assumptions is customarily used by policymakers as the benchmark against which to measure the system's financial health. As noted in Chapter 10, however, this benchmark may be somewhat on the optimistic side.

Under the pessimistic—but not unlikely—set of assumptions, tax income would be sufficient to pay only 59 percent of the promised benefits during the next twenty-five years. During the following 25-year period from 2015-2039, during which most of the baby boomers reach age 65, tax income would be sufficient to pay only 22 percent of the promised benefits. And during the period when the *children* of baby boomers reach age 65 (2040-2064), scheduled tax income would pay for only 17 percent of the promised benefits.

Supplementary Medical Insurance

Chart 21.B and Table 21.3 illustrate the range of projected expenditures for the SMI program under the optimistic, pessimistic, and intermediate sets of alternative assumptions used in the 1990 Trustees Reports. Expenditures include both benefits and administrative costs and are shown as a percentage of taxable payroll for ready comparison with the HI costs. Chart 21.B also shows actual past expenditures.

These SMI projections are unofficial estimates prepared in part by the Health Care Financing Administration and in part by the author. Unfortunately, official cost estimates of the SMI program are made and published by the Trustees for only three years,[1] hence the long-range financial implications

Chart 21.B

Projected Expenditures for Supplementary Medical Insurance Program under Alternative Demographic and Economic Assumptions[a]
Expressed as a Percentage of Taxable Payroll[b]

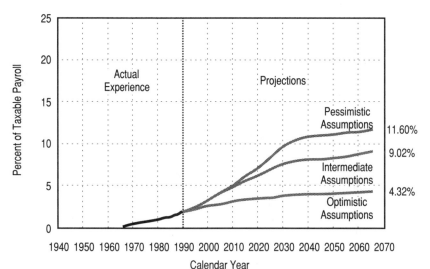

[a] See Chapter 10 and Appendix I for discussion of alternative sets of assumptions.

[b] Although the SMI program is not financed by payroll taxes, its cost is shown for comparative purposes as a percentage of payroll that is taxable for HI purposes. Participation in SMI is optional and is financed by premiums paid by the enrollees, and by general revenues.

of this program are seldom considered. This myopic view is usually justified by the theory that the SMI program is like one-year term insurance and can be terminated by Congress at any time. While it is true that the SMI program, as well as the OASDI and HI programs, can be terminated by Congress at any time, such a termination seems highly unlikely. Furthermore, it seems a real dereliction of responsibility by the Trustees to ignore the long-range future cost of a government program that covers virtually the entire U.S. population over age 65 on the grounds that it can be terminated by Congress. Ironically, the less the attention paid to the long-range costs of a program, the greater the likelihood that it will have be curtailed or terminated because of inadequate advance planning.

The law provides for a financing technique under which approximately 25 percent of the cost is currently paid by "premiums" that are paid by persons eligible for benefit protection and the remaining 75 percent is drawn from general revenue. Under present law, the portion financed by

Table 21.3

Projected Expenditures for Supplementary Medical Insurance Program under Alternative Demographic and Economic Assumptions,[a] Expressed as a Percentage of Taxable Payroll[b]

Calendar Year	Optimistic Assumptions	Intermediate Assumptions	Pessimistic Assumptions
(1)	(2)	(3)	(4)
1990	1.80%	1.80%	1.80%
1995	2.19	2.46	2.46
2000	2.58	3.33	3.33
2010	3.14	4.87	5.11
2020	3.47	6.15	7.11
2030	3.85	7.64	9.71
2040	4.04	8.17	10.84
2050	4.15	8.35	11.10
2060	4.26	8.82	11.43

[a] See Chapter 10 and Appendix I for discussion of alternative sets of assumptions.

[b] Although the SMI program is not financed by payroll taxes, its cost is shown for comparative purposes as a percentage of payroll that is taxable for HI purposes. Participation in SMI is optional and is financed by premiums paid by the enrollees, and by general revenues.

general revenue will increase over time. Yet, despite the high projected future costs, no provision has been made to assure that this amount of general revenue will in fact be available.

Reasons for the Increasing Cost

The cost of Medicare has increased significantly since it was adopted in 1965, and it is projected to continue such escalation for the foreseeable future. Many factors account for this increase, some of which were predictable and some of which were not.

Demographic changes are important determinants of cost, particularly for a pay-as-you-go-financed system. The post-World War II baby boom, followed by lower fertility rates, and increasing longevity, are conspiring to produce a dramatic increase in the over-age-65 population that is eligible for Medicare. In 1965, 9.4 percent of the population was over age 65; by the year 2030—when all the baby boomers have reached age 65—this figure will be about 21 to 24 percent.

Improved medical care technology results in better, but usually more expensive, medical care. Improvements in this technology have been remarkable during the past twenty-five years and can be expected to continue in the foreseeable future.

The increased, ready availability of medical care and the "third-party payor" principle have combined to place tremendous upward pressure on medical care costs. Neither the patient nor the hospitals and physicians have had much incentive to control the utilization of services or to monitor the costs thereof. Legislative and regulatory changes in recent years have attempted to remedy this defect in the system but a patient still has little incentive to be concerned about costs.

Increased litigation and expensive malpractice settlements have raised the cost of medical care in two ways: malpractice insurance costs have increased, and physicians have increased the number and scope of diagnostic tests to protect themselves against allegations of negligence.

Table 21.4 compares the annual increase in average medical care costs with the annual increases in the Consumer

Table 21.4

Comparison of Yearly Increases in Average Medical Care Costs and Consumer Price Index

Calendar Year	Percentage Increase in Average Medical Care Costs[a]	Percentage Increase in Consumer Price Index[b]
(1)	(2)	(3)
1965	2.4 %	1.6 %
1966	4.4	2.9
1967	7.2	3.1
1968	6.0	4.2
1969	6.7	5.5
1970	6.6	5.7
1971	6.2	4.4
1972	3.3	3.2
1973	4.0	6.2
1974	9.3	11.0
1975	12.0	9.1
1976	9.5	5.8
1977	9.6	6.5
1978	8.4	7.6
1979	9.2	11.3
1980	11.0	13.5
1981	10.7	10.3
1982	11.6	6.2
1983	8.8	3.2
1984	6.2	4.3
1985	6.3	3.6
1986	7.5	1.9
1987	6.6	3.6
1988	6.5	4.1
1989	7.7	4.8

[a] The figure for 1965 represents the relative increase in the medical care component of the Consumer Price Increase for 1965 over the corresponding value for 1964, and so on.

[b] The figure for 1965 represents the relative increase in the Consumer Price Increase for 1965 over the corresponding value for 1964, and so on.

Note: Data are based on the Consumer Price Index for All Urban Consumers (CPI-U).

Price Index (including medical care). During the 25-year period from 1964 to 1989, the cumulative increase in medical care costs was 507 percent, compared with a cumulative increase in the Consumer Price Index of 300 percent. Some of this increase in medical care costs—about one-fourth

Chart 21.C

**National Medical Care Expenditures in Calendar Year 1987
by Source of Payment**

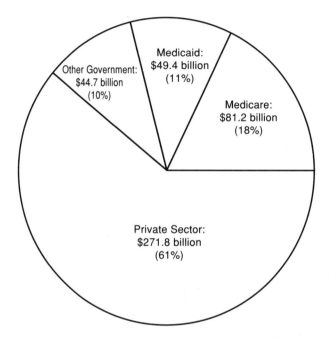

according to some studies—is attributable to qualitative and technological improvements; but it is nonetheless an increase in costs.

Medicare Costs Relative to Total National Medical Care Expenditures

Many of the factors that have increased the total cost of Medicare over the years have also increased the cost of other national health care expenditures: that is, primarily for the population that is less than 65. Total national expenditures for health care have increased from 6 percent of the Gross National Product in 1965—when Medicare was adopted—to 12 percent in 1989. This cost is expected to rise to between 15 and 18 percent of the Gross National Product by the year 2000 and to 30 percent or more by the year 2030 when all the baby boomers have reached age 65. This is in marked contrast to current national health expenditures of 8.6 percent of the Gross National Product in Canada, 8.6 percent in France, 8.2 percent in West Germany, 6.8 percent in Japan, and 6.1 percent in Britain.[2]

Medicare pays for only about 45 percent of the total medical expenses of persons over age 65.[3] And Medicare accounts for only about 18 percent of the total national medical care expenditures for people of all ages. Chart 21.C illustrates the source of payment of national medical care expenditures according to the following categories: Medicare, Medicaid, other government programs, and private sources (for example, payment by employer-provided insurance and individuals).

Accordingly, any resolution of the Medicare "cost problem" will be closely linked with a resolution of the "cost problem" of providing appropriate medical care for the entire population.

Considerations of Fairness

Although Medicare treats everyone alike, not all of its participants receive equal medical care. This is true, if for no other reason, because Medicare does not pay all medical costs; therefore, those who cannot afford to pay these unreimbursed costs probably end up with medical care that is inferior to those who can afford to pay the unreimbursed costs.

People with catastrophic illnesses and those who need custodial care, or long-term care, do not receive the same level of medical care as persons with severe short-term illnesses. Increasing concern is being expressed by the public about these discrepancies.

Questions of fairness inevitably involve the issue of consistency in providing medical care for the over-age-65 population and for the younger population. Approximately 35 to 37 million people—mostly women and children—are not covered by any form of insurance—not even Medicare. Of course, many of these people are eligible for Medicaid (the medical care program for the indigent).

Should there be consistency in the quality of health care and the quality of housing and the quality of nourishing food that is generally available? Or, in allocating national resources, should we emphasize one of these commodities over the others?

Should restoring and maintaining emotional health be accorded the same priority as restoring and maintaining physical health?

The rationing of medical care might appropriately be considered an issue of fairness. Instead of the term "rationing," perhaps it is more useful to refer to "limiting the availability" of medical care. In wartime throughout recorded history, triage has been practiced: that is, the allocation of medical treatment to battle victims according to a system of priorities designed to maximize the number of survivors. But the civilian population, in peacetime, is also subject to the allocation of medical treatment, albeit a different form of allocation. This limiting of the availability of medical care will become more overt in the future and will force us to confront moral and ethical questions we have thus far largely avoided.

The list of "inequities" and "unfairnesses" could go on and on. But what is "fair" and what is "equitable"? Should the same type and level of medical care be available for each and every person regardless of ability to pay? If so, this would be a radical departure from the way we now allocate food, clothing, and shelter, as well as automobiles, vacations, and a host of other items that are virtual necessities of modern life. Is medical care really any different from these other commodities? As difficult as it may be to answer these and other basic questions about fairness and equity, the answers are prerequisite to the formulation of a national policy for providing medical care for America's citizens.

Solutions to Medicare's Problems

Given the nature and extent of the above-stated problems in providing Medicare benefits for the population that is over age 65, as well as the problems in providing reasonable, affordable medical care for the remainder of the population, it would be naive to suggest that there are ready answers; however, several conclusions seem clear.

In considering Medicare reform, we must look beyond the immediate problems of HI and SMI. We must acknowledge that the projected financial deficits in Medicare are symptomatic of complex problems in the overall medical care system for young and old alike. Accordingly, the long-range problems of Medicare cannot be resolved merely by increasing taxes, reducing benefits, redesigning reimbursement procedures, shifting the responsibility and cost of providing medical protection to retirees and their former employers, or any combination of these measures. Such minor tinkering must not be confused with the longer term, major restructuring of our medical care system that is absolutely necessary if we are to have a coherent national health policy.

An important part of this restructuring is that we should place more emphasis on *preventing* illness rather than merely *curing* illness. An important shift in this direction is already under way, as evidenced by official and public acknowledgment of problems caused by the use of alcohol, drugs, and tobacco; recognition of the role of diet in cardiovascular diseases and cancer; and recognition of the healthful benefits of regular exercise. Unfortunately, the role of emotional health in maintaining physical health has yet to be given this same degree of recognition. And we still have a long way to go before the majority of the population accepts and adopts these principles of healthful living.

No matter what steps we take to limit the growth of medical care costs, the nation's consumption of medical care will rise dramatically as an increasingly aged population, as well as the younger population, demands access to the better and more costly medical technology that will be potentially available. But someone will have to produce these medical care services, and those who use them will have to produce other goods and services that can be exchanged for them. In other words, if the nation wants to consume more—be it housing or medical services—it will have to produce more. Accordingly, beginning early in the 21st century, people must begin to work longer and retire later (than their early 60s), thus producing a larger volume of goods and services, including the increased medical care services that the nation will want and require.

In striving to resolve our medical care problems, it will be natural for sentiment to develop for some form of national health insurance. This could work, but it is questionable whether there is anything inherent in a nationally designed and managed system that would not also work in a decentralized, free-enterprise system. Some would say that the very design of Medicare—our existing nationally designed and managed system—is an important cause of some of the same medical care problems that we are now trying to resolve.

It will be tempting to look to other countries for model health care systems. This can be useful but we must remember that any national social insurance system (for medical care as well as any other benefits) is both a reflection and a determinant of that country's social, cultural, and economic structure. If individual freedom of choice is relinquished to attain a uniform social insurance structure, it may soon be relinquished in other areas of life as well.

Conclusion

The problems surrounding the formulation of a coherent national health policy—of which Medicare is only a part—are so many and diverse that this will probably remain as one of the leading domestic issues for the next twenty years or so.

In attempting to resolve the Medicare problem itself, Congress has a tremendous responsibility in deciding exactly which short-range measures and which long-range measures to adopt, and how and when to implement them. Medicare's problems must be viewed from the perspective that Medicare is only a part of the overall medical care system. Also, a lengthy time-perspective must be adopted because much of the action taken will not show tangible results for many years to come—long after the next election.

Voters, as beneficiaries of one of the most advanced medical care systems in the world, have a responsibility to help develop and accept changes in the system that will be in the best long-range interest of the bulk of the population in the future but that may require some sacrifices in the years immediately ahead.

No significant action will be taken by voters or the Congress, however, until the public is more aware of the longer-range social and economic consequences of continuing to pursue today's retirement and medical care policies. The first step then is to sound the alarm and provide the information necessary to help the nation minimize, if not avoid, the social and economic turmoil that appears to lie ahead.

22

What Is the Outlook for Social Security?

The public is frequently given official assurance that the Social Security program is in sound financial condition during the foreseeable future and that there is nothing much to be concerned about. Such statements overlook what dramatic effect the growth in the aged population relative to the active working population shortly after the turn of the century will have on costs. They also ignore the financial condition of the Hospital Insurance program, which is financed by a portion of the Social Security payroll tax. Finally, these reassuring statements ignore the possibility that actual future costs may be closer to those indicated by the pessimistic projections than those indicated by the intermediate projections.

Projections of future costs prepared by Social Security actuaries indicate that the tax rate for the Old-Age, Survivors, Disability, and Hospital Insurance programs will have to rise at least 50 percent and perhaps more than double within the working lifetime of today's young workers; that is, the tax rate will have to rise from 7.65 percent in 1990 to about 12 percent by the year 2035 under the intermediate assumptions and 19 percent under the pessimistic assumptions. The maximum wages to which these tax rates apply are scheduled to increase indefinitely in the future, from the

1990 level of $51,300, in proportion to increases in national average wages. Of course these are just the employee taxes; the employer pays a matching tax. The tax rate for self-employed persons will have to rise from 15.3 percent in 1990 to about 25 percent by the year 2035 under the intermediate assumptions and 37 percent under the pessimistic assumptions.

These projections assume that the Social Security law is not changed (except to increase tax rates enough to pay benefits), that present financing practices are followed, and that current patterns of retirement continue. Such assumptions will probably not materialize, particularly in view of the large projected tax increases as well as the increase that will occur in the average age of the population if the present relatively low birth rates continue. As has been highly publicized in recent years, this aging of the population will result eventually in two—or fewer—workers paying taxes for every one person receiving benefits—in contrast to the present situation of three workers for every beneficiary.

What Changes Lie Ahead?

What kinds of change can be expected in the present law and in the behavior of the population covered by that law because of these projected rising costs, the aging of the population, and various other factors? The following eight points seem to be reasonable expectations for the future. They may or may not be desirable, depending upon your point of view.

First, taxpayers must become accustomed to paying higher taxes for Social Security benefits unless benefits are reduced substantially from current levels. It will just not be possible to pay for the Social Security program in the future with the taxes now scheduled in the current law.

Second, it seems unlikely that the payroll tax will continue to be virtually the only source of tax revenue for the program. Taxpayers are increasingly asking what benefits they receive for their Social Security tax payments. As it becomes more evident that the relationship between taxes and benefits is tenuous for any given individual (that is, the program gives more emphasis to social adequacy than to individual equity), there will be increased resistance to payroll tax rate increases. This will probably result in the use of some form of nonpayroll tax (such as income tax or a value-added tax) for at least one-third of Social Security expenditures sometime early in the next century. It seems unlikely that present Social Security payroll tax rates will be reduced significantly; the new form of taxation will represent additional taxes.

Third, all state and local government employees will eventually become participants in the Social Security program. Perhaps participation will be made compulsory for such employees.

Alternatively, if and when nonpayroll taxes are used to a significant degree to finance Social Security, these employees may insist on being covered by Social Security in an attempt to obtain their money's worth from their general taxes. Also, as the real costs of existing public employee retirement systems become more evident, there may be an inclination to reduce benefits under such systems and to integrate them with the Social Security program. Full participation by all state and local employees would permit a reduction in the average tax rate paid by employees and employers of only about one-eighth percent each.

Fourth, beginning about fifteen to twenty-five years from now, employees will be working longer and retiring at higher ages. This will be a natural development as health and life expectancy improve, and as the growth in the work force slows because of the low fertility rates. For this to be feasible, present socioeconomic arrangements must be revised to make it easier for persons to continue working until advanced ages, perhaps in less strenuous jobs or part-time employment. This development could lessen the financial problems of the Social Security program during the next century since a later effective retirement age, other things being equal, is tantamount to a reduction in benefits. The financial advantage of later retirement, however, could well be offset by increased longevity. Also, further liberalizations in the retirement test as well as scheduled increases in the delayed retirement credit would negate any cost savings resulting from later retirement. (Under present law the normal retirement age will increase gradually from age 65 to age 67 during the period from 2003 to 2027; however, further increases appear inevitable.)

Fifth, social and economic changes in the nation will result in a substantial revision of the program. The changing role of the family unit and of women; changing patterns in the incidence of work, education, and leisure throughout a person's lifetime; lengthening life expectancy and improved health in old age; and increased (or reduced) need to work in order to maintain the desired standard of living—all of these changes and more will require that significant revisions be made in the benefit structure if the evolving economic security needs are to be satisfied appropriately. The net effect of all these changes will not necessarily be an increase in costs.

Sixth, if the nation experiences sustained inflation at relatively high levels, it is likely that the portion of an individual's economic security needs that are met by the private sector will decrease over time; the needs must somehow be met; and the federal government (probably through an expanded Social Security program) will be left as the only entity with the audacity to make unqualified promises to pay benefits seventy-five to one hundred years in the future based upon undeterminable cost-of-living increases. Obviously, the cost of an expanded Social Security program would be correspondingly higher.

Seventh, the Medicare program as well as the nation's entire health care system will be changed beyond recognition during the next ten years. This will be the inevitable result of diverse attempts to make more adequate health care available to society at large, but at the same time prevent total health care costs from continuing to rise as a percentage of the Gross National Product. This restructuring may lead to the consolidation and expansion of Medicare and Medicaid, the nation's two largest health care programs, into a comprehensive national health insurance program.

Eighth, benefits will be reduced by one means or another. Throughout most of Social Security's history, the byword has been extension of coverage and expansion of benefits. Since 1977, however, a surprising number of benefit cuts, not all of them obvious, have been made. Possible future benefit reductions include the following: further increases in the normal retirement age; taxation of a larger proportion of benefits; reduction in cost-of-living adjustments; and interim changes in the Medicare program preceding the eventual shift to national health insurance mentioned above. Medicare program changes might include a shift of medical costs to the individual and his former employer; and a reduction in, and more stringent government control over, Medicare's reimbursement to hospitals and physicians, resulting in a decline in the level of medical care that is offered and, in effect, more rationing of medical care. These benefit reductions will not result in a decrease in overall Social Security costs below today's levels; rather, they will merely retard their inexorable increase.

These eight areas in which Social Security and the behavior of the nation's citizens can be expected to change are stated only in general terms. The exact nature of the changes will depend upon a variety of future events: demographic shifts in the population (affected, in turn, by birth rates, health care developments, and immigration), the nation's economic health, inflation, conditions throughout the world over which we may have little control, and so on. Moreover, public understanding or misunderstanding will play a much more critical role in determining the shape of Social Security in the future than it has in the past—when the payroll tax was relatively low and when the taxpayer was in a less questioning frame of mind. It is obviously preferable for changes to arise from a clearheaded appraisal on the basis of an understanding of our present system rather than from a frenzied cry for change on the basis of misunderstanding and frustration.

Even though a variety of future events—some of which we cannot control—will influence the Social Security of the future, it would be a mistake to be fatalistic. One of the reasons to forecast the future is to enable its change. It is still up to us to shape Social Security so that it is appropriate for tomorrow's environment—so that it provides a system of benefits consistent with our needs and our ability to pay for them.

The outlook for Social Security, then, is whatever we desire—and have the courage to achieve.

23

Can Social Security Be Abolished or Changed Drastically?

More and more often questions are being asked such as, "Can't the Social Security programs be abolished?" or, "Isn't there some alternative to Social Security?" or, "Wouldn't I be better off if I quit Social Security and invested my tax payments in the stock market?" These questions are usually prompted by concern over the seemingly endless rise in Social Security taxes, dissatisfaction with the benefits a particular individual expects to receive in relation to his tax payments, misunderstanding about how the program actually works, general antipathy for any large government program, fear that the present Social Security program is going bankrupt and will be unable to make good on its promises, and so on.

What are the facts? Are there any real alternatives to the present Social Security program?

Without question the present program can be revised and it should be revised—slightly now and significantly later. There are certain practical limits, however, concerning the extent to which changes can be made as well as the speed with which they can be implemented. Complete termination of the Social Security program, as suggested by some, is out of the question.

Some form of national social insurance is absolutely necessary. There is virtually no alternative in a nation that is so large and diverse and that is based on an industrial economy and a highly mobile and dynamic society. The days of the static, agrarian society, built around an extended family with all its attendant mores, are over. In any society it is inevitable that there will be persons unable to work and care for themselves because of conditions virtually beyond their control. In an orderly society, provision must be made in an organized manner for some minimum level of support for such persons. Some form of social insurance must fill this role in modern industrial society.

The present Social Security program, supplemented by an array of welfare programs, is an important element in providing this minimum level of support. To the extent it fills this role, the Social Security program cannot be terminated. It can be revised, consolidated with other components of the total income-security system, or called by another name; but it must continue to exist in one form or another.

The present Social Security program, however, provides not only this *minimum level of support* but also, in some instances, a much higher level of support. This portion of the Social Security program that provides these "supplemental" or "discretionary" benefits is not necessarily essential to the well-being of the nation. Social Security may or may not be the best vehicle by which to provide these "supplemental" benefits depending in part upon:

>   the freedom of choice desired by the people in providing for their discretionary needs;

>   the practical alternative means that are available to provide for such needs; and

>   the differing effect on the economy of these alternative means.

In any event, the portion of the Social Security program that provides for discretionary needs is certainly amenable to study and revision.

In considering any revision in Social Security, an extremely important factor is the long-term promises, expressed or implied, that have been made to millions of Americans who have paid Social Security taxes in the past. In 1990, monthly cash benefits of approximately $250 billion will have been paid to over 40 million people—retired and disabled workers and their dependents, widows and orphans, and dependent parents. One of every seven Americans is receiving a monthly Social Security benefit check. Millions of people who are just a few years from retirement have built their plans around the present Social Security program. Furthermore, over 130 million people have worked and paid Social Security taxes in the past and have some expectation of future benefits.

But that does not mean Social Security cannot be changed. It can be changed, and it can be changed significantly. We are often too quick to say that Social Security is so large and complex and that it has been in existence so long that it will be difficult, if not impossible, to make substantial revisions.

Consider the following important statistics—numbers not called to our attention by those who insist that Social Security should not and cannot have major revisions. The post-World War II generation, approximately 178 million persons under age 45, now (in mid-1990) comprises 79 percent of the total population that is less than age 65. In other words, at least 79 percent of the population that is not yet retired is still young enough to adjust to any retirement policy they decide is appropriate for them. These persons will begin reaching their 60s just sixteen years from now, however, in the year 2006. Thus, it is today that a general framework should be constructed regarding the retirement of this generation—the type and level of benefits to be provided, the source of benefits, the approximate age at which benefits will commence, and so on. In making these choices we need not be influenced unduly by decisions made in the past for different generations of people living under different circumstances. The only reverence we owe these past decisions is to fulfill the promises made to date to our older population.

It is entirely reasonable, therefore, that we give serious consideration to a completely new type of social insurance system for the relatively young segment of our population, even if we continue the present system for the older segment of the population. Significant change is possible if we really want such change.

Remember this astonishing statistic: 79 percent of the present population that is not yet retired is less than age 45. This relatively youthful population of 178 million persons has already had significant influence on our way of life. Are they not entitled also to decide the ground rules that will apply to their retirement, provided only that they not disturb the promises already made to our older population?

24
Social Insurance in Perspective

In view of the information presented in the first twenty-three chapters of this book, as well as the barrage of publicity during the past fifteen years about Social Security's financial problems, one would be tempted to say: "Social Security obviously has a *problem*. Let's identify Social Security's *problem* and fix it."

Following such a line of reasoning, some people assert that benefits are too generous and that they should be reduced. Others insist that the benefits should be maintained—perhaps even increased—and that we must simply increase the taxes enough to pay for these essential benefits. Some people want to remove Social Security from the Federal budget or make other changes in an attempt to "take the politics out of Social Security."

All of these "solutions" betray a misunderstanding of the basic nature of social insurance and its role in the social and economic structure of the nation. In order to develop rational solutions to Social Security's so-called problems, we must step back and view Social Security in a much broader context.

First, consider for a moment the three general questions—let's call them basic economic questions—that any society must answer in organizing its affairs:

(1) What goods and services are to be produced?

(2) What segment of the population is going to produce these goods and services?

(3) How are these goods and services to be allocated among the population?

All societies answer these basic economic questions in a different way, depending upon their particular political, social, and cultural makeup. For example, a free-enterprise, capitalistic society will answer these questions in one way; a socialist society will answer them in another way.

What does all of this have to do with social insurance? Everything. The design of any particular social insurance system depends upon the answers to the above three questions, especially the last two. Ideally, the questions are answered first; then the social insurance system is designed accordingly. Sometimes the social insurance system is designed without considering the three basic questions carefully. In this event, the social insurance system may implicitly help answer the three questions—but not necessarily in the same way as if the questions had been asked and answered directly.

Consider the U.S. Social Security system as an example. The system is in place, and if it is not changed, it will almost certainly require payroll tax rates of two to three times today's levels.

Although such high taxes may be feasible, their assessment would have a marked effect on the standard of living of both the active and retired segments of the population. Active workers would obviously have less discretionary income; but there would also be fewer resources available for improved education, a cleaner environment, improved health care, a better maintained infrastructure of roads and bridges, and so forth. And all of these consequences would flow not from deliberate decisions about how to allocate resources but from the adoption of a social insurance system that turned out to be extraordinarily and unexpectedly costly because of a combination of a baby boom followed by a baby bust, improved but more costly medical care, and longer life spans.

Some would argue that our Social Security system is not an integral part of our economy but that it is a separate system: that workers and their employers paid "contributions" to a "trust fund" as part of an "insurance program" under which they had an "individual account" and thus built up an "earned right" to retirement benefits. In other words, workers bought and paid for their own benefits with their contributions and those of their employer. As explained in Chapter 11, this is simply not true. This illustrates how a social insurance system can be designed and accepted by the voters on the assumption that it answers the three basic economic questions in a certain way; whereas, in fact, it answers those questions in a completely different way.

Therefore, in evaluating Social Security, the first step is to ask and answer the three basic economic questions posed above: in short, how do we want to allocate the nation's resources among alternative uses to satisfy human wants? Implicit in this exercise, of course, is consideration of the question of the extent to which our citizens should have freedom of choice and the extent to which their activities should be regulated. Having answered these questions and thus determined our objectives, we would then ascertain whether the present Social Security system is consistent with those objectives.

If we performed this analytical exercise, we would probably conclude that the retirement age patterns fostered by the present Social Security system will not give us an adequately sized work force in the early 21st century to produce all the goods and services the citizens will want. We would probably conclude that the nation's average retirement age should increase from the early 60s to the late 60s or early 70s by the year 2010 to 2020. This increase in retirement age would help reduce the future cost of Social Security but that would be only a by-product of the primary purpose of establishing an appropriately sized work force.

There would be less agreement on whether our present Social Security system offers the desired level of freedom of choice for our citizens—for the obvious reason that not everyone would agree on the "desired level." In my opinion, the system is not consistent with the principles outlined on pages 155-156 of Chapter 11; namely, that:

An individual should have freedom of choice to the fullest extent possible consistent with the interest of the nation as a whole.

An individual should be afforded maximum opportunity and incentive to develop and utilize his abilities throughout his lifetime.

A government (federal, state, or local) should provide those benefits, and only those benefits, that an individual (acting alone or as part of a group of individuals utilizing some form of voluntary pooling or risk-sharing arrangement) cannot provide for himself. In meeting this responsibility, the government should become involved to the least extent possible consistent with the interest of the nation as a whole.

As noted in Chapter 18, Social Security plays an obvious role in satisfying the population's economic security needs; and, while doing so, is a reflection of our nation's existing social and economic structure. Less obviously—and perhaps more importantly—Social Security is a significant *determinant* of the nation's social and economic structure in the future.

In evaluating our Social Security system we must also keep in mind the point made in Chapter 1; namely, that the government does not pay for Social Security. Stripped to its essentials, Social Security is just an agreement among the people of the nation that one segment of the population will receive certain benefits and that another segment of the population will pay for such benefits. The government may administer and enforce compliance with Social Security, but, in the final analysis, it is paid for by and is for the benefit of the people of the nation. The government is simply the intermediary that carries out the wishes of the people.

Not only are Social Security benefits not *paid for* by the government, they are not *guaranteed* by the government. The payment of future Social Security benefits is the responsibility of future taxpayers, hence *they* provide the guarantee. The present government does, however, define the nature and extent of the future benefits to be paid and thus of the guarantee imposed upon future taxpayers. Today's citizens and taxpayers should do all they can to ensure that the guarantee expected of tomorrow's citizens and taxpayers will be acceptable to them and thus will be honored.

During the past fifteen years (since 1975) Americans have devoted a great deal of time and energy to studying and worrying about Social Security. The concerns are real, not artificial, and indicate that there are serious problems underlying the design of Social Security. The public can no longer be tranquilized by public relations campaigns about how good Social Security is; it is time to develop solutions to the problems.

There is no reason for this country to continue with a social insurance system that is so controversial and unpopular and whose financial status must constantly be debated. Living with such a system is an unnecessary drain on our collective productivity and psyche. It is eminently more sensible for us to design a social insurance system that is understood and perceived as fair and reasonable by the majority of the citizens—one that will support rather than hinder the attainment of a healthy and productive national economy.

Appendix I

Summary of Principal Actuarial Assumptions Used in Cost Projections

Throughout the book, reference has been made to actuarial estimates of the future financial operations of the Social Security program. The purpose of these actuarial projections is not to predict the future, since that is obviously impossible, but rather to analyze how the Social Security program would operate in the future under particular economic and demographic conditions. Because the actual future circumstances could develop in many different ways, it is only prudent to evaluate the program under a variety of different assumed conditions, any of which could be reasonably expected to occur (from today's point of view). Proper use of such projections will facilitate the design and understanding of the Social Security program, as well as help ensure that the program will be able to meet its financial obligations—and thus serve its purpose—in future years.

The official government cost projections for the Social Security program (OASDI and Medicare) are based upon assumptions and methodology explained in detail in the annual reports of the Board of Trustees of the OASI, DI, HI, and SMI trust funds. The same economic and demographic assumptions employed in the 1990 annual reports were used for the financial projections contained in this book. Additional assumptions had to be made, however, in instances when the annual reports did not encompass the same period as the projections in the book. In particular, assumptions had to be made about SMI unit cost increases after the mid-1990s. In this instance it was assumed that costs would increase ultimately at about the same rate as the increase in average earnings of the nation's workers; present rates of increase (which are much higher) were assumed to grade into these ultimate rates by about the year 2015.

Four different sets of economic and demographic assumptions are used in the official Trustees Reports, characterized as alternative I ("optimistic"), alternatives II-A and II-B ("intermediate"), and alternative III ("pessimistic"). These characterizations refer to the effect of a given assumption on Social Security costs, not to the social desirability of a particular trend. For example, an assumption of longer life expectancy is called "pessimistic" since benefits would be paid over a longer period, thereby raising the costs. The alternative sets of assumptions were designed to illustrate a broad range within which one might reasonably expect the actual future experience to fall. Given the past volatility of such factors as inflation, hospital costs, and birth rates, however, there can be no assurance that future experience will fall within the range so defined.

Two "intermediate" sets of assumptions are officially prepared. Alternative II-A is generally based on the Administration's annual budget assumptions and assumes relatively rapid economic growth (by historical standards). Alternative II-B assumes somewhat less robust economic growth and is frequently characterized as the "best estimate" set of assumptions. Alternatives II-A and II-B share the same demographic assumptions. In practice, there is relatively little difference between the cost projections under the two "intermediate" sets of assumptions. For this reason, the projections shown in this book exclude alternative II-A, and alternative II-B is generally characterized as the "intermediate" set of assumptions.

The alternative sets of assumptions underlying the projections shown in this book are summarized in Tables A.1 and A.2. It was assumed that the retirement-age patterns in the future would initially continue the existing trend toward earlier retirement but then change to a pattern of somewhat later retirement, reflecting the scheduled increases in the delayed retirement credit and in the normal retirement age. Assumptions were also made concerning variables such as migration levels (including both legal and illegal immigration), insured status, disability incidence and termination rates, marital status, administrative expenses, the timing pattern of fertility, and many others. The actual future development of all these factors will undoubtedly exhibit fluctuations and considerable variation. Since such cycles and abrupt changes cannot be foretold, the ultimate long-range values of the assumptions shown in Tables A.1 and A.2 are designed to represent the average trend levels that would result if the fluctuations were smoothed out. For the first few years of the projection period, however, an attempt was made to forecast cyclical behavior in the economic factors. The "pessimistic" assumptions, in particular, model two explicit recessions during the first five years before grading into the ultimate, long-term growth assumptions.

Table A.1

Selected Economic Assumptions under Optimistic, Intermediate, and Pessimistic Alternatives, Calendar Years 1990–2065

		Percentage Increase in Average Annual...					
Calendar Year	*Real GNP*[a]	*Wages in Covered Employment*	*Consumer Price Index*[b]	*Inpatient Hospital Unit Costs*[c]	*Real Wage Differential*[d]	*Average Annual Interest Rate*[e]	*Average Annual Unemployment Rate*[f]
(1)	(2)	(3)	(4)	(5)	(6)	(7)	(8)
Past Experience							
1960–64	3.9	3.4	1.3	—	2.1	3.7	5.7
1965–69	4.4	5.4	3.4	—	2.0	5.2	3.8
1970–74	2.4	6.3	6.1	8.7[g]	0.1	6.7	5.4
1975	-1.3	6.7	9.2	18.4	-2.5	7.4	8.5
1976	4.9	8.7	5.7	14.1	3.0	7.1	7.7
1977	4.7	7.3	6.5	8.8	0.8	7.1	7.1

Table A.1 (continued)

Calendar Year (1)	Real GNP[a] (2)	Wages in Covered Employment (3)	Consumer Price Index[b] (4)	Inpatient Hospital Unit Costs[c] (5)	Real Wage Differential[d] (6)	Average Annual Interest Rate[e] (7)	Average Annual Unemployment Rate[f] (8)
			Percentage Increase in Average Annual...				
1978	5.3	9.7	7.6	14.0	2.1	8.2	6.1
1979	2.5	9.8	11.4	10.0	-1.6	9.1	5.8
1980	-0.2	9.0	13.5	15.5	-4.5	11.0	7.1
1981	1.9	9.7	10.2	14.4	-0.6	13.3	7.6
1982	-2.5	6.5	6.0	13.7	0.5	12.8	9.7
1983	3.6	5.0	3.0	8.5	2.0	11.0	9.6
1984	6.4	7.2	3.4	13.6	3.8	12.4	7.5
1985	3.0	4.3	3.5	12.1	0.8	10.8	7.2
1986	3.4	4.3	1.6	6.7	2.8	8.0	7.0
1987	3.7	5.0	3.6	5.9	1.4	8.4	6.2
1988	4.4	5.1	4.0	4.4	1.1	8.8	5.5
1989	2.9	6.3	4.8	7.6	1.5	8.7	5.3
Alternative I (Optimistic)							
1990	2.8	5.7	3.4	5.1	2.2	8.1	5.5
1991	3.7	5.6	3.1	6.6	2.5	7.5	5.4
1992	3.6	5.3	2.8	5.6	2.5	6.6	5.3
1993	3.4	5.0	2.5	5.6	2.4	6.0	5.1
1994	3.3	4.7	2.3	5.2	2.4	5.5	5.1
1995	3.3	4.4	2.1	5.0	2.4	5.0	5.0
1996	3.2	4.3	2.0	4.5	2.3	4.6	5.0
1997	3.2	4.3	2.0	4.5	2.3	4.6	4.9
1998	3.2	4.2	2.0	4.5	2.2	4.7	4.9
1999	3.2	4.3	2.0	4.6	2.3	4.9	4.8
2000	2.9	4.3	2.0	4.5	2.2	5.0	5.0
2010 & later	2.6[h]	4.2	2.0	3.5[i]	2.2	5.0	5.0
Alternative II-B (Intermediate)							
1990	1.9	5.6	4.4	5.5	1.2	8.3	5.5
1991	2.4	5.5	4.5	8.3	1.0	8.2	5.6
1992	2.4	5.5	4.5	7.4	1.0	7.9	5.6
1993	2.1	5.4	4.3	7.6	1.1	7.6	5.6
1994	2.2	5.5	4.2	7.5	1.4	7.3	5.7
1995	2.3	5.4	4.0	7.6	1.4	6.9	5.7
1996	2.3	5.4	4.0	7.4	1.4	6.5	5.7
1997	2.3	5.5	4.0	7.5	1.5	6.4	5.8
1998	2.3	5.4	4.0	7.4	1.4	6.3	5.8
1999	2.3	5.4	4.0	7.5	1.4	6.1	5.8
2000	1.8	5.4	4.0	7.3	1.3	6.0	6.0
2010 & later	1.8[h]	5.3	4.0	6.5[i]	1.3	6.0	6.0

Table A.1 (continued)

Calendar Year	Real GNP[a]	Wages in Covered Employment	Consumer Price Index[b]	Inpatient Hospital Unit Costs[c]	Real Wage Differential[d]	Average Annual Interest Rate[e]	Average Annual Unemployment Rate[f]
(1)	(2)	(3)	(4)	(5)	(6)	(7)	(8)

Percentage Increase in Average Annual...

Alternative III (Pessimistic)

Calendar Year	(2)	(3)	(4)	(5)	(6)	(7)	(8)
1990	-1.3	3.5	4.8	5.4	-1.3	8.4	6.0
1991	0.4	4.5	5.0	8.2	-0.5	8.5	7.0
1992	2.3	6.6	6.7	9.4	-0.1	8.9	6.7
1993	0.7	5.8	6.5	9.6	-0.8	9.3	6.6
1994	-0.7	4.5	5.0	8.5	-0.5	9.0	7.7
1995	3.2	6.8	5.3	10.1	1.6	8.3	7.2
1996	2.1	5.8	5.0	10.0	0.8	7.6	6.9
1997	1.8	5.8	5.0	10.1	0.8	7.3	6.9
1998	1.7	5.8	5.0	9.9	0.8	7.0	6.8
1999	1.7	5.8	5.0	9.7	0.8	6.8	6.8
2000	1.3	5.9	5.0	9.1	0.8	6.5	7.0
2010 & later	1.3[h]	5.8	5.0	8.9[i]	0.8	6.5	7.0

[a] Real GNP (gross national product) is the value of the total output of goods and services in the nation, expressed in constant dollars.

[b] Based on the average of the 12 monthly values of the Consumer Price Index for Urban Wage Earners and Clerical Workers (CPI-W).

[c] Represents average cost incurred under the HI program per inpatient hospital admission. HI unit cost increases are not available prior to 1972.

[d] The real wage differential is the difference between the percentage increase in average annual wages in covered employment and the percentage increase in the average annual CPI.

[e] The average of the interest rates determined in each of the 12 months of the year for special public-debt obligations issuable to the trust funds.

[f] Through 1999, the rates shown are unadjusted civilian unemployment rates. After 1999, the rates are total rates (including military personnel), adjusted by age and sex based on the estimated total labor force on July 1, 1989.

[g] Average for 1972–74. Earlier figures are not available.

[h] This value is for 2010. The annual percentage increase in real GNP is assumed to continue to change after 2010 for each alternative to reflect the dependence of labor force growth on the size and age-sex distribution of the population. The increases in real GNP for 2065 are 2.7, 1.5, and 0.5 percent for alternatives I, II-B, and III, respectively.

[i] This value is for 2010. Under the alternative II-B assumptions, the annual percentage increase in HI cost per admission is assumed to equal the increase in average wages in 2015 and later. For alternative I, unit costs are assumed to grade from 2 percent below the increase in average wages in 2015 to the full wage increase in 2039 and later. For alternative III, assumed unit cost increases grade from 2 percent above the wage increase down to the wage increase during 2015–2039, equalling the wage increase thereafter. The ultimate increases in HI unit costs are thus 4.2, 5.3, and 5.8 percent for alternatives I, II-B, and III, respectively.

Table A.2

Selected Demographic Assumptions under Optimistic, Intermediate, and Pessimistic Alternatives, Calendar Years 1990–2065

Calendar Year	Fertility Rate[a]	Age-Sex-Adjusted Mortality Rate[b]	Life Expectancy[c]			
			At Birth		At Age 65	
			Male	Female	Male	Female
(1)	(2)	(3)	(4)	(5)	(6)	(7)
Past Experience						
1940	2.23	1,532.8	61.4	65.7	11.9	13.4
1945	2.42	1,366.4	62.9	68.4	12.6	14.4
1950	3.03	1,225.3	65.6	71.1	12.8	15.1
1955	3.50	1,134.2	66.7	72.8	13.1	15.6
1960	3.61	1,128.6	66.7	73.2	12.9	15.9
1965	2.88	1,103.6	66.8	73.8	12.9	16.3
1970	2.43	1,041.8	67.1	74.9	13.1	17.1
1975	1.77	934.0	68.7	76.6	13.7	18.0
1976	1.74	923.2	69.1	76.8	13.7	18.1
1977	1.80	898.0	69.4	77.2	13.9	18.3
1978	1.76	892.4	69.6	77.3	13.9	18.3
1979	1.82	864.2	70.0	77.7	14.2	18.6
1980	1.85	878.0	69.9	77.5	14.0	18.4
1981	1.83	853.4	70.4	77.9	14.2	18.6
1982	1.83	827.8	70.8	78.2	14.5	18.8
1983	1.81	835.0	70.9	78.1	14.3	18.6
1984	1.80	828.2	71.1	78.2	14.4	18.7
1985	1.84	830.0	71.1	78.2	14.4	18.6
1986	1.84	822.8	71.2	78.3	14.5	18.7
1987	1.87	813.9	71.3	78.4	14.6	18.7
1988	1.91	809.5	71.5	78.4	14.9	18.7
1989	1.93	802.5	71.6	78.6	14.9	18.8
Alternative I (Optimistic)						
1990	1.94	797.0	71.8	78.6	15.0	18.8
1995	2.00	777.6	72.4	78.9	15.0	18.8
2000	2.06	765.9	72.8	79.0	15.0	18.8
2005	2.11	755.8	73.0	79.2	15.1	18.8
2010	2.16	745.7	73.2	79.3	15.1	18.9
2015	2.20	736.2	73.4	79.5	15.2	19.0
2020	2.20	727.0	73.5	79.6	15.3	19.0
2025	2.20	718.0	73.7	79.8	15.4	19.1
2030	2.20	709.3	73.9	79.9	15.5	19.2
2035	2.20	700.8	74.0	80.0	15.6	19.3
2040	2.20	692.6	74.1	80.2	15.6	19.4

Table A.2 (continued)

Calendar Year	Fertility Rate[a]	Age-Sex-Adjusted Mortality Rate[b]	Life Expectancy[c]			
			At Birth		At Age 65	
			Male	Female	Male	Female
(1)	(2)	(3)	(4)	(5)	(6)	(7)
2045	2.20	684.5	74.3	80.3	15.7	19.5
2050	2.20	676.7	74.4	80.4	15.8	19.6
2055	2.20	669.1	74.6	80.6	15.9	19.7
2060	2.20	661.6	74.7	80.7	16.0	19.8
2065	2.20	654.4	74.8	80.8	16.0	19.9
Alternative II-B (Intermediate)						
1990	1.93	804.0	71.6	78.7	15.0	18.9
1995	1.93	766.0	72.0	79.3	15.3	19.2
2000	1.92	734.2	72.6	79.9	15.6	19.5
2005	1.91	701.8	73.5	80.4	15.8	19.7
2010	1.91	678.6	74.1	80.7	16.0	19.9
2015	1.90	660.4	74.4	81.0	16.2	20.1
2020	1.90	643.4	74.7	81.3	16.4	20.4
2025	1.90	627.3	75.0	81.6	16.6	20.6
2030	1.90	611.7	75.3	81.9	16.8	20.8
2035	1.90	596.8	75.6	82.2	17.0	21.0
2040	1.90	582.5	75.9	82.5	17.2	21.2
2045	1.90	568.9	76.2	82.8	17.4	21.5
2050	1.90	555.7	76.5	83.0	17.6	21.7
2055	1.90	543.1	76.7	83.3	17.8	21.9
2060	1.90	531.0	77.0	83.6	18.0	22.1
2065	1.90	519.3	77.3	83.8	18.2	22.3
Alternative III (Pessimistic)						
1990	1.92	812.6	71.7	78.8	15.1	18.9
1995	1.85	769.7	72.0	79.8	15.7	19.6
2000	1.78	749.1	71.8	80.4	16.1	20.2
2005	1.72	693.3	73.0	81.2	16.5	20.6
2010	1.65	632.0	74.9	82.0	16.9	21.0
2015	1.60	594.9	75.9	82.7	17.3	21.4
2020	1.60	568.0	76.5	83.2	17.7	21.8
2025	1.60	544.4	76.9	83.8	18.1	22.3
2030	1.60	522.1	77.4	84.3	18.5	22.7
2035	1.60	500.8	77.9	84.8	18.9	23.1
2040	1.60	480.4	78.3	85.3	19.3	23.5
2045	1.60	460.9	78.8	85.8	19.7	23.9
2050	1.60	442.3	79.3	86.4	20.1	24.3

Table A.2 (continued)

Calendar Year	Fertility Rate[a]	Age-Sex-Adjusted Mortality Rate[b]	Life Expectancy[c]			
			At Birth		At Age 65	
			Male	Female	Male	Female
(1)	(2)	(3)	(4)	(5)	(6)	(7)
2055	1.60	424.7	79.8	86.9	20.5	24.8
2060	1.60	407.9	80.3	87.4	20.9	25.2
2065	1.60	392.0	80.8	87.9	21.3	25.6

[a] The average number of children who would be born to a woman in her lifetime if she were to experience the observed age-specific birthrates and if she were to survive the entire child-bearing period. The ultimate total fertility rate is assumed to be reached in 2014.

[b] The annual number of deaths per 100,000 persons in the enumerated population as of April 1, 1980, if that population were to experience the death rates by age and sex specified for the selected year.

[c] The average number of years of life remaining for a person if that person were to experience the mortality rates, by age, specified for the selected year.

Note: The figures shown in Tables A.1 and A.2 for 1989 and earlier represent actual experience as estimated at the time the 1990 Trustees Reports were prepared. Certain of these figures are subject to later revision, based on more accurate data.

Appendix II

Summary of Principal Social Security Amendments after January 1, 1990

The Social Security benefit provisions contained in this book are those in effect on January 1, 1990. These benefit provisions form the basis for the 1990 Annual Reports of the Boards of Trustees of the Old-Age and Survivors Insurance, Disability Insurance, Hospital Insurance, and Supplementary Medical Insurance Trust Funds, submitted to the Congress on April 18, 1990, and hence form the basis for the benefit cost and tax income projections presented herein. In November 1990, Public Law 101-508, the Omnibus Budget Reconciliation Act of 1990, was enacted, including the following benefit and financing provisions that might affect statements contained in this book or otherwise be of interest to the reader.

1. *Increase in Hospital Insurance (HI) Contribution Base.* The maximum amount of earnings subject to the HI portion of the Social Security tax was increased to

$125,000 for 1991, with automatic increases as average wages rise thereafter. The maximum OASDI contribution base rose to $53,400 for 1991 in accordance with the existing law's provision for automatic increase. Formerly, the maximum contribution base was the same for both OASDI and HI.

2. *Increase in Premium for Supplementary Medical Insurance (SMI) Portion of Medicare.* The monthly SMI premium (for Part B of Medicare) was increased to $29.90 in 1991, $31.70 in 1992, $36.60 in 1993, $41.10 in 1994, and $46.10 in 1995.

3. *State and Local Coverage.* Beginning July 1, 1991, mandatory OASDI coverage was extended to state and local government employees not participating in a public employee retirement system (except students employed by the educational institution which they attend). Participation in the HI portion of Social Security was already required of such employees by existing law.

4. *Improvement in Earnings and Benefit Statements.* Statements concerning past earnings on which Social Security taxes have been paid and potential benefits must be sent each year to all workers covered by Social Security, beginning no later than October 1, 1999. Currently, such statements are sent only upon request by a worker.

5. *Intelligible Social Security Notices.* All Social Security notices issued on or after July 1, 1991 must be written in clear and simple language and must contain an address and telephone number of a field office that serves the individual (presumably to clarify any unintelligible information in such notice).

Notes

Chapter 1

1. The dollar amounts in this paragraph relate to all the benefits usually thought of as Social Security: Old-Age and Survivors Insurance, Disability Insurance, and Medicare (Hospital Insurance and Supplementary Medical Insurance).

2. These and other figures throughout the book are based on the 1990 Trustees Reports (intermediate II-B assumptions) unless otherwise noted.

3. Self-employed persons are considered to be their own employer and thus pay both the employee and the employer tax; but such taxes are payable only on 92.35 percent of net self-employment earnings, up to the maximum taxable earnings base. Both self-employed persons and regular employers receive an income tax deduction for the "employer" portion of the tax.

Chapter 2

1. *Social Security Handbook*, U.S. Department of Health and Human Services, Social Security Administration, SSA Publication No. 05-10135, October 1988.

2. Ibid., p. 2.

3. For many years, the government agencies administering these programs also referred to them, collectively, as "the Social Security program." This practice began to change following the Social Security Amendments of 1983. At that

time, the Old-Age, Survivors, and Disability Insurance program was brought back into long-range "actuarial balance" but the Medicare program was not. Thereupon, public officials made numerous reassuring statements about the financial health of "Social Security" in an attempt to restore public confidence. For these statements to be valid, however, it was necessary to exclude the Medicare program from the term "Social Security program," a practice that has generally been followed ever since by the agencies and many analysts and commentators.

4. For purposes of Chart 2.A, workers in covered employment include those eligible for Old-Age, Survivors, Disability, and Hospital Insurance. This ignores certain employees who are paying only the Hospital Insurance portion of the Social Security tax and are thus acquiring eligibility for such benefits but not for Old-Age, Survivors, and Disability Insurance benefits: federal civilian employees who were hired before January 1, 1983, and who are not covered by Old-Age, Survivors, and Disability Insurance; state and local government employees who were hired on or after April 1, 1986, and who are not covered by Old-Age, Survivors, and Disability Insurance; and state and local government employees who were hired before April 1, 1986, who are not covered by Old-Age, Survivors, and Disability Insurance, and whose government entity elected Hospital Insurance coverage on their behalf.

5. For purposes of Chart 2.B, workers not in covered employment include those not eligible for the full range of Social Security benefits. See Note 4 of this chapter for more details on certain federal, state, and local government employees who are eligible for some, but not all, Social Security benefits. In addition to these noncovered employees, there are approximately 300,000 active railroad employees who are not included in Social Security but who are covered by their own railroad retirement system. For all practical purposes, however, these railroad employees may be considered to be covered by Social Security. They receive benefits at least equal to those provided by Social Security as a result of a special minimum guaranty provision. In addition, there is

a "financial interchange" between the two systems that places the Social Security program in the same financial condition that it would have been in if railroad employment had always been covered directly by the Social Security program.

6. This figure includes the resident population of the fifty states and the District of Columbia, American Armed Forces and certain civilians overseas, and the residents of Puerto Rico, Guam, American Samoa, the Virgin Islands, and the Northern Mariana Islands. These groups comprise the total population eligible to participate in the Social Security program.

7. Daniel R. Waldo, Sally T. Sonnefeld, David R. McKusick, and Ross H. Arnett, III, "Health expenditures by age group, 1977 and 1987," *Health Care Financing Review*, Summer 1989.

8. Social Security payroll taxes are shared approximately equally by employees and employers, when viewed in isolation from the entire system of taxation; however, in the 1970s the earned income tax credit (EITC) was enacted to relieve the Social Security tax burden on low-income individuals who maintain a home for one or more dependent children. In 1990 the EITC is 14 percent of the first $6,810 of earned income, or adjusted gross income, whichever is greater. The EITC is phased out as such income increases above $10,730 per year and reaches zero when such income reaches $20,264. Accordingly, individuals who maintain a home for one or more dependent children and whose income is less that $20,264, in effect, pay less Social Security payroll tax than is apparent. These earnings amounts change each year to keep pace with changes in the cost of living.

9. *The Budget of the United States Government, Fiscal Year 1991.*

Chapter 3

1. At first, early retirement prior to age 65 was not permitted, and there was no adjustment for benefits lost due to later retirement. These provisions were added through subsequent amendments.

2. The basic formula for the Primary Insurance Amount is as follows, for someone who reaches age 62 in 1990 or who dies or becomes disabled in 1990 before reaching age 62:

90 percent of the first $356 of Average Indexed Monthly Earnings (AIME), plus

32 percent of the next $1,789 of AIME, plus

15 percent of any remaining AIME in excess of $2,145.

The dollar amounts in the formula are indexed to reflect future changes in national average wages; however, the percentage factors are fixed and do not vary over time. Accordingly, the formula for the Primary Insurance Amount is "weighted" in favor of lower income workers. This is one of several means by which Social Security provides benefits based on "social adequacy" as distinguished from "individual equity."

3. Many people express confusion and concern that earned income may affect benefits, but unearned income does not affect benefits. This apparent anomaly is discussed in Chapter 12.

Chapter 4

1. W. Rulon Williamson and Robert J. Myers, "Revised Cost Estimates for Present Title II." Unpublished study, Actuarial Study No. 12, October 1938, Social Security Board, Office of the Actuary.

2. The results of using the more optimistic "II-A" assumptions—which, for simplicity, are not presented in this book—do not differ materially from those of using the "II-B" assumptions. All projections were based on the Social Security benefit provisions in effect on January 1, 1990. Most of the projections were obtained from the 1990 Trustees Reports or unpublished estimates prepared by actuaries in the Social Security Administration and the Health Care Financing Administration in conjunction with the preparation of the Trustees Reports. In cases where particular estimates were not available, the author has prepared his own estimates on the basis of the 1990 Trustees Reports assumptions.

3. As mentioned before, the SMI program is not financed by the Social Security payroll tax; it is financed primarily

from general revenue (currently 75 percent) and enrollee premiums (currently 25 percent). Since SMI costs are properly included as "Social Security costs," they have been shown as a percentage of taxable payroll in order to have a uniform basis for comparison.

Chapter 5

1. In 1989, total Social Security income exceeded total program expenditures by a substantial margin ($410.5 billion versus $336.8 billion, respectively). Payroll tax income alone amounted to $342.6 billion, more than total expenditures. While it is not possible to ascertain exactly which revenue sources were used to meet current costs and which were not, it is reasonable to assume a pro rata share of each revenue source was expended. This assumption has been made in this chapter, for purposes of discussing payroll tax versus general revenue financing for Social Security.

2. Self-employed persons pay Social Security taxes on 92.35 percent of their net self-employment earnings, up to the maximum taxable earnings base, and can deduct half of such taxes as a business expense in computing income taxes.

3. Social Security payroll taxes are shared approximately equally by employees and employers, when viewed in isolation from the entire system of taxation; however, in the 1970s the earned income tax credit (EITC) was enacted to relieve the Social Security tax burden on low-income individuals who maintain a home for one or more dependent children. In 1990 the EITC is 14 percent of the first $6,810 of earned income, or adjusted gross income, whichever is greater. The EITC is phased out as such income increases above $10,730 per year and reaches zero when such income reaches $20,264. Accordingly, individuals who maintain a home for one or more dependent children and whose income is less that $20,264, in effect, pay less Social Security payroll tax than is apparent. These earnings amounts change each year to keep pace with changes in the cost of living.

4. J. Douglas Brown, *The Genesis of Social Security in America*, Industrial Relations Section, Princeton University, Princeton, N.J., 1969, p. 13.

5. Ibid., p. 14.

6. Arthur M. Schlesinger, Jr., *The Age of Roosevelt*, vol. 2, *The Coming of the New Deal*, Houghton-Mifflin, 1959, pp. 308–9.

7. In the 1991 SMI Trustees Report, projected expenditures are shown for a ten-year period. Presumably, this practice will continue in subsequent reports.

8. The SMI projections shown in Table 5.4, under the intermediate "II-B" assumptions of the 1990 Trustees Report, are based on an unpublished study by the actuarial staff of the Health Care Financing Administration.

Chapter 6

1. For additional discussion of this general question of advance funding of social insurance, please see: Carolyn L. Weaver, *Social Security's Looming Surpluses*, AEI Press, Washington, DC, 1990.

Chapter 7

1. As noted in Chapter 6, the trust funds for the Old-Age, Survivors, and Disability Insurance program will begin to exceed this contingency fund level in the early 1990s and will become quite large during the early years of the 21st century if the law is not changed. Even so, the financial stability of Social Security will still depend upon the ability and willingness of the nation's workers and employers to pay the taxes necessary to support the benefit payments. This dependence on future taxes will not change unless the trust funds invest "outside" the government: that is, other than in government bonds.

2. *1990 Annual Report of the Board of Trustees of the Federal Old-Age and Survivors Insurance and Disability Insurance Trust Funds* (House Document No. 101-175, 101st Congress, 2nd Session, 1990).

3. The report includes two intermediate projections, labeled alternative II-A and alternative II-B. Both alternatives are based upon the same set of demographic assumptions;

however, alternative II-A reflects more robust economic growth than does alternative II-B. In this chapter, the term intermediate projections refers to those based upon the alternative II-B assumptions.

4. In most years the OASDI program has been operated on what may be characterized as a current-cost basis, since the trust fund balances have been relatively low. Should the trust fund balances in fact increase as implied by Chart 7.A, the program would more properly be described as "partially advance-funded," at least for the next thirty to fifty years.

5. This computation, as well as those throughout the chapter, is based on a "real rate of interest" of 2.0 percent. For example, in the case of the intermediate assumptions, the assumed 6.1 percent interest rate is comprised of a "real rate of interest" of 2.0 percent, compounded with an assumed 4.0 percent annual increase in the Consumer Price Index.

6. *1990 Annual Report of the Board of Trustees of the Federal Hospital Insurance Trust Fund* (House Document No. 101-174, 101st Congress, 2nd Session, 1990).

7. *1990 Annual Report of the Board of Trustees of the Supplementary Medical Insurance Trust Fund* (House Document No. 101-173, 101st Congress, 2nd Session, 1990).

8. In the 1991 SMI Trustees Report, projected expenditures are shown for a ten-year period. Presumably, this practice will continue in subsequent reports.

9. In recent years, Congress has acted to keep the proportion of SMI costs met by premiums from falling below 25 percent. Under present law, these temporary provisions expire in 1991, and the percentage increase in the SMI premium will again be limited to the general benefit increase for OASDI (i.e., the benefit increase attributable to the CPI increase). If Congress were to set the premium percentage at 25 percent on a permanent basis, then the SMI actuarial deficit (as defined in the text) would be 4.58 percent of taxable payroll or $6,100 billion.

10. It is only coincidental that the estimated unfunded accrued liability of $12 trillion is approximately equal to the estimated actuarial deficit of $13.2 trillion. As noted earlier, these two concepts are fundamentally different.

Chapter 9

1. In the 1991 SMI Trustees Report, projected expenditures are shown for a ten-year period. Presumably, this practice will continue in subsequent reports. Eventually, perhaps, the projection period will be extended further.

Chapter 10

1. This effect occurs because higher assumed fertility leads to greater numbers of projected workers over much of the 75-year projection period. It also leads eventually to more beneficiaries, but only toward the end of the projection period. During most of the period, the higher assumed fertility results in a greater increase in workers than in beneficiaries, with a resulting reduction in the cost of the program as a percentage of taxable payroll.

2. Finis Welch, "Dissenting Opinion Regarding Birth Rate Assumptions," *Final Report of 1990 Panel of Technical Experts* (Appendix F), Quadrennial Advisory Council on Social Security, September 1990.

3. *1990 World Population Data Sheet*, Population Reference Bureau, Inc., Washington, D.C., and *1990 Annual Report of the Board of Trustees of the Federal Old-Age and Survivors Insurance and Disability Insurance Trust Funds* (House Document No. 101-175, 101st Congress, 2nd Session), 1990.

4. Gregory Spencer, "Projections of the Population of the United States, by Age, Sex, and Race: 1988 to 2080" *Current Population Reports Series P-25, No. 1018*, U.S. Department of Commerce, Bureau of the Census, January 1989.

5. See, for example, the *Final Report of 1990 Panel of Technical Experts*, Quadrennial Advisory Council on Social Security, September 1990. After extensive analysis of this issue, the panel recommended a significant reduction in the assumed productivity increases.

Chapter 11

1. The examples used in this chapter are drawn from an unpublished update, produced in July 1990, of the following study: Orlo R. Nichols and Richard G. Schreitmueller, "Some Comparisons of the Value of a Worker's Social Security

Taxes and Benefits," Actuarial Note No. 95, HEW Publication No. (SSA) 78-11500, April 1978.

2. The calculations were based on standard actuarial mathematics, and they attempted to account for each of the appropriate factors that can influence the results. For example, the probabilities that a worker would die before becoming eligible for retirement benefits or, conversely, that he would live far into old age were accounted for. Similarly, the worker's chances of becoming disabled in any given year were included. The changing value of the dollar (inflation) and the "time value of money" (interest) along with changes in average wages were also accounted for.

3. These examples were derived from the updated study mentioned in Note 1 but do not necessarily conform to specific examples given in the study.

4. If the program is partially advance-funded in the future, it will complicate the analysis of equity among generations, as discussed in Chapter 6.

5. This relationship might not hold, of course, if taxes are increased in the future, or benefits reduced, in an effort to address the long-range financial imbalance projected for the OASDI program.

Chapter 13

1. The specific "low earnings" assumption used for illustrative purposes herein, and by the Trustees of the Social Security program, is 45 percent of average annual wages.

2. As used herein, "replacement ratio" is based on gross income before and after retirement and ignores the effect of income taxes.

3. Although public sector benefit plans would appear to be subject to Internal Revenue Service laws and regulations for "qualified" plans, as a matter of practice such laws and regulations have not been consistently enforced.

Chapter 14

1. In the Social Security Amendments of 1983, Congress enacted a limited procedure for restricting benefit increases. Specifically, when OASDI Trust Funds fall below a certain

point, the automatic benefit increases are based on the smaller of the increase in wages and the increase in prices. When the trust funds return to a less critical level, beneficiaries receive "catch-up" benefit increases. This provision has never been activated, since assets have exceeded the minimum threshold in every year since the legislation was enacted.

Chapter 15

1. This percentage refers only to those eligible for Old-Age, Survivors, and Disability Insurance benefits; and Medicare benefits: Hospital Insurance and Supplementary Medical Insurance benefits. This ignores certain employees who are paying only the Hospital Insurance portion of the Social Security tax and are thus acquiring eligibility for such benefits but not for Old-Age, Survivors, and Disability Insurance benefits: federal civilian employees who were hired before January 1, 1983, and who are not covered by Old-Age, Survivors, and Disability Insurance; state and local government employees who were hired on or after April 1, 1986, and who are not covered by Old-Age, Survivors, and Disability Insurance; and state and local government employees who were hired before April 1, 1986, who are not covered by Old-Age, Survivors, and Disability Insurance, and whose government entity elected Hospital Insurance coverage on their behalf. This percentage will increase over time as a higher percentage of federal civilian employees become covered on a mandatory basis. See Chapter 2 for additional information on this subject.

2. The Social Security Amendments of 1983 included a special "windfall elimination provision" designed to help prevent persons whose primary work was not covered by Social Security from receiving unduly generous benefits from Social Security.

Chapter 17

1. In 1987, Medicare benefit payments on behalf of persons aged 65 and older covered approximately 45 percent of their total medical expenses. (Daniel R. Waldo, Sally T. Sonnefeld,

David R. McKusick, and Ross H. Arnett, III, "Health expenditures by age group, 1977 and 1987," *Health Care Financing Review,* Summer 1989.)

Chapter 18

1. A topic of considerable debate in the economic world concerns the effect the temporary partial-advance-funding of the OASDI program has on national savings. While many economists believe that OASDI financing surpluses *can* contribute to increased national savings, few conclude that this is actually happening at this time. In particular, to the extent that OASDI surpluses merely support higher deficits in other government accounts, there is no reduction in government "dissaving"—a major factor in the nation's current low rate of savings.

Chapter 20

1. Based on a study by Alex Inkeles, Ph.D., of Stanford University, and Chikako Usui, Ph.D., of Tulane University, as reported in the April–May 1990 issue of *Modern Maturity* magazine.

Chapter 21

1. In the 1991 SMI Trustees Report, projected expenditures are shown for a ten-year period. Presumably, this practice will continue in subsequent reports.

2. International comparisons of health care expenditures must be interpreted carefully. The following book presents an interesting discussion of this subject: Joseph L. Bast, Richard C. Rue, and Stuart A. Wesbury, Jr., *Why We Spend Too Much on Health Care*, The Heartland Institute, Chicago, IL, 1992, pp. 19–27.

3. In 1987, Medicare benefit payments on behalf of persons aged 65 and older covered approximately 45 percent of their total medical expenses. (Daniel R. Waldo, Sally T. Sonnefeld, David R. McKusick, and Ross H. Arnett, III, "Health expenditures by age group, 1977 and 1987," *Health Care Financing Review,* Summer 1989.)

Index

About the Author

A. Haeworth Robertson was Chief Actuary of the United States Social Security Administration from 1975 to 1978, the period during which attention was first directed toward the significant financial problems that lie ahead. He resigned shortly after the 1977 Amendments to Social Security were passed, believing he could more effectively provide the information necessary to bring about further rational change by working on the "outside." In 1981 he completed *The Coming Revolution in Social Security* (Reston 1981), a comprehensive exposition on United States Social Security, its problems, and proposed reforms. During the past fifteen years he has written and lectured widely, giving special emphasis to interpreting and clarifying the financial status of Social Security.

While Chief Actuary of Social Security, he received two awards—the Commissioner's Citation and the Arthur J. Altmeyer Award—for distinguished service in managing the affairs of his office and in explaining Social Security's financial complexities in an easy-to-understand way to the Administration, the Congress, and the public.

Mr. Robertson's actuarial career began in 1953 when, as an officer in the United States Air Force, he served with a special unit of the Department of Defense appointed to prepare an actuarial study of the military retirement system for the 83rd Congress. Since then his entire career has been devoted to personal security programs of one kind or another. In addition to serving as Chief Actuary of Social Security, he worked twenty-five years as a consulting actuary dealing with private and public pension plans; five years in organizing, operating, and serving as president of a life insurance company; and six years as an international consultant on social insurance programs, which involved assignments in Switzerland, Barbados, Ghana, Lebanon, and the Philippines.

319

Mr. Robertson received his undergraduate degree in mathematics from the University of Oklahoma in 1951, where he was a Phi Beta Kappa, and his graduate degree in actuarial science from the University of Michigan in 1953. He is a Fellow of the Society of Actuaries and a Fellow of the Conference of Consulting Actuaries. He is also a member of the American Academy of Actuaries, the United Kingdom's Institute of Actuaries, the International Actuarial Association, the International Association of Consulting Actuaries, and the National Academy of Social Insurance.

Mr. Robertson has served as a member of the Board of Governors and as a Vice President of the Society of Actuaries, and as a member of numerous committees and advisory groups dealing with social insurance and private and public employee pension plans. In 1984 he was selected for a ten-year term and named first chairman of the Department of Defense Retirement Board of Actuaries, a three-person board appointed by the President to oversee the financial operation of the United States military retirement system and report thereon to the President and Congress—a fitting appointment as this is the same retirement system with which he began his actuarial career in 1953.

Mr. Robertson currently resides in the Washington, DC area, where he is President and Founder of The Retirement Policy Institute, Inc., a Washington-based nonprofit research and education organization devoted to the study of national retirement policy issues. He is listed in *Who's Who in America* and *Who's Who in the World*.

About the
Retirement Policy Institute

The Retirement Policy Institute is a Washington-based, nonprofit, nonpartisan research and education organization founded in 1986 by A. Haeworth Robertson, former Chief Actuary of the Social Security Administration, to conduct a program of research, analysis, and public education regarding:

> The demographic, economic and social trends that may require changes in current retirement policies.

> The development of reform proposals and policy alternatives in such areas as Social Security, Medicare and Medicaid, private pension and health benefit systems, and personal savings.

> The macroeconomic, social, and other governmental policies that are needed to maximize long-term economic growth and individual welfare in an aging society.

> Trends with respect to public opinion, voter awareness, and political interest concerning the above topics.

The Retirement Policy Institute has been designated by the Internal Revenue Service as a Section 501(c)(3) tax-exempt organization.

This book was set on an Apple® Macintosh® IIsi, using Aldus PageMaker® 4.0. Body text is 11 point Bitstream® Century Schoolbook, widened to 105%. Chapter numbers and titles and part titles are 24 point Adobe® New Century Schoolbook Bold Italic; chapter subheadings are 11 point Adobe New Century Schoolbook Italic. The size of the type page is 26 by 45 picas. The text paper is Springhill regular finish, sixty pound, offset paper. Book design by Valerie L. Robertson. Linotronic output by ICCA Graphic Services.

To Help Increase Understanding of Social Security

Social Security: What Every Taxpayer Should Know is for everyone concerned about the role that Social Security will play in their own future financial security, as well as the financial security of the nation.

If this book has given you facts and perspectives that help you understand Social Security better and thus enables you to take a more informed position in the ongoing public debate about the future of the system, perhaps you would consider giving copies to your friends and neighbors. People tend to pay more attention to a book if someone they know recommends it or gives it to them. One thing seems certain: more widespread understanding of Social Security is essential if we are to have a system that is considered to be fair and reasonable by the majority of our citizens.

Additional copies of this hardcover edition of *Social Security: What Every Taxpayer Should Know* are available at the following prices:

Single copy $ 40.00	5 to 9 copies $ 30.00
2 to 4 copies 35.00	10 to 24 copies 25.00

25 or more copies $ 20.00

FREE shipping for orders pre-paid by check or credit card.

Mail order form to:
RPI Publications • P.O. Box 240242 • Charlotte, NC 28224

Please send me _____ copies of *Social Security: What Every Taxpayer Should Know* for a total of $ _____ .

I understand I may return books within 15 days for a full refund if not satisfied.

[ ] Check enclosed   [ ] Visa   [ ] MasterCard

Card#_____ Exp. Date_____

Signed_____

Name _____

Address _____

_____

City _____ State _____ Zip _____

To Help Increase Understanding of Social Security

Social Security: What Every Taxpayer Should Know is for everyone concerned about the role that Social Security will play in their own future financial security, as well as the financial security of the nation.

If this book has given you facts and perspectives that help you understand Social Security better and thus enables you to take a more informed position in the ongoing public debate about the future of the system, perhaps you would consider giving copies to your friends and neighbors. People tend to pay more attention to a book if someone they know recommends it or gives it to them. One thing seems certain: more widespread understanding of Social Security is essential if we are to have a system that is considered to be fair and reasonable by the majority of our citizens.

Additional copies of this hardcover edition of *Social Security: What Every Taxpayer Should Know* are available at the following prices:

Single copy	$ 40.00	5 to 9 copies	$ 30.00
2 to 4 copies	35.00	10 to 24 copies	25.00
	25 or more copies	$ 20.00	

FREE shipping for orders pre-paid by check or credit card.

Mail order form to:
RPI Publications • P.O. Box 240242 • Charlotte, NC 28224

Please send me _____ copies of *Social Security: What Every Taxpayer Should Know* for a total of $ _____ .

I understand I may return books within 15 days for a full refund if not satisfied.

[ ] Check enclosed   [ ] Visa   [ ] MasterCard

Card#_____ Exp. Date_____

Signed_____

Name _____

Address _____

_____

City _____ State _____ Zip _____